ESSENTIALS OF
MAHAMUDRA

ESSENTIALS OF MAHAMUDRA
Looking Directly at the Mind

Khenchen Thrangu Rinpoche

WISDOM PUBLICATIONS • BOSTON

Wisdom Publications
199 Elm Street
Somerville MA 02144 USA
www.wisdompubs.org

© 2004 Thrangu Rinpoche
All rights reserved.

No part of this book may be reproduced in any form or by any means, electronic or mechanical, including photography, recording, or by any information storage or retrieval system or technologies now known or later developed, without permission in writing from the publisher.

Library of Congress Cataloging-in-Publication Data
Thrangu, Rinpoche, 1933–
    Essentials of Mahamudra : looking directly at the mind / Khenchen Thrangu Rinpoche.
        p. cm.
    Includes bibliographical references and index.
    ISBN 0-86171-371-0 (pbk. : alk. paper)
    1. Mahāmudrā (Tantric rite) 2. Spiritual life—Bka'-rgyud-pa (Sect) I. Title.
BQ7699.M34 T474 2004
294.3'4435—dc22

                                      2003027190

Cover design by Elizabeth Lawrence.
Interior design by Potter Publishing Studio. Set in Centaur 11.5/17.

Wisdom Publications' books are printed on acid-free paper and meet the guidelines for permanence and durability of the Committee on Production Guidelines for Book Longevity of the Council on Library Resources.

Printed in the United States of America

CONTENTS

Preface	VII
1. Introduction	1

Part I. Meditations Shared by Other Traditions — 13

2. The Shared Tradition of Shamata and Vipashyana	15
3. The Shared Tradition of Shamata Meditation	31
4. The Shared Tradition of Vipashyana Meditation	45
5. Eliminating Doubts Concerning Vipashyana Meditation	63

Part II. Mahamudra Meditation — 71

6. The Origins of Mahamudra	73
7. The Preparatory Practices for Mahamudra	93
8. Mahamudra Shamata Meditation	101
9. Mahamudra Vipashyana Meditation	119
10. Eliminating Doubts about Vipashyana	137
11. Mind As It Is and Coemergence	149
12. Eliminating Flaws That May Arise in Mahamudra	169
13. Maintaining Mahamudra in Meditation and Postmeditation	181
14. Eliminating Obstacles to Mahamudra	209
15. The Practice of Utterly Releasing	219

16. Bringing Obstacles to the Path	229
17. How Realization Dawns	239
18. How We Should Practice	251
Notes	257
Glossary	261
Table of Tibetan Terms	265
Index	269
About the Author	275

PREFACE

Twenty-five hundred years ago, the Buddha taught that one can attain true, lasting happiness by examining and working with one's own mind. This message is as valuable today as it was then, for though we are now engulfed by material wealth, we are no more happy or secure. The root of this dilemma is the mind that keeps looking outside and grasping at external pleasures in order to achieve some measure of happiness. This method is futile, for a sure basis for stability can only be established within. Looking within is done through meditation.

There are two main types of meditation: tranquility (Skt. *shamata*) and insight (Skt. *vipashyana*). These two approaches—calming the mind and developing wisdom—form the basis for all other forms of meditation, including the mahamudra meditation taught in this book. *Mahamudra* is the examination of the nature of mind itself, what is called "looking directly at the mind." Deceptively simple, it is actually an extremely advanced form of meditation that requires years of practice to develop. Nonetheless, due to its universal applicability and directness, it is a particularly valuable technique for people in our modern times who want to pursue Buddhist practice while making a living or raising a family.

Mahamudra has been practiced in Tibet since the twelfth century, particularly within the Kagyu lineage of Tibetan Buddhism. Most mahamudra manuals are simply instructions on what to do, with little or no explanation about the rationale behind the practices. Since the method of just following instructions without asking why is not compatible with the Western approach to learning, a more contextual presentation is valuable for us here in the West. Fortunately Tashi Namgyal (*Bkra shis rnam rgyal*, 1512–87), a great scholar and meditator of the sixteenth century, wrote a detailed explanation of both the fundamental reasons behind mahamudra meditation and its practice entitled *Moonlight of Mahamudra* (*Nes don phyag rgya chen po'i sgom rim gsal bar byed pa'i legs bshad zla ba'i 'od zer*). *Essentials of Mahamudra* is a commentary on Tashi Namgyal's text.

Between 1990 and 1995, Thrangu Rinpoche taught on mahamudra in five retreats held at Big Bear Lake in California. This book is based on teachings from the second through fifth of those retreats.

Thrangu Rinpoche holds the highest degree within Tibetan Buddhist studies and was requested by the Sixteenth Karmapa, the head of the Karma Kagyu lineage, to set up the curriculum for the lamas of the Karma Kagyu lineage. Thrangu Rinpoche is not only an eminent scholar of Buddhism, he is also recognized as having the realization of the practice of mahamudra. Thus he is well qualified to teach on this topic. In addition, Thrangu Rinpoche has taught thousands of Westerners in over thirty countries in the past two decades, and is very skillful in conveying the Buddha's message to Western ears.

Technical Notes

The chapter breaks generally follow the outline of Tashi Namgyal's text, but doing so consistently would have proved very awkward. In addition, Thrangu Rinpoche occasionally addresses topics that are not mentioned in the root text, and for this reason some of the subheadings within the chapters are not contained in Tashi Namgyal's outline.

Since these teachings are an amalgamation of more than one course, there was a certain amount of repetition in the transcripts. This has been minimized through editing, and what remains is there in order to retain the progression of Rinpoche's presentation based on the root text.

Tibetan and Sanskrit words are rendered phonetically within the body of the book. For those interested, Tibetan transliteration is provided in a glossary at the back.

The numbers that appear in brackets throughout the book refer to the page of the English translation of Tashi Namgyal's text, translated by Lobsang P. Lhalungpa as *Mahamudra: The Quintessence of Mind and Meditation*. Originally published by Shambhala Publications in 1986, it can be found also in a 2001 Indian reprint available from Motilal Banarsidass.

Acknowledgments

I'd like to express my thanks to the many people who helped make this book possible. Over the years the following people have worked on correcting and editing this commentary: Peter Barth, Susan Chapman, Sandy Garison, Bill Lawless, Terry Lucas, Donna McLaughlin, Arline Mathieu, Laurie Milner, and Lama Tashi Namgyal. Needless to say, any errors that remain in this text are my own.

It has been my great privilege to work with Thrangu Rinpoche's teachings for many years, and in particular to assist in making his mahamudra teachings available to the world. May the instructions here be of benefit to all beings.

Clark Johnson

INTRODUCTION

Mahamudra Practice

There are many great Buddhist traditions, and of these the teachings of mahamudra are particularly helpful in these modern times. The reason I think that the mahamudra teachings are especially relevant and beneficial today is that we find ourselves in situations that are quite similar to those in which the great practitioners of mahamudra found themselves many centuries ago. The eighty-four great adepts, or *mahasiddhas*, who lived in India in the second to twelfth centuries found it necessary do spiritual practice in conjunction with their worldly activities. For instance King Indrabhuti ruled a large kingdom and was surrounded by great luxury. Yet he received mahamudra instructions, practiced them while ruling his kingdom, and achieved the supreme accomplishment of mahamudra— enlightenment in one lifetime. Similarly the great scholar Nagarjuna, who composed many treatises on the meaning of emptiness, achieved the supreme accomplishment of mahamudra while carrying out vast responsibilities and difficult work. Other mahasiddhas were cobblers, arrow makers, sweepers, and even practitioners of such humble occupations as grinding sesame seeds. All of them combined their practice of mahamudra with whatever activities they were engaged in. There was, for them, no contradiction between the work that they had to do and the practice of mahamudra; no conflicts came up between Dharma practice and worldly activities. Thus the tradition of mahamudra arose and flourished.

Here in the West people are engaged in a great variety of occupations and thus experience a great diversity of thoughts. The practice of mahamudra allows each person to live as they wish, do the work that they want to do, and at the same time, without any contradiction, practice Dharma.

One of the best things about mahamudra practice is that it is peaceful and gentle, and there isn't a great danger of making terrible mistakes or creating a practice situation that can harm us. In contrast some other special practices can yield profound results if practiced well but involve the danger of unwanted complications. One such practice is known as the dark retreat, which entails doing contemplative practice while staying in a dark room for a month or so. If it is done properly it yields profound realization, but if it doesn't go well there is the danger of creating even greater difficulties for the person. Another example is the practice of going without food for seven or fourteen days. If done correctly it brings about the realization known as *extracting the essence*, but if done incorrectly it causes one to become sick and extremely unhappy.

The practice of mahamudra is free from such dangers and complications. It is simply a matter of looking at our mind, recognizing its nature, and remaining within that recognition. The mahamudra instructions penetrate right to the essence of the teachings, and if they are followed there is no risk to body or mind.

Moonlight of Mahamudra

Once we decide to study and practice mahamudra, the question of how to approach the teachings arises. There are a great many texts on the practice of mahamudra—some extremely vast and some quite concise. Most practitioners in the West have gone to school and have been taught analytical thinking, and they want to learn the reasons for doing the practice.

Therefore I have selected the text *Moonlight of Mahamudra* by the great practitioner and scholar Tashi Namgyal. This text is not only a compilation of the quintessential instructions on mahamudra, it also explains them in such a way that we can understand the purpose of the practice. From my own experience I have found this text extraordinary.

When the Sixteenth Karmapa came to America for the first time in 1974, a student of his, Mr. Shen, asked, "What text would be of great benefit to students in the West if it were translated? I will sponsor it." His Holiness the Karmapa replied that *Moonlight of Mahamudra* would be extremely beneficial. When I heard that he had selected this book, I saw it as proof of the utter clarity of the Karmapa's remarkable enlightened mind. In accordance with the Karmapa's wish the text was translated by Lobsang Lhalungpa with the help of Dezhung Rinpoche and published as *Mahamudra: The Quintessence of Mind and Meditation*. I've heard that some students think that there are problems with the translation. This may be the case, as it is difficult to translate some of the subtleties of the thought. However it seems to me that the essential points have been translated well and that they can be understood with careful reading.

I thought that if I were to teach this text in a slow and careful manner over a number of years, it would allow students to understand its meaning and get at something very essential in Buddhist practice. It seemed to me that this must have been the Sixteenth Karmapa's intention when he recommended that the text be translated, studied, and used as a basis for practice. Although the Karmapa passed into nirvana many years ago, his hope and his instruction regarding this text remain. In presenting an explanation of *Moonlight of Mahamudra* I feel that I am offering some service to him.

The texts on the Middle Way, or *Madhyamaka* in Sanskrit, such as *The Root Verses on the Middle Way* by Nagarjuna and *Entrance into the Middle Way* by Chandrakirti, explain the perfection of wisdom (Skt. *prajnaparamita*). These texts set forth the correct view of the way things exist and provide very clear explanations of the nature of reality. However they don't explain how to meditate. The Madhyamaka texts explain the view and allow us to develop great faith and understanding of the Dharma, but they don't address how we can actually meditate to gain a direct understanding of the view.

Moonlight of Mahamudra is different in that it explains very clearly how to meditate by developing the practices of *shamata*, or tranquillity meditation, and *vipashyana*, or insight meditation. It shows how these meditations allow us to rest our mind evenly in order to see the basic nature of reality. In addition *Moonlight of Mahamudra* describes many levels of meditation experience. If you are new to the practice of meditation and want to know how to begin, the text describes how to begin. If you have practiced meditation and given birth to some results and wish to know how to proceed, the text talks about that also. If you have developed some genuine meditation and encountered obstacles and difficulties, the text explains where these obstacles come from, what they are, and how to get rid of them. All these explanations are presented with great clarity. That is why the Sixteenth Karmapa said that this is the best book to translate for Western students.

Reasons to Meditate on the Nature of Mind

[6] It is important to know why we practice meditation. There are two main types of meditation: analytical meditation and placement meditation. The Madhyamaka school has given us extensive, clear explanations of how external things or phenomena are actually emptiness. In analytical meditation we meditate on these reasons and arguments; however it is very difficult to actually meditate on the emptiness of phenomena. In the tantric, or *Vajrayana*, tradition of Tibet, rather than meditating on the nature of external phenomena, we meditate on mind itself. The technique of mahamudra meditation is essential and unique to the Vajrayana tradition.

Tashi Namgyal, who lived four hundred years ago in Tibet, observed that, in his day, there were those who practiced meditation but did not understand the true nature of phenomena, and those who knew the true nature but did not practice meditation.[1] He said that it is important to combine the practice of meditation with analytical understanding of the teachings. Therefore both the explanation of the view and the explanation of the practice are taught in *Moonlight of Mahamudra.*

The first Jamgon Kongtrul Rinpoche, Lodro Taye, said that a person without the view of how to practice meditation is like a person with no hands trying to climb a mountain. On the other hand someone who understands the view but doesn't practice is like a wealthy person who is a miser and does not use his money to help himself or others. But if a person has the understanding of the view and also practices the view, he or she is like a great garuda bird that uses both wings together to travel freely and effortlessly through space. If we combine the wisdom of listening to the teachings with the wisdom of meditation, we will surely arrive at the final truth.

The reason for teaching meditation on the true nature of the mind is that all phenomena are just mind. This means that external appearances, such as images, sounds, smells, tastes, and tangible objects, are merely mind, and internal objects, such as feelings and thoughts of pleasure, pain, attachment, and anger, are also just mind. All of these various experiences of mind and body come back to mind itself.

When we say that we "meditate on the mind," we are referring to the true nature of mind, or the way the mind is. In the Vajrayana tradition the teacher points out the nature of the mind to the student; this pointing-out is called *semtri* in which *sem* means "mind" and *tri* means "leading someone." So *semtri* means "leading the mind to knowing the mind as it is."

The first teaching of mahamudra is that "all phenomena are mind" or "all dharmas are mind." This teaching is presented first because the nature of the mind is most important in mahamudra. In the Mind Only, or *Chittamatra*, school of Buddhism the notion that everything is mind is explained in great detail. The view that all appearances—mountains, houses, trees, and so forth—are just mind is expounded in a set of logical arguments. However when it comes to practice, we aren't very concerned whether these appearances are mind, for it does not matter much for meditation. When we practice mahamudra, what we are concerned with are our mental states. We are concerned with feelings of pleasure and pain. We are concerned with aspects of the mind that are beneficial to us, such as faith, confidence, compassion, and the aspiration that all beings attain enlightenment. We are also concerned with what is harmful, such as the disturbing emotions (Skt. *klesha*) of great attachment, hatred, and ignorance, with discursive thought and our holding onto a self. If we meditate on the mind we can understand the mind as it is. With this understanding whatever good qualities need to be developed will be developed, and whatever negative qualities need to be abandoned will be abandoned. Along the way good qualities, such as faith and confidence in the Buddha, the Dharma, and the Sangha, the energy to practice, love, and compassion, will become stronger and stronger. At the very end of this path wisdom will be unveiled. All of this just through understanding the mind as it is.

We can try to discover the nature of mind by studying logical arguments, or we can rely on the authority of the scriptures. For example the *Lankavatara Sutra* says:

> All things appear as perfect reality to the mind.
> Apart from the mind, no reality as such exists.
> To perceive external reality is to see wrongly.

In the *Samputa Tantra* it says:

All things, external and internal,
are imputed by the mind.
Apart from the mind nothing else exists.

Problems from Not Meditating on Mind

[9] Is it helpful to know the true nature of mind but not practice meditation? It is somewhat helpful, but just knowing it is not going to allow us to abandon the various negative emotions, such as desire and hatred, and achieve complete enlightenment. This is the great problem with not meditating on the true nature of mind.

[10] *Moonlight of Mahamudra* explains the importance of meditating on the thought that all appearances are mind by first discussing the faults of not meditating in this way and then discussing the benefits of actually doing this meditation. The Buddha and many learned adepts of the tradition have given the faults of not meditating. For example in the *Treasury of the Abhidharma*, Vasubandhu gives an example of a bank teller who spends all day counting hundreds of thousands of dollars and stacking the money into piles. The teller has a great deal of money but can never do anything with it because it doesn't belong to him. Similarly you can listen to all these valuable teachings and tell others about the miseries of cyclic existence or samsara and the great qualities of liberation, but if you have never actually meditated on them they are useless to you.

In the *Gandavyuha Sutra*, the Buddha compared a person who knows a great deal about the Dharma but doesn't put it into practice to a doctor who knows a great deal about medicine but doesn't apply it when he or she becomes sick. If we know a lot of Dharma but don't practice, it will not be very beneficial.

The reason we need to practice meditation is that we have many disturbing emotions. If we do not practice, these disturbing emotions will arise and remain in us. Mere knowledge is not sufficient. The great Indian saint

Shantideva spoke to this fact when he said that the mind is the hub of our existence in much the same way that the hub is the central part of the wheel, holding all the other parts together. If you don't understand this essential point about the mind, then even though you want happiness you will not be able to achieve it.

Benefits from Meditating on Mind

Many sutras and other texts extol the benefits of meditation. They all say essentially the same thing: It is far more beneficial to meditate for just one day than it is to listen to teachings and analyze them for eons and eons. It is also far more important to meditate for a short period of time than to engage in vast virtuous and beneficial activity for a very long time. This does not mean that there is no benefit or meaning in other practices. On the contrary it is extremely beneficial to listen to the teaching of the Dharma and to think about the meaning of what one has heard. However the practice of meditation surpasses the benefit of any other type of practice that can be done.

Questions

QUESTION: I am tormented by the lack of time I have to practice because of my work. This makes me angry at work. It is a serious attachment problem, and I would like to know how to work with it.

RINPOCHE: What you described is quite familiar. It is really a matter of the balance of meditation and postmeditation. By meditation I mean sitting down somewhere and drawing attention to the mind. If we have the aspiration to meditate for a long time and are busy and have other things to do then we get up and go do them while practicing postmeditation. This makes our meditation continuous. Whether we are speaking with someone or working on a particular task, we bring mindfulness and alertness to the activity so that our mind is not fluttering here and there in great distraction. When we are able to bring meditation into postmeditation through this practice of mindfulness, work and meditation cease to be contrary.

If we don't combine meditation and postmeditation, meditation will be one thing and work will be something else, and they will fight with each other. We will feel that we can't work when we meditate and we can't meditate when we work. But if we bring this practice of alertness and nondistraction of mind into all of our actions, work and meditation will go together. In fact we will find that meditation and postmeditation begin to stimulate one another: the more we practice meditation in our actions, the easier our meditation on the cushion will be. Then we will be able to easily carry that good meditation experience back into our work. Meditation and postmeditation will begin to help one another so that we do not have the feeling that we have to flee from work, and working itself will become a way of subduing and overcoming the disturbing emotions, the wildness, dullness, lack of clarity, and instability of mind.

QUESTION: Could you please explain the main differences between dzogchen and mahamudra?

RINPOCHE: There are differences in the lineage of transmission and in the skillful methods (Skt. *upaya*) of these two meditations. But if we are speaking of exactly what they are, there is no difference: both are practices leading to recognizing mind as it is.

The lineage of dzogchen, which in Sanskrit is *mahasandhi* and means "the great completion" or "the great perfection," began with the teacher Garab Dorje, who passed it to Trisina, who passed it down from teacher to student. The lineage of mahamudra, which in Sanskrit means "the great symbol," or the "the great seal," began with Saraha, who passed it to Nagarjuna, who passed it down to Shawari, and so forth. The lineage of dzogchen that came to Tibet was mostly associated with the Nyingma lineage, while the lineage of mahamudra was mostly associated with the Kagyu lineage, with Marpa, Milarepa, Gampopa, and so on.

Both dzogchen and mahamudra are methods for meditating on the mind. In the Kagyu lineage supplication we say "all thoughts are dharmakaya." The guru can point out the nature of mind to us; in the mahamudra tradition, we then meditate in terms of that. In the tradition of dzogchen, we make a distinction between mind (Tib. *sem*) and awareness (Tib. *rigpa*). *Rigpa* has the connotation of knowing and recognizing, of having understood true nature; *sem* has the connotation of not having recognized the true nature. So the technique or method of dzogchen is to separate *sem* from *rigpa* and, knowing that *sem* is not the true nature of mind, to come to *rigpa*, the knowing or fundamental mind.

In *An Aspirational Prayer for Mahamudra* composed by the Third Karmapa, Rangjung Dorje, there is a verse that says:

> It doesn't exist, even the victorious ones haven't seen it.
> It is not nonexistent because it is the basis of all samsara and nirvana.
> This is not a contradiction because this is the unity of the middle way.
> May we realize the true nature of mind, which is free from all limitations and extremes.

Similarly, in *An Aspirational Prayer for Dzogchen* by Jigme Lingpa, there is a verse that says:

> It doesn't exist, even the victorious ones haven't seen it.
> It is not nonexistent because it is the basis of all samsara and nirvana.

> This is not a contradiction because this is the unity of
> the middle way.
> May we realize the ground of dzogchen.

So we see that there is little difference between mahamudra and dzogchen.

It should be noted that the Third Karmapa was the teacher of the great Nyingma master Longchenpa. He also wrote one of the most precious teachings of the Kagyu lineage called the *Karma Nyingtig;* a *nyingtig* is a dzogchen style of teaching. So the Third Karmapa was not only an author of mahamudra teachings but of dzogchen teachings as well.

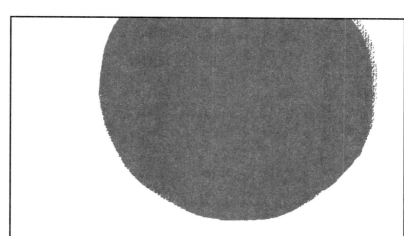

Part I

MEDITATIONS SHARED BY OTHER TRADITIONS

THE SHARED TRADITION OF SHAMATA AND VIPASHYANA

What Are Shamata and Vipashyana Meditation?

[15] We will begin by explaining the meditation of shamata and vipashyana that is common to all Buddhist practices, and in later chapters we will discuss the shamata and vipashyana meditation that is particular to mahamudra. In this text the word *samadhi* (Tib. *tingedzin*) is used to cover all types of meditation. While many different levels and types of meditation are described in the Buddhist texts, all of them can be included within shamata and vipashyana meditation.

If our mind is continually restless, being carried away by thoughts like a flag waving helplessly in the wind, it is very difficult for spiritual growth to occur. In contrast if we can place our mind somewhere and rest it there, we can become accustomed to whatever is taking place within it.

The practice of shamata is the practice of allowing our mind to rest and be peaceful in this way. However it is not enough to stop and relax with this peacefulness. It is also important to develop vipashyana, or insight meditation, which is a clear and intense seeing.

We might believe that shamata and vipashyana are very ordinary meditations because teachers talk about them all the time. In fact they are extremely important and extraordinary. Suppose a teacher gives us the mind transmission, pointing out the nature of our mind when we are at the beginning of our path. We have this wonderful experience and think that something fantastic has happened to our meditation, but the next day the experience might not be so clear, and the following day, even less clear. After a year we might recall, "Well, last year my meditation was really great." This happens when we have no steadiness of mind. Shamata helps us stabilize our insights, and for this reason it is the foundation of meditation. In the beginning, it is of little importance whether we have fantastic experiences in meditation or whether everything is quite ordinary. We just let these experiences be and learn to focus on letting the mind be steady, firm, and still. We let the mind come to rest.

The Root of Shamata and Vipashyana

[17] There are three primary causes of successful shamata and vipashyana meditation: discipline, listening to the instructions, and reflecting on the instructions. What ethical discipline we take up depends on our station in life. If we have taken the vows of a monk or a nun, we follow the discipline of the monastic orders. If we are working in the world and living as a householder, we engage in a different discipline. If we follow the discipline that is appropriate to our station in life, then, along with listening to and reflecting upon the instructions, we will be able to clear away the obstacles to meditation and develop genuine understanding of and confidence in our practice. This will lead to the birth of true meditation in our being.

To maintain discipline we need devotion, which is a secondary cause of shamata and vipashyana.[2] The Tibetan word for devotion is *mögu; mö* means longing, admiration, and interest, and *gu* means respect. This suggests that what we have devotion for is distinctive, special, or superior, and so elicits our great longing and respect for and faith in it. The principal focus of our devotion is mahamudra itself. We have an intense longing and respect for mahamudra meditation because mahamudra can tame our mind and liberate it from its bondage. Our devotion is also toward our root guru and lineage gurus, for without wholeheartedly relying on our gurus it is impossible to give birth to the mind of mahamudra. With devotion we can give rise to mahamudra naturally and thereby receive the guru's blessings. In the Vajrayana we practice guru yoga to give rise to such devotion.

The accumulation of merit is another secondary cause of shamata and vipashyana. Merit is gathered by way of our body, speech, mind, and wealth. The accumulation of merit by way of our body includes helping others materially and doing physical actions of devotion, such as offering prostrations to our guru, the Buddha, the Dharma, and the Sangha, or working to promote the Dharma. The accumulation of merit by way of our speech includes doing supplication chants and reciting mantras, or offering completely unbiased advice to help others. The accumulation of merit by way of our mind involves cultivating love, compassion, and bodhichitta, which is the commitment to become enlightened oneself so that one can help all sentient beings become enlightened. We can also accumulate merit by meditating on a *yidam*, a deity representing an aspect of the enlightened mind. The accumulation of merit by way of our wealth includes helping someone who is poor or making offerings to the Buddha, the Dharma, and the Sangha to help the Dharma flourish.

Obstacles to Shamata and Vipashyana

[19] There are an almost limitless variety of thoughts that are obstacles to shamata and vipashyana. These thoughts can be grouped into five different classes.

The first class includes two elements that differ in quality and content but are similar in effect. The first element is excitement or mental agitation, which means being so joyful and agitated about something that your mind is completely distracted; the second is sadness or remorse, which means thinking that everything has gone wrong and becoming completely discouraged. Although excitement and sadness are experienced differently, they both prevent the mind from resting in meditation.

The second class of obstacles consists of mental heaviness and falling asleep. Mental heaviness feels as though the mind were enveloped in darkness. While these elements are different, one can lead to the other—being heavy or dull of mind often leads to sleep.

The third class consists of overwhelming doubts: we deliberate so much among various possibilities that we cannot make a decision.

The fourth class includes discursive thoughts of attachment or desire: we feel so strongly that there is something that we must have that our attachment creates a problem for practicing meditation.

The fifth class includes thoughts of revenge or wanting to harm others. We feel that others have treated us badly and so we must get back at them by addressing them in a nasty or harsh way. When we feel jealous and wish to harm someone, our mind becomes unclear and cannot rest.

Remedies to the Obstacles of Shamata and Vipashyana

[21] These five obstacles to shamata and vipashyana can harm our practice. If our mind is steady they make it unsteady; if our mind is clear, luminous, and unobstructed, they make it dull and obstructed. If we can identify the obstacles to meditation, we can use various antidotes to clear them away. Not identifying them is like shooting an arrow without a target. What are we trying to hit? To eliminate the obstacles, we must first identify them.

The remedy for the first obstacle, wild or excited mind, is meditation upon impermanence. When we feel things are going well, we become happy and our mind becomes excited. The thought of impermanence—remembering that it will end—settles our mind down. We should also remember impermanence when we are feeling remorse or sadness. Whatever it is that we feel regret about has passed, so there is no point in continuing to cling to it. If we can cease bringing it to mind, our mind will become clear and bright, and we will be able to proceed with our meditation.

The second obstacle, a mind that is heavy and dull, can be dispersed by thinking about the good qualities of the Buddha, of the Dharma, and of meditation. Such thoughts help us feel joyful, and clear away this mental heaviness. Sleepiness, the other element of this obstacle, can be remedied by meditating on the sense of luminosity.[3] When we meditate on the sense of brilliance, our sleepiness will subside.

The remedy for the third obstacle, doubt, is to settle the matter with one-pointed mind. Rather than incessantly deliberating, "Is it like this or is it like that? Is it good or is it not so good?" we investigate with a concentrated mind to settle the matter once and for all.

The fourth obstacle, the continual desire for more acquisitions, is very negative, because even if we get what we want, we never feel satisfied, we never feel we have enough. If we realize that there is no satisfaction to be had from material things we will feel some contentment and will not be tortured by this continual longing for more.

The remedy for the fifth obstacle, wishing to harm others, is love—wishing that others have happiness and that they are free from suffering. We must realize that, just as we want happiness, others also want happiness. Just as we do not want suffering, others do not want suffering. Wishing harm to others is a pointless, destructive act. Even if someone who has harmed us were to suffer terribly, it would not benefit us one bit. There is not always justice and fairness in our world, but harming others does not level the score. In fact, we only harm ourselves when we seek revenge. Instead, we should develop kindness toward others and the wish to help them, no matter who they are or what they have done to us. When we think about these things carefully, we are then able, bit by bit, to pacify the malevolent attitude of wanting to harm others.

Remedies for Dull and Excited Mind

[23] There are other ways to talk about the various obstructions to meditation and the remedies for them. Another classification that is particularly helpful divides the remedies into two: those for heavy or sinking mind (Tib. *jingwa*) and those for excited or wild mind (Tib. *göpa*).

The reason the mind becomes heavy is that we have lost the longing and admiration for meditation. The most effective remedy for this is to reflect on the good qualities of the enlightened ones and to develop great longing to become like the Buddha. Recognizing that meditation is the pathway to enlightenment, our longing and admiration for meditation will increase. We can also enliven the factor of luminosity. Intelligence, or *prajna*, is very clear and sharp; more than knowledge, it is the very quality of knowing, and this quality is sometimes referred to as luminosity. Contemplating the essential points of meditation or the essential points of Dharma lights the fire of prajna. The luminosity of prajna dispels the darkness and heaviness of mind. Similarly, to arouse our joy and delight, we can remember that at last we have the inconceivably good fortune to practice meditation and the Dharma. This joy leads to exertion, which also increases the luminosity of mind.

An excited mind is an instance of the mind being very attached to or passionately stuck on something. The basic remedy for this attachment is remembering impermanence. Thinking that all things come to an end causes us to become less attached and less excited.

We can also work with a dull or excited mind through specific physical activities. If our mind is dull and heavy, we can get up, walk around, and then come back and practice again. This will help to clear away the heavy feeling. If our mind is wild, we can do prostrations; the physical exertion will calm us down.

The True Nature of Shamata and Vipashyana

[26] Shamata and vipashyana are not the same thing in all Buddhist traditions. Even though the names are the same, the meaning is not. For example, the way that shamata and vipashyana are practiced in the Buddhist Hinayana traditions is unlike the way they are practiced in the Buddhist Vajrayana tradition.

In the Vajrayana tradition, vipashyana meditation is an indispensable key to abandoning the disturbing emotions and achieving genuine happiness, the qualities of enlightenment, and genuine wisdom. Understanding vipashyana is important because normally we place great value and importance on the appearance of external phenomena. We are happy when we feel that external phenomena are in order and miserable when external phenomena are not as we expect. Relying on the external world for happiness only leads to unhappiness. Instead, we need to understand the internal world of the mind. If we have happiness of mind, our environment will appear to us like a palace of the buddhas, no matter where we are. Without happiness of mind we will feel no pleasure, even if we are living in a palace of gold and silver. If our mind is peaceful and free from fear, we will experience our world as a peaceful, nonthreatening place. Whatever pleasure or pain we experience is our own mind. That is why the mind is the most important thing to understand.

There are two aspects to mind: mind as it appears (Tib. *nanglug*) and mind as it really is (Tib. *ngelug*), its true nature. Mind as it appears is cyclic existence, *samsara*. When we look at samsaric mind, we find many coarse and obstinate thoughts with strong elements of pride, envy, desire, anger, and ignorance. When these disturbing emotions dominate our mind, our body and speech follow accordingly, and we accumulate negative karma. This then causes us further mental anguish.

But if we look carefully, we see that the mind's nature is not entirely covered with disturbing emotions. In the sutra tradition mind is explained as having buddha essence, or buddha nature (Skt. *tathagatagarbha*). This buddha nature is a potential within us, like a seed from which all the good qualities of the Buddha can grow. This essence of the enlightened one exists within us like pure gold, but it is obstructed by distorted and painful states of mind, such as attachment, aggression, and ignorance. For buddha essence to manifest, we must abandon these disturbing emotions.

Upon hearing about buddha essence we might think that the disturbing emotions are external and buddha essence is within us, or that the disturbing emotions are extraneous and buddha essence is essential. We could examine these thoughts in meditation by asking: Where does this mind dwell? Is it outside the body, inside the body, or some place in between? Does it have a form or is it formless? If it has a form, what is its color and shape? If it doesn't have a form, then what exactly do we mean by mind? When we analyze in this way, we do not find anything that we can point to and say, "That's mind." We do not find any place in particular where thoughts exist.

There are two ways that we can look at our mind: after the fact or experientially. We can look at a strong thought of attachment or aggression after it has left, but we can never catch hold of it because it has already passed. Or we can look at our mind experientially, by looking at the present state of our mind, not thinking about the future or the past. We can look at our present mind to see if a thought, such as attachment or aggression, is occurring, and ask, "What is the manner of its birth?" If we determine that it was not born from something within us, we can ask, "How did it get there? How did that come about?" When we look for the origin of thoughts, we never find anything.

The reason that we can't find mind when we look for it is that mind doesn't have an essential nature of its own. This nonexistence is what the Buddha called emptiness, or *shunyata*. This emptiness does not need to be verified through complicated philosophical reasoning; it is simply the nature, or essence, of the mind. Both peacefulness and disturbing emotions arise from mind's nature. And this is not solid and dense; rather, it is empty of inherent existence. Because it is empty, its nature cannot be harmed and does not become defective or degrade with age and illness. Because buddha nature is essentially free from fault, we need not fear anything whatsoever. This peace, which is characteristic of mind, is also known as emptiness.

When we say that the mind is empty, we do not mean that it is a void in the way that space is empty. Space is indeed empty, but it does not have the ability to know, to see, or to reflect. Space is a "dead emptiness." When we say that the nature of mind is emptiness, we mean that the mind is not a solid or fixed entity. It cannot be found, no matter where we look. Nonetheless it has the ability to understand and reflect. This ability to think and know is what we mean when we speak of the mind's luminosity.

In the sutras, this luminosity is called *buddha essence*. Buddha essence is the union of wisdom and space. But this space is an alive space (Skt. *dhatu*), connoting spaciousness, vastness, and reality. We call this spaciousness "emptiness," and by *wisdom* we mean "the luminosity of the mind." We might think that because the mind is empty it could not have the ability to know. But actually emptiness and luminosity are not contrary. While the mind is empty, it is luminous. And just as it is luminous and aware, so it is entirely empty.

When we say the mind is empty, we do not mean that it ceases or is nonexistent. Suppose we feel tremendous aggression toward someone. If we look for where the thought and feeling of hatred come from, we do not find anything. Similarly, if we look to see where thoughts and feelings of pain and sadness come from and where they are now, we do not find anything. Yet, despite our inability to find the mind, the mind is luminous, it has the capacity to know. Thus we say the mind is naturally the union of luminosity and emptiness. Resting our mind evenly in the recognition of this is called *vipashyana*.

When we practice this meditation, we experience something like the sun among the clouds: When the sun is shining in a cloudy sky, sometimes we see the sun very clearly and sometimes the clouds obscure and block it. Similarly when we are meditating upon the mind, upon this union of luminosity and emptiness, sometimes we see it clearly and sometimes it fades away. The reason it fluctuates is that we do not have sufficient shamata. We have become accustomed to discursive thoughts and easily fall into them. To develop stable clear vision we need to become accustomed to the nondiscursive mind. The way to do this is, simply, to meditate again and again and again.

Types of Shamata and Vipashyana

[29] There are several classifications of shamata and vipashyana meditation. Shamata includes two types: the worldly shamata of simply resting one's mind and the shamata that goes beyond worldly concerns and is influenced by bodhichitta. In the *Samdhinirmochana Sutra*, the Buddha set forth three categories of vipashyana. The first is vipashyana that has arisen from valid cognition: we use reasoning and logic to analyze the nature of phenomena. The second is vipashyana that is the process of seeking the view: through the practice of looking into our own minds we establish what the view actually is. The third is vipashyana that arises from meditation: having decisively found the view, through meditation we arrive at a nonconceptual vipashyana that is called direct perception.

The Sequence for Practicing Shamata and Vipashyana

[32] There are two different traditions concerning the sequence of practicing shamata and vipashyana: the sutra tradition and the tradition of the siddhas. Most of the sutras say that we must practice and attain excellent

shamata before practicing vipashyana. Shantideva reflects this view when he says that we must first make our mind peaceful and relaxed through shamata. When our mind is relaxed, we can begin to develop vipashyana to see the reality, or *dharmata*, of things. In this way, we abandon the disturbing emotions.

The siddhas, however, both sought meditation from within the view of vipashyana and sought the view from within meditation. Having first understood things as they are, some siddhas were then able to develop the very steady mind of shamata in order to stabilize that recognition. More commonly, however, they also first established a relaxed and stable mind and on that basis proceeded to recognize the true nature of phenomena.

[33] It makes no difference whether we seek meditation in terms of the view or seek the view within meditation. Both shamata and vipashyana are very important, and we need to practice both. If we try to practice vipashyana without having achieved shamata, our insight into the nature of phenomena will not be stable. It is like the flame of a butter lamp in the wind: we cannot see very much in the light of a flickering flame. On the other hand, if we try to practice shamata without vipashyana, we will achieve a relaxed, peaceful, happy, and steady mind, but we will not abandon the disturbing emotions at the root. If we cannot abandon these kleshas, our wisdom will not increase. While we may focus on either shamata or vispashyana at first, we ultimately need to develop them simultaneously because we need both of them equally to attain realization.

Usually we begin with the practice of shamata, using an appropriate object of observation. Frequently this object is our breath, but it could be any visualized object. Once we develop shamata, the guru may point out the nature of our mind to us, and if we understand it, that is extremely good. But we need the stability of mind that is developed through shamata to meditate for a long period of time, without distraction, upon the reality that has been recognized. Merely knowing the mind is not enough; it is necessary to join that recognition with the ability to meditate on it for an extended period. When we can do both, it is possible to eliminate the various faults of the mind, such as the disturbing emotions, and give rise to the extraordinary good qualities, such as the wisdom of the enlightened ones.

Results of Shamata and Vipashyana

[37] As a result of practicing shamata, our mind becomes peaceful and relaxed, and we are able to weaken the disturbing emotions. Vipashyana is the way in which realization unfolds; it is a matter of abandoning some habits and adopting others. While the final goal is achieving complete enlightenment, buddhahood, other good results also come from having developed vipashyana. The pain and discomfort that we experience in our everyday life result from not having control over our own mind. If we achieve shamata and vipashyana, our mind becomes independent, no longer under the influence of confusion and the disturbing emotions. We then have the power to create a pleasurable life for ourselves.

It is said that the fruition of shamata is a pure mind, undisturbed by false conceptions and emotional afflictions. The fruition of vipashyana is intelligence, or *prajna*, and pure wisdom, or *jnana*. *Jnana* is the wisdom that knows the true nature of phenomena. This is the final wisdom at the level of complete enlightenment. At this stage, our prajna intelligence has become so vast that we develop a second type of wisdom called "the wisdom that knows the variety of phenomena."

Questions

QUESTION: Rinpoche, how do we deal with the sluggishness, pain, and physical exhilaration that occur in meditation? How do we approach or use our mind so that it does not reflect those physical sensations?

RINPOCHE: If we feel joy and enthusiasm for meditation and have no doubt about wanting to practice meditation, heaviness of the body will not pose an obstacle. If we feel lazy and don't have a strong wish to meditate, the body will feel heavy or restless. The body and mind appear to be separate but, in fact, the mind is dominant and can overcome the situation of the body. For instance, after Milarepa had been in retreat for eighteen months, Marpa, his teacher, visited him and said, "You have been meditating for eighteen months. Why don't you take a break and rest a little bit?" Milarepa replied that he had no need to rest, that meditation was rest. Milarepa had such a great love of and longing for meditation that he was joyful to be able to practice. With such enthusiasm, his body posed no obstacle. Meditation itself was whatever rest he required.

QUESTION: I am unclear how doubt differs from regret.
RINPOCHE: Maybe a better way to say regret is "feeling ill at ease." For instance, you might be meditating and thinking quite vividly about what you did yesterday, turning it over in your mind and saying, "Boy, I really messed that up. That was terrible." Or you you might not be thinking about it explicitly, but you are still affected by it, like an aftertaste. That is what I called regret, or feeling ill at ease. Doubt, on the other hand, is actively turning some option over in your mind, thinking, for example, "I don't know if this is a good meditation to be doing. Maybe I should be doing this other practice." You are all wrapped up in debating with yourself. That is the difference between doubt and regret.

QUESTION: How do we purify our obscurations and ill deeds?
RINPOCHE: The practices common to both the sutra and mantra traditions say that it is important to develop an attitude of remorse or regret for what we have done. Realizing that we have done something that was harmful to ourself and probably harmful to others as well should give rise to regret. While feeling this regret, and not just wallowing in it, we do what

are known as the *four powers of purification*. The first of these is simply recognizing that what we did was negative. This is called the *power of regret*. The second involves casting it out, becoming thoroughly involved in the remedies, that is, activities that establish within us the roots of what is beneficial. This is called the *power of banishing*. The third is called the *power of the basis*, which means that we generate devotion in the presence—either actual images or visualized ones—of the Buddha, the Dharma, the Sangha, and our root guru. We realize that it is not enough to confess our ill deeds to ourselves; we need to confess them to our teacher and to the Three Jewels as well. Finally, having confessed, we should not think, "Oh well, that is enough." We generate the resolve that, from this moment on, we will not engage in any negative activities and will only engage in virtuous and beneficial activities. This is the *power of resolve*. These four powers of purification are common to the sutra and the mantra traditions.

In the mantra tradition there is in addition the practice of Vajrasattva, in which we visualize Vajrasattva on top of our heads and supplicate Vajrasattva, exposing our ill deeds and requesting Vajrasattva to purify them. As a result, a stream of healing nectar passes from Vajrasattva into our body and mind, filling them and clearing away the ill deeds and obstructions. At the end of the practice we generate the firm feeling and conviction that indeed these things have been purified, and Vajrasattva melts into us.

QUESTION: Rinpoche, this notion of suppressing emotions is something we don't like in Western culture. If someone tells us to suppress things, we don't want to do it.

RINPOCHE: What Western psychology means by suppressing thoughts or emotions is very different from what we are talking about here. We are trying to understand the nature of the situation, and this means knowing the reason for holding onto something. For instance, getting angry and exploding at another person probably won't help a situation. Realizing this clearly, with wisdom, we simply endure the situation. If we understand the reason for biting our tongue, our mind actually relaxes. That is very different from saying don't suppress something.

QUESTION: Rinpoche, could you say something about "mind appears, yet it is empty; it is empty, yet it appears"?

RINPOCHE: The best way to describe the mind as apparent and yet empty at the same time is through the example of a dream. When you dream of an elephant, does an elephant appear to your mind? Indeed it appears very clearly. Is there an elephant there? No. This appearance of an elephant in your dream is a union of appearance and emptiness. It appears, yet it does not exist. It does not exist, yet it appears. It is the same with all external phenomena. Similarly, when we say the mind does not exist, we do not mean that the continuum of the mind is severed, or that the mind stops. The mind exists, it is aware, it knows. At the same time it cannot be found, it is empty. Emptiness and appearance occur simultaneously; they are not different things. If we understand the example of the appearance of something in a dream, it is easier to understand how the mind appears yet does not exist, and does not exist yet appears.

QUESTION: In your talk you said that we could use our occupation as a way of overcoming the disturbing emotions. I was thinking that we don't always do what we want at work.

RINPOCHE: It is very important to develop mindfulness and alertness in postmeditation so that when you are working, you are mindful and very aware of what you are doing. If you are writing a letter, you pay attention to the letter, not letting your mind stray to something else. If you are speaking to someone, you pay attention to that conversation and don't let your mind wander to something else. That way work does not need to be detrimental to the development of mindfulness and alertness.

The mindfulness and alertness that one experiences in meditation and in postmeditation come about through different techniques. But they are the same in terms of being mindful and aware. This is the development of shamata in postmeditation. There is also the development of vipashyana in postmeditation, which is to look right into the thing itself to see what it is. Whatever one is experiencing, whatever one is thinking, whatever one is feeling, one asks, "Where does this come from? Where is it?" This is difficult for a beginner, but as you become more familiar with it, it can be quite helpful.

THE SHARED TRADITION OF SHAMATA MEDITATION

[39] In the last chapter we discussed the meditation of shamata and vipashyana that is common to all Buddhist traditions. In this chapter we will concentrate on the shamata, or tranquillity meditation, shared by all traditions.

Preparation for Shamata

In *Moonlight of Mahamudra*, it is explained that the preparation for shamata is done to "bind the doors of the five senses" so that the mind does not scatter wildly. The Buddha said that if we eat too much, we become sleepy and our mind is distracted. Therefore, to prepare for shamata, we ought to divide our stomach into three parts and fill one third with food, one third with drink, and one third with our breath. That way, while meditating, our breathing will not be noisy and we will not be sleepy or distracted.

It is important to avoid distractions when we are developing shamata. Going to an isolated place to practice is helpful because there is little to distract us there, and our mind can relax. If we are unable to remain in an isolated place, we can go on a retreat now and then to develop some experience of shamata. Once we have had this experience, it will not be an obstacle to be in a busy situation. We will be able to bring the experience of shamata into our ordinary lives and continue our practice, increasing it further and advancing to a higher level.

Objects of Focus in Shamata

[40] There are four different classes of objects that we can focus on when developing shamata: vast or pervasive objects of observation, objects of observation for purifying behavior, objects of learning, and objects of observation to eliminate the disturbing emotions.

With the first class, *pervasive objects of observation*, we develop shamata by focusing on something extremely vast that pervades all phenomena.

With the second class of objects, *objects of observation for purifying behavior*, we focus on individual disturbing emotions, or kleshas. If we are dominated by desire, for instance, we can reduce attachment by meditating on ugliness and recognizing the impurity of our bodily substances. If we are dominated by hatred, we can meditate on love and compassion. If dominated by ignorance, we can meditate on interdependent origination. If dominated by pride, we can meditate on the composition of the body—recognizing that the solid parts are the earth element, the fluid parts are the water element, the heat or metabolic functions are the fire element, and the moving functions are the air element. When we realize that our body, which is the basis for pride, is just an aggregation of elements, our pride diminishes. These meditations on ugliness, love and compassion, interdependence, and the composition of the body in terms of the four elements weaken the disturbing emotions, and our meditation becomes clearer and steadier.

Most of us, however, are dominated not by one, but by several disturbing emotions. Our main problem is that we have many thoughts. In this case it is appropriate to meditate on the inhalation and exhalation of the breath. This meditation is not directed to any single disturbing emotion but to all of them and to the thoughts that we experience endlessly.

By meditating on the breath, our thoughts decrease. This is the best-known meditation and the one that most of us do.

Objects for learning, the third class of objects to focus on, are objects that enable our prajna to increase. Because we tend to be very attached to things, we have many problems. One of the reasons we develop strong attachment is because we feel that our physical bodies and our mental selves are solid, stable, and steady. In fact, they are not. The Buddha gave many teachings on the nature of the mental self and the physical body. In these he presented four sets of objects for learning: the five aggregates, the eighteen elements, the twelve doorways of perception, and interdependent relationships.

The first of these objects of learning is the aggregates, or *skandhas*. *Skandha*, a Sanskrit term meaning literally "pile" or "heap," connotes a "collection" or "aggregation." The Buddha taught that a person is a collection of body and mind, and that the body is a collection of the four elements of earth, water, fire, and air. Specifically, the person is the aggregation of the five psychophysical skandhas—of form, feeling, perception, compositional factors, and consciousness. By studying and meditating on our five skandhas we see that we are a collection of many different things that are piled together, with new things being added and other things being discarded all the time. Therefore the psychophysical self is not stable at all. Recognizing this instability, we become skilled in understanding that a person has no inherent nature. When we realize that the five skandhas are without essence, our attachment to our body and mind is greatly reduced.

The eighteen elements are the second set of objects for learning. These include the six sensory objects, the six sense organs, and the six consciousnesses. The six sensory objects are visual forms, sounds, smells, tastes, tangible objects, and mental phenomena. The six sense organs, which negotiate the relationship between each consciousness and its objects, are the eye, ear, nose, tongue, body, and mind, or mental, sense organ. Finally, the six consciousnesses are the those of the eye, ear, nose, tongue, body sensations, and mental consciousness. These eighteen objects describe our perception and the composition of our world in a thorough way. The reason for developing an understanding of these elements is to see the interrelationship of cause and effect, that is, when a cause occurs, an effect follows. Knowledge of this process allows us to abandon what is undesirable and unhelpful.

The third set of objects for learning is called the twelve doorways of perception (Skt. *ayatana;* Tib. *kyeche*). These are often translated "sense fields," but the syllables of the Tibetan word are very meaningful. The first syllable, *kye,* means "to be born" or "to be generated," and the second syllable, *che,* means "to increase." These twelve sense fields are the six senses together with the six consciousnesses. A sense faculty coming into contact with a sensory object opens the doorway of perception and generates sensory consciousness and the development of mental consciousness. Studying how these consciousnesses come about enables us to see that the entire process of perception is empty, having no essential nature of its own.

Interdependent relationships compose the fourth set of objects for learning. This is very simple: every event happens in dependence upon another event. When we understand this we realize that everything is changeable. Good situations are not fixed as good, and bad situations are not fixed as bad; pleasant things will not always remain pleasant, and unpleasant things will not always remain unpleasant. If phenomena had an essence or solid nature, they would remain the same forever. However, because phenomena arise in dependence on other phenomena, they are empty of an essence, and so are impermanent and changeable. This means that we can change any situation.

[41] The fourth and final object of focus in shamata practice is *objects of observation to purify the disturbing emotions.* The method for purifying

disturbing emotions that is common to Buddhist and non-Buddhist traditions is to recognize the faulty nature of disturbing emotions, to realize that they are not beneficial to us or to anyone else. We then realize that the absence of disturbing emotions creates peace and gentleness, which are extremely beneficial to us and to others. When we clearly understand the destructive aspect of the disturbing emotions and the great advantages of freedom from them, disturbing emotions will naturally subside.

The uncommon method for purifying disturbing emotions is in relation to conventional and ultimate truth.[4] First we develop understanding of the four noble truths: We realize that samsara is misery and that the root of samsara is the disturbing emotions. We realize that the actions that arise from such disturbing states of mind result in suffering. We understand further that by overcoming these disturbing emotions and the actions that arise from them, we achieve liberation, which is the cessation of suffering.

Then, through meditating, we abandon the disturbing emotions in a final way. In the creation stage of Vajrayana practice, we visualize the body of a Buddha as our object of observation. Visualizing a deity in front of us or visualizing ourselves as the deity is a very special kind of practice because it brings the blessings of the deities that we visualize. When practicing meditation using other objects of observation, our thoughts come and go; by the time we notice this, our meditation has been disturbed and the thought has already gone. But when we visualize the body of the Buddha, our mind is held to it. We see thoughts quite clearly at the moment they arise; we see our meditation disturbed and brought back again. Therefore using a deity as an object is very special.

For some people, the visualization comes clearly and for others it does not. This is because of differences in the subtle channels in our bodies and the subtle energies that flow in those channels.[5] Actually, it is not terribly important whether or not the visualization comes clearly, because the practice of visualizing deities is not done to establish the clarity of the visualization but to calm the mind and develop confidence and faith in the practice.

The Object of Observation for a Beginner

[43] With what object of observation should a new student begin? Generally speaking, it is easier for a beginner to meditate on an external object than the internal mind.

In the creation stage, there are two principal objects of focus: deities and the breath. We can meditate on a particular yidam deity such as Avalokiteshvara or Vajrasattva, or if we are doing the preliminary practices (Tib. *ngondro*), we can meditate on Vajradhara. By focusing on a deity we develop greater and greater stability, and the resting increases. Otherwise we can develop stability of mind by simply holding our mind on the breath. This way of meditating is common with the sutra tradition. When meditating upon the breath, however, the mind is erratic; it wanders and we bring it back again and again. When meditating upon a deity, the mind is continually engaged and active. This is because the mind visualizes many details: the deity's face and arms, the color of the deity's body, the ornaments the deity wears, the objects the deity holds, the letters that are placed in various spots on the deity's body, the wheel of mantra that appears in a certain spot in the deity's body. Our mind becomes extremely stable as we hold it to these visualized aspects. Thus this is a special way of doing shamata meditation.

When we are practicing meditation we are working on the level of the sixth consciousness, the mental consciousness. When we speak about the mind, it has two aspects: mind (Tib. *sem*) and mental factors (Tib. *semjung*). "Mind" in this case is basic awareness, the simple quality of knowing. Mental factors are, figuratively speaking, companions that give the mind a particular color or flavor. What we normally understand as thoughts are actually these mental factors. What is it that actually looks at the object? It is the mental factor of mindfulness (Tib. *drenpa*) that keeps us from becoming distracted. Without such mindfulness there can be no samadhi. If mindfulness fails, the mind wanders. What is it that knows whether or not the mind has wandered? It is the quality of alertness (Tib. *shezhin*), which has the sense of knowing what is occurring in the mind in the present. These two are of great importance to the practice of meditation.

The great Shantideva praised mindfulness and alertness by saying that meditators should value them more than their own lives. He said, "I place my palms together to express my respect for mindfulness and alertness and for those who have developed them."

Maintaining a Visualized Image with Mindfulness

[44] It is said that when we first practice shamata our mind resembles a crazy elephant that runs amok and does a lot of harm. Whether we use the body of a deity or our breath as the object of our observation, we need to hold our mind to that object and stay with it. How do we go about tying our mind to the object of observation? To prevent an elephant from running all over the place we tie it to a stake with a rope. Likewise, using mindfulness as our rope, we tie this crazy mind to the object of observation.

It is essential that we do not hold the mind too tightly or too loosely with the rope of mindfulness. If we hold our mind too tightly to the object of observation, it doesn't stay; instead it jumps somewhere else, and when we bring it back, it jumps somewhere else again. On the other hand, if our mindfulness is too loose, we forget that we are practicing meditation; our mind just wanders off and doesn't return. So it is important to practice mindfulness without being too tight or too loose.

Methods of Developing Shamata

There are four general methods for developing shamata: the eight impediments,[6] the nine stages, the six powers, and the four applications. The eight impediments will not be discussed here. We will begin with the nine stages of settling the mind, the method most commonly used.

THE NINE STAGES OF RESTING THE MIND

[47] *Ornament of the Sutras* by Maitreya gives nine stages of resting the mind that allow shamata meditation to arise. These nine stages can be considered a progressive series of steps in the development of shamata. The first stage, *placement*, involves placing our mind on a particular object. This might be an external object or an internal visualization. Whatever it is, the first step is simply to place our mind on it.

Initially we place the mind on an object for a brief duration. When we are able to extend that period of time somewhat, we arrive at the second stage, called *continually placing*. At this stage, our mind continues to wander. With alertness we realize this, then simply bring our mind back to the object and hold it there with mindfulness. We do this without thinking that the mind has wandered or that this is bad. We simply bring the mind back and place it again.

The third stage is called *placing again*. The mind still wanders, and we bring it back again and again. The main roadblock at this stage is attachment to thoughts. Thoughts arise and we think, "This is a very important thought. I have to think about it. I must not forget this." Thinking this way, the thought comes back again and again, and instead of practicing shamata, we increase our attachment to thoughts. To explain how to deal with this, the great meditators of the past used the example of a pig that has gotten into a flower garden and wants to eat all the flowers. The person in charge of the garden should be there with a stick, and as soon as the pig enters the garden, the person should rap the pig firmly on the snout. If the pig starts eating the flowers before it is hit on the snout, it will be many times more difficult to get rid of the pig. Similarly when thoughts arise in meditation, we have to cut the attachment to them at the very moment they appear. We need to sever it on the spot.

The fourth stage of resting the mind is called *placing closely*. When we meditate and develop some samadhi, we have the sense that our mind has become larger. When thoughts arise within this vast mind, we sense them as very subtle and small. It is as though something in that great space moved ever so slightly. Because our mind has become much larger, these thoughts might escape our notice. To tame the mind further, we actually constrict it by focusing on these small, moving things.

The fifth stage is called *taming* or *subduing*. When our meditation is going well, we feel joy, lightness, enthusiasm, and relaxation. We then think about the extraordinary qualities of meditation, realizing that these are very beneficial for us and for others. Thinking about the good qualities of meditation causes the mind to rest and stabilize further.

The sixth stage of resting the mind is called *pacifying*. We tamed the mind somewhat in the previous stage in response to the lightness we felt in meditation. Still there is some tendency for the mind to wander. The principal problem at this stage is that we are attached to those distractions and wanderings of the mind. When we recognize the faults and disadvantages of such distractions, they are naturally pacified.

The first six of the nine methods work mainly with the wildness of the mind. Even when mind has been brought into an undistracted state at the seventh stage of *thoroughly pacified*, there can be faults, which are mainly concerned with the obscurations of mind. When we are under the influence of these faults, our mind is not clear. At this stage we recognize the distractions and faults of the mind that occur, such as attachment or discouragement, and apply the appropriate antidote. To eliminate the obscurations, it helps to reflect on the good qualities of the Buddha, the good qualities of meditation, and so on.

The eighth way of resting the mind is *one-pointedness*. In the first seven stages we proceeded through the power of mindfulness and alertness. In the eighth stage exertion is required. With further exertion the mind becomes quite pure.

This brings us to the ninth stage, called *placing (the mind) evenly*. Because of what has been accomplished in the first eight stages, the mind simply rests evenly, naturally, and under its own power.

THE SIX POWERS

[48] The development of these nine stages of resting the mind are paralleled by the development of the six powers given in the *Stages of the Shravaka*.

The first power is *hearing*. Due to hearing the instructions of the guru we enter the first stage of placement. We hear the instructions and bring them to our practice, placing our mind on the object of observation.

The second power is *contemplating*. We contemplate the instructions, which brings us to the second stage of continual placement.

The third power is *mindfulness*, which is associated with the third and the fourth stages of bringing the mind to rest. Much of the power of mindfulness is that we do not forget what we have heard and contemplated during the practice of shamata. We notice if our effort to practice decreases and return the mind again to the practice of shamata. As mindfulness increases, it leads to the fourth stage of close placement.

The fourth power, *awareness*, is associated with the fifth and sixth stages of taming and pacifying the mind. Through the power of awareness we are able to understand the good qualities of meditative stabilization and the faults of our mind being distracted.

The fifth power is *effort*, or *exertion*. This is associated with the seventh and eighth stages of thoroughly pacifying the mind and making the mind one-pointed. Through effort we are able to dispel the faults of heaviness and obscuration of mind. With the mind free of these thoughts, we pass to the ninth stage, a state of equipoise associated with the sixth power, the power of *familiarity*.

THE FOUR MENTAL APPLICATIONS

[49] The development of the nine stages of the mind coming to rest is also paralleled by the four mental applications or engagements. The first application, called *forcibly engaging*, is related to the first two stages in which we have to force our mind on an object of observation.

The second mental application, called *interrupted engaging*, is related to the third, fourth, fifth, sixth, and seventh levels of the mind coming to rest. At these stages our practice is still interrupted by thoughts and we have to continually bring the mind back.

The third application, called *uninterrupted engaging*, is related to the eighth stage of settling the mind. Mindfulness and alertness have come to maturity, so the mind does not wander but stays with the object uninterruptedly.

The fourth application, called *spontaneous engaging*, is related to the ninth stage of settling the mind. In this stage we do not need to apply any methods or antidotes. The mind simply rests in a state of equipoise.

The correspondence among the nine stages, the six powers, and the four engagements is summarized in the table on the next page.

Questions

QUESTION: Rinpoche, you said that if we feel pain or sadness we should look to see where the feeling came from. When I look into those places I find external causes, like a marriage that just ended or a doctor saying that there is a disease. Those causes don't disappear; they just seem to keep coming up, making it very difficult for me to meditate.

Correspondence of the Powers, Stages, and Engagements

SIX POWERS	NINE STAGES	FOUR APPLICATIONS
1. Hearing the teachings	1. Placement	1. Forcible mental engagement
2. Contemplating the teachings	2. Continual placement	
3. Memory of mindfulness	3. Resettling the mind	2. Interrupted mental engagement
	4. Intensely settled engagement	
4. Power of awareness	5. Taming the mind	
	6. Pacifying the mind	
5. Power of exertion	7. Thoroughly pacifying the mind	3. Uninterrupted mental engagement
	8. One-pointed mind	
6. Power of familiarity	9. Resting in equanimity	4. Spontaneous mental engagement

RINPOCHE: There is a distinction between the conditions of the relative world and the mahamudra practice of looking directly into the object itself. As you say, there are various things we experience in our mind and body that arise in dependence upon external conditions. There is a connection between these external events and our inner experience, but that connection is not what we are talking about here. What we are talking about is the painful feeling itself. We try to look right into that pain and ask where it came from. Where did the pain start? Where is it now? What is it?

We ask the same questions with an illness. Of course, there are various situations and causes for illness, but what we are talking about is the actual feeling of pain. If I pinch my hand hard, it hurts. What is that pain? Where is that feeling and where does it come from? We are looking right at it, not trying to trace its interdependent origination. We are trying to look at the feeling itself, straight in the face. It is not something that exists inherently, so where does it come from? What is the actual nature of the pain?

QUESTION: Rinpoche, could you give some examples of pervasive objects of meditation?
RINPOCHE: This refers principally to meditating without having any particular point of reference or support, such as a visualization of a buddha. Meditation with visualization causes the mind to become narrowed. When the mind does not have a particular basis in meditation it becomes extremely relaxed and vast. This meditation is pervasive in the sense that nothing is excluded.

QUESTION: In the fourth stage of placing closely, where there is a lot of space, when small thoughts occur, do you just decide that you are not interested in them and so they just dissolve?
RINPOCHE: The little thoughts that arise at this point are talked about as the movement of thought from below. There is the sense that something small rises up from somewhere below one's self. These thoughts need to be stopped in order to bring the mind to the complete development of shamata. The way they are stopped is through focusing on them. It has nothing to do with the thoughts in particular; they simply serve as messages that we need to focus and concentrate more upon the object of meditation.

QUESTION: Rinpoche said that yidam practice in the Vajrayana is superior to the practice of focusing on the breath because our mind doesn't wander in yidam practice. My mind wanders in visualizations, so how am I to understand this?
RINPOCHE: Meditating upon the breath or upon some visualized object

is a way of developing one-pointedness of mind. While it is a very effective way to proceed, it is somewhat boring. In contrast when you meditate upon the deity, it is very interesting. There are many things to look at, such as the face, the hands, the ornaments, the clothing, and held objects, so there is always a sense of something fresh and new going on. In that way, it enhances the stability.

THE SHARED TRADITION OF VIPASHYANA MEDITATION

Types of Vipashyana Meditation

[51] There are three types of vipashyana: worldly vipashyana, Hinayana vipashyana, and Mahayana vipashyana. Vipashyana is made up of the Sanskrit syllables *pashyana*, which means "see," and *vi*, which means "intensely." When *vi* was translated into Tibetan as *lhag*, it carried the sense of "beyond" or "surpassing." Thus the Tibetan word for vipashyana, *lhagtong*, means "insight that is not seen by ordinary persons." The vipashana practioner passes beyond what ordinary people see.

In the first type of vipashyana, *worldly vipashyana*, we cultivate the four levels of concentration of the form realms and the four levels of absorption of the formless realms. We achieve the special insight that the lower levels are relatively coarse and agitated compared to the higher levels, which are less coarse and more peaceful.

Hinayana vipashyana surpasses worldly vipashyana. By meditating on the four noble truths—the truths of suffering, of the origin of suffering, of the cessation of suffering, and of the path to liberation—we develop understanding of egolessness. We see that conceptual consciousness, or "I," does not exist. This is called "seeing the selflessness of persons."

Mahayana vipashyana involves meditation on the two truths: conventional truth and ultimate truth. In addition to seeing the nonexistence of self in persons, we realize the nonexistence of a self in all phenomena. Through reasoning and analysis, we come to understand that phenomena lack inherent existence; like illusions or dreams, they have the nature of emptiness.

The study and understanding that we acquire through these three forms of vipashyana will greatly facilitate our practice of mahamudra.

Vipashyana of the Sutra Path

In the practice common with the sutra path we use reasoning to examine and analyze phenomena. We recognize that all phenomena lack any true existence and that all appearances are interdependently related and arise without any inherent nature. They are empty yet apparent, apparent yet empty. We understand this through inferential reasoning and develop certainty by meditating on what we have understood. Through a process of gradual familiarization we develop direct realization, that is to say, we see the true nature of phenomena, or dharmata, in a direct manner. The realization at this point is stable and firm; however, getting to this point takes a very long time.

On the inferential path we use knowledge (Skt. *prajna*) rather than wisdom (Skt. *jnana*) as the path. We develop certainty about emptiness over a long period of time. The sutras speak of practice that goes on for three countless eons, during which time we accumulate vast stores of merit, purify all ill deeds and obscurations, and listen to the teachings of the Dharma again and again. Gradually, we come to realization.

Vipashyana of the Mahamudra Path

In the path of mahamudra we proceed using the instructions concerning the nature of mind that our guru gives us. This is called "taking direct perception, or direct experience, as the path." With the blessings of the guru, the nature of mind is pointed out. We are introduced to it and see it directly. This is a rapid path. In the tradition of the Vajrayana, particularly that of mahamudra, we speak about achieving the state of realization in one lifetime and with one body.

When we talk about realization of mind as it is, there is no difference between the sutra or mahamudra path. In either case it is dharmata, or reality as it is, that is realized. In both cases it is realization of the mind itself. The only difference is in the speed of this realization.

Vipashyana in Different Buddhist Schools

[53] The Buddha gave teachings in three stages called the "turnings of the wheel of Dharma." In the first turning, the Buddha taught the four noble truths—the truth of suffering, the truth of the origin of suffering, the truth of the cessation of suffering, and the truth of the path—for the sake of arousing confidence and aspiration in new practitioners.

In the second, or intermediate, turning of the wheel of Dharma, the Buddha gave careful and full explanations of transcendent knowledge (Skt. *prajnaparamita*). These teachings include the explanations of the emptiness of persons and the emptiness of phenomena.

In the final turning of the wheel of Dharma, the Buddha taught the definitive meaning. While the intermediate and final turnings are largely identical in meaning, there is a difference in the manner of instruction and the way in which reality, dharmata, is described. In the intermediate turning, the Buddha emphasized emptiness, or shunyata; in the final turning, he taught that wisdom pervades this emptiness, and in this way he taught about buddha essence or buddha nature.

Different traditions of commentary arose that clarified various aspects of the Buddha's teachings. Asanga was the principal exponent of and commentator on the final turning of the wheel of Dharma, and Nagarjuna was the principal person to clarify and expound on the intermediate turning of the wheel of Dharma. Asanga founded the Mind Only

(*Chittamatra*) school, and Nagarjuna founded the Middle Way (*Madhyamaka*) school. The Madhyamaka school later divided into the *Rangtong* ("empty of self") tradition and the *Zhentong* ("empty of other") tradition. All of these teachings agree that emptiness is the nature of all phenomena and that all sentient beings possess buddha essence.

All Phenomena Are Mind

How do we practice the teaching that all phenomena are nothing more than mind? According to this teaching, objects that appear to be external phenomena are nothing more than appearances to our mind; they do not truly exist.

Through logical arguments, Nagarjuna demonstrated that phenomena are neither single nor multiple. For instance when we think "my body," we believe that we are referring to a single thing that exists. In fact "my body" refers to my head, my right hand, my left hand, my right leg, my left leg, and so forth. There is no body that is separate from those parts. Nor are any of these parts "my body." Rather my head is my head, my hand is my hand, and so on. This so-called "body" doesn't exist.

The more finely we analyze, the more substances we find. Suppose we consider "my head." My head is composed of my eyes, my ears, my nose, my tongue, my teeth, and so on. "My head" is just a designation for the collection of these many different parts. We can continue this analysis to ever more subtle levels until we finally reach the smallest of particles. Yet, even the smallest particle, such as an atom, has an eastern direction, a southern direction, a western direction, and a northern direction. It is a collection of these different directions. Therefore we can never locate the true nature of external phenomena.

What about internal phenomena, or mind? There are two methods of reasoning that demonstrate that appearances are merely mind. The first is called *the certainty of simultaneous observation*. When a glass full of water appears to my mind, the glass that appears and the eye consciousness perceiving that appearance are always together. There is no such thing as a glass that is not appearing to a consciousness or a consciousness observing something when there isn't anything there to observe. Object and subject happen simultaneously.

The second reasoning is called *luminous and knowing*, which means that the only way to demonstrate that anything exists is to show that it has appeared to someone's consciousness. Except for objects that are perceived in my eye, ear, nose, tongue, or body consciousness, or in somebody else's consciousness, there aren't any phenomena whose existence can be proved. Something must be the object of some consciousness for it to exist. These two logical arguments show that all phenomena are mind.

Nagarjuna also gave reasonings to explain how conventional phenomena, or appearances, exist. Even though phenomena lack existence on the ultimate level, on the relative level there are conventional appearances because of interdependent origination. For instance, the body is no more than a collection of parts, yet it appears in the mind. Similarly, even though the head is nothing more than a collection of parts, nevertheless there is the appearance of a head. The Buddha used the example of a chariot to demonstrate the reasoning of being one or many. If we analyze a chariot, we find it has two wheels, an axle, and a carriage. We can analyze each of these parts and ask if it is the chariot. For example, is one wheel the chariot? No, it is a wheel. Is this other wheel the chariot? No, it is the other wheel. Is the axle the chariot? No, it is the axle. Is the carriage the chariot? No, the carriage is that part in which a person rides. We can then ask if there is something separate from these pieces that is the chariot? The answer is no, because the chariot is made up of these pieces. A similar argument can be made about our body and mind. There is no self separate from our body and mind, nor are the various components of our body and mind the self. This is because body and mind are multiple. Are all these collective parts of body and mind me? No. Is there something separate from them that is me? Again, the answer is no. And so the Buddha taught the inherent nonexistence of self.

The Buddha also taught that there were lifetimes prior to the present birth and there will be lifetimes subsequent to our present lifetime. It may seem that these two teachings are contradictory. After all, if there is no self how could there have been former or future lifetimes? If there is no self to accumulate actions and experience the fruition of these actions, how could rebirth happen? Reincarnation, however, that takes place merely in terms of the continuum of the mind. One might argue that the continuum of mind is the self, but there is a difference. The continuum of the mind has the nature of cessation, then birth, then cessation, then birth, and so on. Something comes to life and then it ceases, then something else is born and then it ceases. Consider, for instance, the mind of a young child, the mind of an adolescent, and the mind of an aged person. These three stages of a person's life are connected by the continuum of mind, but at each stage, the mind is not similar. For instance, the games that fascinate and delight a young child are not very interesting to an adult, and the work that is interesting to an adult is not anything that a child enjoys. So in their character, the mind of a child and the mind of an old person are extremely different. Unlike an unchanging self, the mind of a child and an adult are the same as a mere continuum, but that is all.

The Story of Asanga and Vasubandhu
Asanga, who clarified the third turning of the wheel of Dharma, established the Mind Only school. This the story of Asanga. In the fourth century C.E., a great number of Buddhist treatises, many Abhidharma texts in particular, were destroyed in a fire in the library at the famous monastic university of Nalanda. A nun named Tsawai Tsultrim, who was an emanation of a bodhisattva, felt very strongly that the teachings of the

Abhidharma should be restored and strengthened so that they would not disappear. As she did not feel able to do this work herself, she gave up her vows as a nun and gave birth to two sons, Asanga and Vasubandhu. It was the tradition at that time for the sons to follow in the occupation of their father. When Tsawai Tsultrim's sons asked her what work their father did so that they could follow in his occupation, she told them, "I did not bring you into this world for that purpose. You must exert yourselves to sustain and expand the teachings of the Abhidharma."

Asanga and Vasubandhu were able to greatly benefit the Hinayana and Mahayana Abhidharma teachings. Asanga practiced for twelve years seeking to meet Maitreya, who was in the sambhogakaya realm of Tushita. After twelve years Asanga met Maitreya face to face and accompanied him to the Tushita realm, where he received what are known as the five treatises of Maitreya. Asanga then composed his own commentaries on these treatises. Vasubandhu became a student of a very learned Kashmiri teacher named Zangpo and received the Hinayana Abhidharma teaching from him. Vasubandhu composed what are known as the twenty sets of doctrines of Maitreya, which demonstrate that phenomena are nothing more than appearances of mind and that the nature of phenomena is emptiness.

The traditions of Nagarjuna's Middle Way and Asanga's Mind Only schools passed to Tibet, where the Rangtong and Zhentong schools allowed students to listen to expositions of the Dharma and think about them very carefully. Through study students developed true skill and sharpness of knowledge about the Middle Way and the Prajnaparamita. This brought them great confidence that indeed emptiness is the nature of phenomena and that wisdom is the nature of emptiness. By combining the study of emptiness and of buddha nature with the practice of bringing direct experience onto the path through mahamudra and dzogchen meditation, they were able to proceed in an effective, steady, and unerring manner, and achieve the fruition of great spiritual accomplishment.

General Meditation on Selflessness of Persons

[54] The sutras speak about the selflessness of persons and the selflessness of phenomena. We will first discuss the selflessness of persons.

We all have disturbing emotions, which need to be eliminated. If we simply think, "I am no longer going to give rise to disturbing emotions," the disturbing emotions continue to arise. This is because we believe in and hold onto a self, which is the basis of these disturbing emotions. For instance, when someone harms us and we think they harmed "me," hatred will arise. Desire arises by thinking "*I* need that." Jealousy arises because we think that some condition or honor should not be "theirs" but "mine." Pride arises because of the thought that "I" am better than another person. Ignorance is a very cloudy state of mind, but basically it is thinking "I" and not seeing things as they truly are, which in turn gives rise to the other disturbing emotions.

[56] Whenever we think "me" or "mine" there is some object of reference. Sometimes "I" refers to the body and sometimes it refers to the mind. We take that self to be real, to be something that actually exists. But, as we have seen, there is no such thing as a self. Instead there are merely the five aggregates of form, feeling, perception, compositional factors, and consciousness that are gathered together. If we understand that completely, we realize there is no self. When we realize the nonexistence of a self, the disturbing emotions, which depend upon that notion of self, are destroyed. Therefore, we must meditate on the selflessness of the person.

There are two aspects to the way we conceive of the self. One is to think "I" and the other is to think "mine," or that which belongs to "me." While thinking "I" is the principal aspect, thinking "mine" is somewhat easier to understand. We might think of something very small, such as a bowl or an article of clothing, as being "mine." Or we might think of something larger, such as a house, a friend, or even a country as being "mine." We might think that everything from California to New York is "my" country, even though it obviously is not.

This conception of "mine" leads to a lot of pain. For instance, suppose we are in a restaurant and, across the way, a waiter drops a glass, which falls to the ground and breaks. We might think, "Too bad, somebody broke a glass." But if our own glass falls to the ground and breaks and all the water spills out, it is be a different matter because that glass of water is "mine." It can be very upsetting. Yet there is nothing in a glass—not its color, shape, or any inherent properties—that makes it mine. It is just a glass. Similarly, there is nothing about the water in the glass that makes it my water. It is just water. Nevertheless we become confused and feel a great deal of pain when "my" glass breaks. That feeling of unhappiness comes from thinking "mine."

Various objects might serve as a basis for this notion of "mine." It might be our body—we might think of everything from the top of our head down to the soles of our feet as being "my" body. We might identify with our mind, thinking that mind is "me" and the body is "mine." Or, it might be the other way around—we might think the body is "me" and the mind is "mine." We might locate ourselves somewhere in the upper part of our body and regard our feet as "my" feet. We might regard our head as "mine" and the rest of our body as "me." Or we might regard our skin as "my" skin, so that "I" am inside "my" skin.

This continual shifting of self shows that there is no such a thing as "me" or "mine." Rather, "me" is many things gathered together. Understanding this and gaining real confidence in this understanding leads us to the nonconceptual, direct realization of selflessness.

When we get a sense of the nonexistence of the self, we might feel afraid. However, there is no need for fear. If the self were to exist, we could be harmed, but since the self does not exist, there is no "I" to be harmed. With the complete realization that the self does not exist comes great courage, and fear simply disappears.

General Meditation on the Selflessness of Phenomena

[64] The second kind of nonself is the selflessness of everything else, including external things such as trees, rocks, and mountains and internal things like our thoughts and feelings. This selflessness of phenomena is also called the nonself of dharmas. *Dharma* has many meanings, but in this particular context it means all appearances of the world. We usually believe that phenomena are solid and permanent, with some essential nature of their own, but the Buddha taught that phenomena are empty of inherent existence, that is, they do not have a real, independent nature.

To realize that all dharmas are emptiness, we must carefully follow a path of reasoning and analysis. In the sutras, the Buddha gave logical arguments that enable us to realize that all dharmas are emptiness. These arguments were then elaborated on and explained clearly and fully in treatises by great masters such as Nagarjuna. Some of these arguments are simple to follow and will be presented below.

The Interdependence of Phenomena

One of the arguments for emptiness is made on the basis of interdependence. By showing that one thing arises in dependence upon something else, which arises in dependence upon something else, and so on, we can see that things do not have solid reality of their own. Because things are dependently originated, they cannot be inherently existent. Nevertheless, the eye consciousness sees visual forms, the ear consciousness hears sounds, and so on. How, we may wonder, can these these things be empty? Doesn't saying they are empty mean that they don't really exist?

Let us consider a simple example. If we see a two-inch stick of incense next to a four-inch stick of incense, we say that the two-inch stick is the short one and the four-inch stick is the long one. If we ask one hundred people which stick is the short one and which is the long one, they would all agree with us. Suppose we then bring out a six-inch stick of incense, put it next to the four-inch stick, and remove the two-inch stick. The stick that was previously the long one would now be the short one, and the new stick would be the long one. Everyone who looked at it would agree that the four-inch stick is now the short one and the six-inch stick is the long one. This illustrates that objects don't have an inherent "shortness" or "longness." Rather, this quality is dependent upon other conditions. That is the way it is with all things—whatever nature they appear to have actually depends upon other things.

And so it is with such qualities as beautiful and ugly, good and bad, big and small, and so on. Each of the qualities is inseparable from emptiness. A piece of incense appears to be long in one moment and short in another. At the same moment that it is short, it is long. Short and long coexist. At the same time that a piece of incense appears long, it is empty of being long. This indicates the way in which all things are empty yet apparent, apparent yet empty. Emptiness and appearance exist together.

The Argument of Single and Multiple

We might think that, while the argument of interdependence applies to relative categories such as long and short, there are some things that are not comparisons, such as the substance of the incense stick itself. Consider the example of a hand. If I hold out my hand, it does the work of a hand. If I put another object next to it, it still appears as a hand. We can see it with our eyes as a solid, single object. If we examine it closely, however, we can discern that it is designated as a hand only through the gathering together of many different things, as we saw with the Buddha's example of the chariot above. We can ask, is the thumb the hand? No, it is the thumb. Is the index finger the hand? No, it is the index finger. It is the same with the third, fourth, and fifth fingers. Is the palm the hand? No, it is the palm of the hand. Is the skin the hand? No, it is the skin. If we look for something that is the hand, we don't find it. Yet the hand appears and functions.

We might think, "Okay, the hand doesn't exist, but what about an individual finger?" We then carry out the same analysis on a finger. What is the finger? Is the first joint a finger? Is the second joint a finger? What about the third? The answer is always "no." There is really no finger there; rather, there are different pieces that are gathered together. What is seen as a finger is the interdependence of these pieces.

It is the same with everything we see and experience. All things are composite. They do not exist as substantial selves. We can apply this reasoning to any part of our body and to all external phenomena. The Tibetan word for composite is *duje,* which means, "made of many things gathered together." Since all phenomena are composites, they are apparent yet empty, empty yet apparent.

[64] Mental consciousness is also a composite. It consists of the eye consciousness, the ear consciousness, the nose consciousness, the tongue consciousness, or the body sensation consciousness. It has many different moments: past, present, and future. It is newly born in every moment. There is no moment from the past that exists now and no moment now that will exist in the future.

Emptiness is not void like space—space cannot be made into anything, does not change, and cannot give rise to good qualities. While the dharmadhatu is not a concrete thing, it appears as everything through the interdependent relationship of phenomena. Through interdependent relationship all relative phenomena appear. This emptiness that we call dharmadhatu is the possibility for anything to appear. Yet the thing that appears does not exist. The emptiness is not separate from the appearance. The appearance is emptiness.

Not realizing the emptiness of appearance, we become confused and we become attached to objects. The root of that attachment is that we have not realized emptiness. To overcome our attachment we meditate upon the emptiness of those objects and realize that the nature of all phenomena is dharmadhatu—it is nothing in itself yet it appears as everything. Understanding this and resting our mind evenly there is called the view of mahamudra.

Even though we are practicing mahamudra meditation, we need to understand the view that is common to the sutra and mantra traditions. When we meditate, we have some experiences that we perceive as good and other experiences that we fear may lead us astray. By understanding the view that is common to the sutra and mantra traditions, we can evaluate these experiences appropriately. Proper analysis allows us to develop certainty in our understanding of the way things exist. Such inferential realization is extremely helpful and beneficial. We can then determine if our experience is similar to what is taught in the sutras and commentaries (Skt. *shastras*). If it is not, we can see that we have done something different and haven't realized the view of emptiness. If it is, we can say that our experience is just like that of the Buddha.

Of course it is possible that listening to the teachings can obstruct our meditation practice. Indeed, if we have heard a lot about emptiness or luminosity, it is possible that, when we sit down to meditate, we may fabricate some sort of emptiness or luminosity with our mind that will obstruct the reality that we want to realize. Rather we must rest evenly in whatever experience we have, and place our confidence in that experience. Our meditation upon emptiness or luminosity must not be conceptual because the result will merely be fabricated.

It is not a matter of taking something that is not empty and making it empty, or taking something that has no luminosity and making it into luminosity. This is the nature of whatever appears to the mind. Maitreya said there is nothing to be cleared away and nothing to be constructed.

In other words, we do not have to manufacture good qualities; rather, we realize that things are authentic, genuine, and correct just as they are. We see the genuine as the genuine and then choose liberation.

Questions

QUESTION: Rinpoche, why is the selflessness of persons always taught before the selflessness of dharmas? It seems to me that it is easier to experience interdependent origination than to understand how the skandhas work.

RINPOCHE: When the Buddha taught, there were a great many other traditions and teachers who spoke about emptiness. But these teachers did not understand the nonexistence of the self. If we do not understand the emptiness of the person, we cannot understand the emptiness of dharmas properly. For that reason the Buddha taught about impermanence, emptiness of persons, and so forth. Once we understand that a person lacks a self, we can proceed to understand the nonexistence of all other dharmas.

From another point of view, the main thing to be abandoned is the disturbing emotions. To abandon the disturbing emotions, we must understand the nonexistence of the self. If we can realize this, then the disturbing emotions will gradually disappear. When we have cleared away the disturbing emotions, we can go further and eliminate the obscurations of knowledge, which is done by understanding the emptiness of all phenomena.

QUESTION: Could you briefly explain how it is that earth, water, fire, and air are the nature of emptiness?

RINPOCHE: Earth, water, fire, and air are explained by Vasubandhu in *Treasury of the Abhidharma*. The way that the four elements are described in the Abhidharma and the way they are generally understood are not the same. In the Abhidharma, earth is that which is hard and has the quality of solidity, water is that which is fluid and has the quality of moistening, air or wind has the quality of motion, and fire has the quality of ripening. It is not quite the same as when we say the earth is this solid thing we live on, water is like a body of water, fire burns, and wind blows things back and forth.

For example, the earth appears in this world as very solid and large, yet it is a composite of many very small particles. Whatever we look at is composed of many, many, many particles—like many grains of sand. Earth exists as all these individual separate things, not as one thing. From this point of view the earth is not truly existent. It is something that is not free from being either single or multiple; it is an interdependent relationship. In a similar way we can analyze anything big or small and, with reasoning, demonstrate that it is empty.

QUESTION: I am confused by the example of the hand. My understanding is that if you really break it down, you end up with the elements of earth, air, fire, and water.

RINPOCHE: Yes, that is true. If we analyze it thoroughly we come down to earth, water, fire, and air. When we analyze the hand, it comes down to that which is solid, that which is moistened, that which is ripening, and that which is moving. The parts of the hand that are hard and obstructing are the earth element of the hand, and there are a good many of these little particles. The water element of the hand causes its cohesion. During the life of a person, the hand changes greatly from childhood to youth to maturity to old age. What causes it to change is the fire element. Then you can move your hand around and that is the air or wind element. *Treasury of the Abhidharma* talks about a mass of eight tiny particles. It is said that in the smallest element an atom is composed of eight particles. These eight particles are earth, water, fire, wind, visible form, smell, taste, and tangibility, which are the qualities and properties of the smallest physical thing, which we could call an atom. Without those we don't have anything at all.

QUESTION: I think that the word *emptiness* causes a lot of problems for Westerners. When I hear emptiness, it means nothing. Does not "empty of intrinsic nature" mean beyond the duality of subject and object?
RINPOCHE: Yes. The definition of the word doesn't matter a lot. The point is to overcome our strong fixation on conceptualization. When it is said that things are empty, it means that things do not exist in the way they seem to exist. It is our fixation on them that must be overturned. As I said before, emptiness does not mean a blank emptiness or space. It is not a dead emptiness. Emptiness is the possibility for everything to appear. It is the possibility for anything whatsoever to happen.

In the impure state of sentient beings, what is meant by emptiness is that dharmata—the reality that is beyond the confusion of samsara—is the nature of samsara and nirvana. In the pure state of enlightened beings, emptiness means the wisdom, or *jnana,* of the buddhas. In the impure state we speak about the inseparability of appearance and emptiness. In the pure state we speak of the five wisdoms of a buddha, which are the inseparability of luminosity and emptiness. These wisdoms are entirely ungraspable, yet they appear. The nature of their appearance is nondual, yet they appear.

The union of appearance and emptiness seems contradictory in that when there is appearance we do not see dharmata. We might think that dharmata cancels appearance but, in fact, these two are not contradictory to one another. Appearance and dharmata coexist and are inseparable.

Likewise, when we speak about luminosity and emptiness, we say these two coexist, are simultaneous, and do not contradict each other.

QUESTION: I don't understand why we would, for example, ask to be born in the buddha pure realm of Dewachen in the Chenrezig practice if everything is actually empty.

RINPOCHE: You need to make a distinction between the conventional truth, or things as they appear, and ultimate truth, or things as they are. Ultimately there is no self, but relatively we do indeed perceive the self as a solid object. The five aggregates that make up our continuum of body and mind do appear. In this context there are former lifetimes and later lifetimes, with continuity from one to another. All this appears even if ultimately it does not exist.

It is helpful to think of the example of a dream. Suppose you are asleep and dreaming of a tiger, and you become afraid that the tiger is about to bite you. Now suppose someone with clairvoyant powers sees that you were dreaming of a tiger and that you were afraid. This person feels compassion, wakes you up, and says, "Don't be afraid, the tiger is just a dream." It is just like this with the things we experience in former and later lifetimes. Birth and death, the skandhas, and karma are happening to us, and that is the way things appear. If none of these appearances were going on, it wouldn't be necessary to practice the path. But since they are, it is necessary to get help. Because we have not realized the ultimate nature of phenomena, these appearances arise.

QUESTION: Could Rinpoche describe the difference between the first and second logical arguments establishing all appearances as mind? Also isn't the first argument, the certainty of simultaneous observation, like the question, "If a tree falls in the forest and there is no one around to hear it does it make a sound?"

RINPOCHE: Originally, the Buddha gave these two logical arguments in a sutra. Later Dharmakirti set forth the arguments in the treatises on valid cognition. The logical argument called the *luminous and knowing* states that all sorts of appearances arise but never in the absence of mind; that is to say, appearances appear only in the perspective of mind. If the qualities of luminosity and awareness aren't present, there are no appearances. That's the main point. The other reasoning elaborates on the first by pointing out that, within the arising of appearances in an observing consciousness, consciousness and appearance always happen simultaneously. It is a meeting of consciousness and appearance. If there is no mind there, there is nothing to meet. So the two always happen simultaneously.

This leads us to the question: If a tree falls and nobody hears it, was there any sound? The argument just presented is about mind only and is made in the context of alaya consciousness. *Alaya consciousness* has sometimes been translated as "universal consciousness," or compared to Jung's collective unconsciousness, but those interpretations are wrong. The alaya consciousness is something that exists within the continuum of each person; it is like the repository for latencies, or traces (Tib. *bagchag*), of whatever experiences we have had, rather than a universal consciousness. I call the alaya consciousness the "mind-basis-of-all" (Tib. *kunzhi namshe*), because it is a mental entity of consciousness as well as the basis of all the other consciousnesses. The alaya consciousness gives rise to the six consciousnesses—the eye, ear, nose, tongue, body, and mind consciousnesses. Various phenomena then appear to these consciousnesses. These appearances arise from that same predispositions within our own alaya consciousness.

Regarding trees falling in the forest, there has to be some latency in our own mind to enable such an event to take place. Yet at that time, since there is no one there, no sound is perceived by anybody's ear consciousness. Nevertheless, there must be predispositions within the alaya consciousness of various people for that sound to occur, even if at the time there is no manifestation of sound.

ELIMINATING DOUBTS CONCERNING VIPASHYANA MEDITATION

Analytical and Placement Meditation

[70] Vipashyana can be viewed in terms of four aspects: view, meditation, action, and fruition. View serves as the foundation, or ground. We arrive at the view by listening to the teachings and reflecting upon what we have heard. In so doing, we begin to understand what we should meditate upon. However, the view alone is not sufficient. It needs to be joined by action, so that our understanding and experience increase. Together, view, meditation, and action bring us to the fruition of vipashyana. The question now is, How do we sustain the view in meditation?

The siddhas have described the practice of sustaining the view in meditation in many different ways. Essentially, the view in meditation is a discussion of the merits of analytical meditation (Tib. *chegom*) and placement meditation (Tib. *joggom*). Analytical meditation is the meditation of the *pandita*, or scholar. In analytical meditation we investigate and analyze. Placement meditation is the meditation of the *kusali*, or simple person. In placement meditation we allow our mind to rest in equanimity without doing any investigation or analysis.

Analytical Methods of Vipashyana

[72] Some people say that shamata consists of placement meditation only, and that the practice of analytical meditation harms the practice of shamata. They also say that vipashyana consists of analytical meditation only, and that there is no practice of placing and resting the mind in it. However, Tashi Namgyal says that this view is incorrect and indicates a lack of experience in meditation.[7]

In general, shamata is meditation in which the mind is placed somewhere and rests there. But when we practice shamata, we also investigate to see how the meditation is going, while being mindful of the shamata itself. "Is it going well? Is it not going well? Which antidote needs to be applied?" This checking of our mind as we are practicing is analysis.

Likewise if vipashyana were only analytical meditation it would not be authentic. If we only analyzed and never placed the mind and allowed it to rest in what we have understood, vipashyana would not lead us to abandon the kleshas, and we would not develop a definite and certain understanding. So there is placement meditation within vipashyana.

We can see that both shamata and vipashyana involve analytical and placement meditation. Having said that, however, it is fair to say that shamata is mainly a matter of placing the mind and doing only limited analysis, while vipashyana is mainly a matter of analyzing and less of placing the mind.

The Practice of Analytical and Placement Meditation

[75] According to one view, we should listen to or study many explanations of the scriptures and then analyze them carefully with reasoning to develop a clear and definite understanding of emptiness and the interdependent relationship of phenomena. Having developed such understanding, we should then place our mind in an even meditative state, without analysis. According to this view, it is best to alternate analysis

with resting the mind so that our vipashyana does not degenerate into shamata.

Again, Tashi Namgyal says this view is not correct. He states that the analysis of valid cognition (Skt. *pramana*) is not the same as seeing phenomena directly. What appears to our mind has been created by our mind and is not authentic meditation. Instead, Tashi Namgyal says, we should listen to the instructions, think about them, and analyze what we have heard in the same way that we show a racetrack to a horse. If we want a horse to follow a certain course, we first show the track to the horse so that it knows where to go once the actual race begins. Likewise, we listen to and reflect upon the teachings so that we know the way to go correctly and are able to develop the prajna to achieve certainty and confidence. The prajna that arises from hearing and contemplating the teachings, however, is not sufficient. We also need the prajna that arises from meditating. We meditate on the dharmata that exists with things themselves.

Lama Gotsangpa explained that while, ultimately, analytical meditation and placement meditation have the same destination, placement meditation proceeds more quickly. Therefore, the great gurus of the lineage, such as Naropa and Maitripa, who were extremely learned, depended mainly on the quintessential instructions and meditated by settling the mind in equipoise. Likewise, we need to listen to and think about the various teachings on the true nature of phenomena, but when it comes to practice, we need to depend upon only the most quintessential instructions of the siddhas and meditate in that manner.

There are three incorrect views that are identified and refuted in *Moonlight of Mahamudra*. The first incorrect view is what was mentioned above—that when we practice shamata, we do not need to perform any analysis, and when we practice vipashyana, we do not need to place the mind in equipoise. In fact, in shamata we need to investigate and analyze our meditation to determine how to clear away the afflictions, distractions, and thoughts that arise. We need to employ the various methods for bringing the mind to a state of rest, and that involves analysis within our meditation. Similarly, in vipashyana, even though the emphasis is on the development of prajna, we must set the mind in a state of equipoise to do this.

The main problem for beginning meditators is wildness of mind. Just focusing on the shamata practice of calming the mind helps settle the mind's wildness. When our shamata practice is going well, we can then work with the obstacles of mind using investigation and analysis.

The second incorrect view is that we should alternate between shamata and vipashyana. According to this view, we first practice the methods for calming the mind and then analyze to develop certainty about the view. But if we do this, our shamata and our vipashyana will oppose each another. It is better to find the view and then to settle into equipoise within the view.

A third incorrect view, asserted by Sakya Pandita, is that the mahamudra meditation of Gampopa was basically the meditation taught by the Chinese master Hashang Mahayana.[8] Briefly, Hashang taught that the way to practice meditation is simply to abandon all notions of good and bad and not think about anything at all. The practice taught by Hashang, however, is not at all like the practice of mahamudra taught by Gampopa.

Meditation on Mind Itself

[77][9] When we speak about dharmata, or things as they really are, we are speaking about the absence of the confusion and mistaken appearances that ordinary people experience most of the time. When we talk about the mind itself (Tib. *semnyi*), or mind as it is, we are referring to the inseparability of luminosity and emptiness. If we just meditate without having identified dharmata, the meditation will make us more peaceful, gradually causing us to understand the view, but it will not cut the root of the disturbing emotions. We will not abandon what must be abandoned to reach

enlightenment. Therefore, we need to find out what dharmata is and rest our mind there. When we meditate on external phenomena, dharmata is covered and hidden. But when we meditate on mind itself, we are meditating on the naked form of emptiness. And that is what we mean when we talk about bringing direct perception to the path. It is meditation upon the mind itself.

Questions

QUESTION: Rinpoche, you said that when we attain the equanimity of mind, we see the world as a safe place. How do we combine the equanimity of mind with the need to have discrimination and avoid danger?
RINPOCHE: What you have described is certainly true of the relative world, the world of conventional truth, or *kundzob denpa,* which comes about through the interdependent relationship of one thing to another due to the latencies that have been established with our own mind. For instance, if you put your hand in a fire, the fire will indeed burn your hand. Thinking, "Oh, it is just emptiness," is not going to help very much. This is not because emptiness is not the nature of the fire or of your hand. It is because you have not realized that emptiness. Because you have not realized emptiness, the fire will burn your hand.

What I was really talking about were feelings that you experience in your mind, which don't have to depend upon what is going on in the outer world. For instance, having tremendous wealth does not guarantee that you will feel happy. And people who are poor are not necessarily miserable. There is no necessary correlation. If you are happy mentally, it doesn't matter whether you have or don't have a lot of things.

As you say, at this point the world is not entirely safe. This is because we have not realized the reality of this world; we have not realized dharmata. Not having realized the reality of phenomena, we have to deal with the relative world. We live in the relative world because we have not understood the mind as it is and we have not actualized the mind's deep nature. Because we have not achieved such siddhi and actualized such ultimate wisdom, we are not able to change things right away.

QUESTION: Could you explain the relationship between alternation of shamata and vipashyana, and wildness and heaviness of mind?
RINPOCHE: Dullness and wildness of mind are problems for the practice of shamata. They are also problems that we experience when we practice vipashyana. So if we are practicing shamata and heaviness of mind occurs, we should encourage ourselves by remembering that buddha nature exists, thinking of the good qualities of a buddha, and so forth. If wildness is the principal problem in our shamata practice, we should think about impermanence and the suffering of samsara, generating some discouragement about the things we are getting excited about. Realizing that samsara is entirely futile should pacify our wildness. Wildness could also come into our meditation when we are practicing vipashyana and we have actualized the true nature of mind. If wildness begins to afflict our meditation of vipashyana, we should look right into that wildness to see just what it is. If heaviness and obscurations come into our practice of vipashyana, we should look right into their nature in the same way.

QUESTION: I am a doctor. Many people come to me with a memory that is causing great pain. It might be a memory of something that happened a long time ago, such as neglect or abuse from a parent, relationship loss, or divorce. They go to the psychologist and say, "I have this memory and my whole life is not working because of it." They work for years on one memory and nothing is really gained. How can we help people who have a persistent memory that causes emotional pain that eventually becomes physical pain?
RINPOCHE: Yes, it does happen as you describe. Through the power of

various predispositions or latencies there is a lot of distress in our mind that becomes distress in our body. Having those predispositions leads to a situation of difficulty and anxiety.

What can one do? We talk about precious human birth, which is endowed with freedom from bad conditions and engendered with good conditions. It can be very helpful to think about the significance of having such an opportunity. We have the capacity to do almost anything, but we don't recognize this or remember that we have a precious human birth. Our heads begin to spin and we don't know that this is the actual situation. So we begin to think that there is this thing that we have to have, and if we don't have it, we become very discouraged. We do not notice the tremendous range of options, the great variety of paths, that are open to us. We can let our mind become vast and very spacious. Furthermore, the past is over and done. We can't do much about whatever has happened, whether it was helpful or unhelpful. So I don't think there is a whole lot of benefit in dwelling upon the past.

QUESTION: Could you explain interdependent origination further?
RINPOCHE: The argument of interdependent origination is the reasoning of the dependence of one thing upon some other thing. It shows that there is nothing that can set itself up without dependence on something else. For instance, when you are standing here, this is here and that is there. But if you were to go to the other side of the room, what is "here" would become "there." We can look at this from many points of view and apply it to many different situations. In the end what is demonstrated is that there is no such thing as here or there because they depend on each other. Interdependent origination is a reasoning that demonstrates emptiness.

The other logical argument establishes that appearances are just appearances of mind. For instance, yesterday you saw a patch of blue and you remember that. When you remember the blue, you don't just remember blue, you also remember the scene of blue, you remember the knower apprehending blue and the qualities associated with the experience of seeing the blue. This shows that whenever you remember something, you remember both what you saw and the seeing of it. It shows that these two are inextricably tied together, and that what appeared to be an appearance of something external to the perceiving consciousness was not actually external but was of the same entity as the perceiving consciousness.

Principally what is being demonstrated in the case of dependent arising is how one thing depends upon another for its identity. And in the case of this simultaneity, what is being taught is how the apprehended object and the apprehending subject occur only together. This demonstrates that what seem to be external appearances are really just appearances of the mind.

Part II

MAHAMUDRA MEDITATION

THE ORIGINS OF MAHAMUDRA

We have been discussing the stages of shamata and vipashyana that are common to the sutra and mantra path. Now we will discuss those practices specific to mahamudra, the uncommon practices.

The Definition of Mahamudra

[92] First of all, we need to have confidence in mahamudra, which arises from knowing the extraordinary and good qualities of mahamudra. These qualities are illustrated in the Sanskrit term itself: *maha* means "vast," "very large," and "pervading everything," and *mudra* means "seal," in the sense of the seal that a king places on a document so that nothing passes out of its sphere. Mahamudra then is the seal for all phenomena and the dharmata, the reality, of all things. There are no objects that pass beyond mahamudra or exist outside it because it is the reality of everything. Thus, mahamudra has the meaning of a great seal.

The literal translation of *maha* in Tibetan is *chenpo* and the translation of *mudra* is *gya*. When the Tibetan translators translated the term mahamudra, they added a third syllable, *chag*. This syllable is honorific, indicating that mahamudra is not an ordinary object but something worthy of respect. *Chag* is also the honorific word for "hand." We use the honorific word *chag* instead of the ordinary word *lagpa* when we speak about the hand of a guru or king who is able to benefit beings. For example, a guru sometimes bestows an empowerment by touching a person with his or her hand. Likewise, a lama bestows blessings with just the touch of his or her hand, and an accomplished person composes Buddhist treatises by hand to help purify the minds of ordinary people. People in positions of authority, such as kings, work with their hands to clear away obstacles. Thus, the word *chag* is used to indicate the transformation of something from an impure state to a pure state. *Chag* also indicates something that has capacity, potency, and ability. In the context of mahamudra, it indicates that through mahamudra we are able to discard all impurities, such as the disturbing emotions, so that our being becomes pure, and all good qualities increase and expand.

There are many different names for mahamudra. In the context of the Middle Way, or Madhyamaka, school it is called the ultimate, suchness, or unsurpassable wisdom. In the context of the Dzogchen school, it is called Kuntuzangpo in Tibetan, which means "all good," and Samantabhadra in Sanskrit. In the context of fruition it is called dharmakaya. These different names all mean the same thing.

Maitripa explained in the *Seven Yogas:* "What is mahamudra? It passes beyond the mind of ordinary people, it is luminous, it is without conceptuality, and it is like space."

Types of Mahamudra

[95] The nature of mahamudra is that it pervades everything: external things and mind, ourselves and others. At the same time it cannot be identified and labeled.

There are three kinds of mahamudra: ground mahamudra, path mahamudra, and fruition mahamudra. *Ground mahamudra* is the nature of all phenomena. It is there from the very beginning; it is there even when we have not realized it. From the point of view of experience, ground mahamudra is mind as it is. From the point of view that ground mahamudra pervades everything, it is reality, things as they are. Sometimes it is called the jewel of the mind, sometimes it is called *tathagatagarbha*, or buddha essence. It is the same whether we are suffering or doing well because mahamudra pervades all sentient beings in precisely the same way.

And yet, at the relative level we may temporarily be unable to realize ground mahamudra due to adverse circumstances or obstacles. To overcome these adverse circumstances and correct our confusion, we need to purify our understanding of mahamudra and accustom our minds to it. This is *path mahamudra*. The guru introduces us to this mahamudra; we recognize it, meditate upon it, and become familiar with it. In path mahamudra, our realization of mahamudra becomes clearer.

Path mahamudra leads us to *fruition mahamudra*. At this stage our realization of mahamudra is complete and continuous. We realize every facet of it brilliantly and lucidly.

In the *Uttaratantra*, Maitreya described three different situations. The first, called *impure*, refers to the state of sentient beings. This is ground mahamudra. The second, called *impure and pure*, refers to state of partial realization of mahamudra. This is path mahamudra. The third, called *extremely and thoroughly pure*, refers to the state of complete realization of mahamudra. This is fruition mahamudra.

The Importance of Mahamudra

[96] The problem of not understanding mahamudra is set forth for the purpose of arousing confidence in mahamudra.

In *Guide to the Bodhisattva's Way of Life*, Shantideva discussed the six perfections (Skt. *paramitas*): generosity, discipline, patience, exertion, stable concentration, and wisdom. He said that the subduer, by which he meant the Buddha, taught these for the sake of prajna. Prajna, in this context, is the wisdom that realizes things as they are. Shantideva said that although we might do many hundreds of thousands of other practices, such as recitation of mantras, all of them are simply methods for realizing mahamudra. These other practices are beneficial in terms of bringing us to the point of being able to realize mahamudra, but if we do not realize mahamudra, we will not achieve the final fruition. If we realize mahamudra, however, we will achieve that fruition.

In the *Mahamudra Subtle Drop Tantra*, the Buddha said that if we realize mahamudra we become Vajrasattva:

> He who does not understand mahamudra
> is not a realized one, however illuminated.
> He will not achieve supreme fulfillment
> without perfectly understanding
> the essence of mahamudra.

To achieve the final state, we must understand mahamudra. That is the great benefit of knowing mahamudra and the great fault of not understanding it.

The Origin of Mahamudra in the Sutras

[97] The Buddha described mahamudra in various sutras, sometimes calling it mahamudra and sometimes not. Whatever name the Buddha used, the meaning was the same: phenomena are naturally pure and sealed as primordially liberated. This is how mahamudra is described in the sutras.

The Origin of Mahamudra in the Tantras

There are four sets of tantras in the Vajrayana. The first three, called the lower tantras, are kriya tantra, charya tantra, and yoga tantra, or in English, the action tantra, performance tantra, and union tantra. The higher tantras are the anuttarayoga tantras, or unsurpassable yoga tantras, which are the main texts of the Vajrayana. Mahamudra is taught in all four sets of tantras. It is taught in every tantra in the unsurpassable yoga tantras, and in the lower tantras it is spoken of as the "hand seal"—just as you seal something closed with your hand, so too phenomena are sealed with their true nature, emptiness.

In addition, mahamudra is sometimes spoken of in terms of the four seals, or mudras. These are the samaya seal, the wisdom seal, the action seal, and the great seal, or, in Sanskrit, the samayamudra, the jnanamudra, the karmamudra, and the mahamudra (or dharmamudra).

The anuttarayoga tantras are divided into three subdivisions: father tantras, mother tantras, and nondual tantras. The mahamudra is taught in all of these subdivisions. In particular there is the extraordinary uncommon presentation given in the *Kalachakra Tantra*, which belongs to the nondual section of the highest yoga tantras. In the context of Kalachakra, mahamudra is spoken of as "the emptiness possessing the supreme of all aspects," indicating that it is the basis of all phenomena. It is also called "the supreme unchanging bliss," because upon realizing it, we pass beyond changeable samsara and arrive at unchanging bliss.

Mahamudra is also taught in the *Mahamudra Subtle Drop Tantra*, which is not among the four sets of tantra but is instead part of the spiritual songs *(doha)* literature.[10] In this particular context, *subtle drop* (Skt. *bindu*, Tib. *tigle*) means "without change."

So, mahamudra is taught in all the sets of tantras, especially in the fourth and highest set. It is elaborated particularly in the *Kalachakra Tantra* and the *Mahamudra Subtle Drop Tantra*.

Eliminating Mistaken Perceptions

[105] Some scholars have attempted to refute mahamudra. They say that mahamudra is mistaken because there are some who give instructions and practice the meditation of mahamudra without understanding what they

are doing. Indeed, there is a danger if mahamudra is practiced in an incorrect way. These criticisms, therefore, are of those who use the name mahamudra without understanding its meaning. For instance, Sakya Pandita said that meditating upon mahamudra would probably lead one to take rebirth as an animal or in the formless realm. He said this to encourage those who have an incorrect understanding to discard their misunderstanding. It is necessary to reply to that statement because there are some who, without recognizing its intent, will simply take it to mean that mahamudra is a useless meditation. We can see, however, that both the refutation and the reply to that refutation have a purpose.

The Sutras and Tantras in Mahamudra

[109] The text then discusses the way in which the profound meaning of all the sutras and tantras is included within mahamudra. For instance, the emptiness that is realized with transcendent knowledge, which is taught in the second turning of the wheel of Dharma, is included within mahamudra. The buddha essence that is taught in the third turning is also included within mahamudra, as are the quintessential instructions of the completion stage of the Vajrayana. If we understand mahamudra, we will see how all of these are included within it.

Gampopa said that there are three different paths with different practices, but these three paths have the same nature. These are taking inference as the path, taking blessings as the path, and taking direct experience as the path. Taking inference as the path refers to, for instance, the various reasonings set forth in the Madhyamaka that show that all things are neither single nor multiple. Taking blessings as the path refers to, for instance, meditation upon the body of a deity or the practices involving the subtle channels and subtle energies. Taking direct perception as the path is mahamudra. Mahamudra is pointed out to us, and we recognize it, become accustomed to it, and take direct experience as the path.

We can also classify the different paths into three groups: the paths that abandon the ground, paths that transform the ground, and paths that recognize the ground. The first path of abandoning the ground is the vehicle of transcendent action of the sutra vehicle, in which some things are abandoned and others are remedies for those things to be abandoned. The second path, transformation of the ground, refers to the practices of the Vajrayana in which we purify our body and mind by meditating on our body being a deity. Our body is thus transformed into the pure body of the deity, and our mind is transformed from discursiveness into wisdom. In the third path, recognizing the ground, is mahamudra. We know that we do not need to abandon or transform the ground; rather, we know it as it is. When we know the ground as it is, we recognize all appearances as the magical display of the mind. Thus, mahamudra is a matter of using direct perception as the path. This is also called the quick path.

The Good Qualities of Mahamudra Practitioners

Since the teaching of mahamudra is extraordinary, the lineage of transmission of this teaching must also be extraordinary and distinctive. The text describes the lineage of transmission by first explaining the way in which the Buddha came to India and turned the wheel of Dharma so that the Dharma flourished, and how both the Dharma and the teaching of mahamudra spread.

Distant Lineage of Mahamudra

[116] There are a number of stories recounted in the text about people in India who had very unusual experiences and high realization of the practice of mahamudra.

The Buddha taught mahamudra in the *Mahamudra Subtle Drop Tantra,* the *Glorious Unblemished Tantra,* and the *Thoroughly Abiding Tantra.* The Buddha gave the mahamudra teachings near the end of his life. After the Buddha passed away, the great bodhisattvas Manjughosha and Avalokiteshvara gave these teachings to Saraha.

When Buddha taught mahamudra, he said that in the future there would be great bodhisattvas who would practice and propagate this teaching. In particular, he named Saraha and Nagarjuna. It came to pass that the great bodhisattva Manjushri appeared as a bodhisattva named Ratnamati, and the great bodhisattva Avalokiteshvara appeared as a bodhisattva named Sukhanata. These two bodhisattvas gave the mahamudra teachings to Saraha, who achieved immediate liberation, becoming a siddha, or accomplished person. Saraha served as the source through which the mahamudra spread and flourished in India. He passed the mahamudra teachings to Nagarjuna who, prior to meeting with Saraha, was a pandita, or scholar. After meeting with Saraha, Nagarjuna became a great adept, actualized mahamudra, and lived as a siddha. Nagarjuna passed the lineage of quintessential oral instructions on the practice of mahamudra to Shavari. Shavari not only received the teachings directly from Saraha, but also met the same two bodhisattvas, who were emanations of Manjughosha and Avalokiteshvara respectively, in a visionary manner and received the mahamudra teachings directly from them.

Maitripa heard of Shavari and his tradition of oral instructions and, with profound faith, immediately went to southern India to meet with him. Maitripa underwent tremendous difficulties and hardships on his journey. Eventually he succeeded in meeting Shavari and received all the mahamudra instructions in their complete form. Maitripa then went to central India, where he disseminated these teachings to others. This transmission is known as the distant lineage of mahamudra.

The Close Lineage

[116] There is also a close lineage of mahamudra that begins with Tilopa, who received the teachings of mahamudra from Vajradhara.

> **The Distant Lineage of Mahamudra**
>
> BUDDHA SHAKYAMUNI
>
> Taught mahamudra teachings without using "mahamudra" terminology in a number of sutras, especially the *King of Meditation Sutra*.
>
> SARAHA
>
> Received the mahamudra teachings from Buddha's disciples, Avalokiteshvara and Manjughosha, who appeared as the bodhisattvas Ratnamati and Sukhanata.
>
> NAGARJUNA
>
> Received the mahamudra teachings from Saraha and achieved enlightenment.
>
> SHAVARI
>
> Received the teachings from Saraha and the two bodhisattvas, Ratnamati and Sukhanata.
>
> MAITRIPA
>
> Received the teachings on mahamudra from Shavari.
>
> MARPA
>
> Received mahamudra teachings from both Maitripa and Naropa and brought them to Tibet.

The Buddha has three bodies: the dharmakaya, the sambhogakaya, and the nirmanakaya. The Buddha Shakyamuni was a *nirmanakaya*, or emanation body, which is the body visible to ordinary beings. He is called a *supreme* emanation body because he gave the teaching to achieve enlightenment, turned the wheel of Dharma, demonstrated the way of passing into nirvana, and so forth. After his death that particular supreme emanation body no longer existed. However, his mind continued. The Buddha's mind is of the nature of wisdom, or the wisdom dharmakaya.

That wisdom knows the full variety and the nature of all phenomena and is endowed with positive qualities such as compassion. This wisdom dharmakaya did not pass into nirvana but remained, so that fortunate students are still able to meet with it. In that way, it is called the *vajra dharmakaya* in which "vajra" means unchangeable. This dharmakaya also appears in the form of the sambhogakaya. In the sambhogakaya, the Buddha appears like Vajradhara, who is depicted on the scroll paintings, or *tangkas*, with a dark blue body, one face, two arms, and wearing the customary ornaments. It is possible for students with ability and good fortune to meet with that sambhogakaya emanation. There is, however, no difference between the sambhogakaya and the nirmanakaya Buddha who appeared in this world.

Tilopa met directly with the sambhogakaya Vajradhara, received the instructions on mahamudra from him, and achieved realization. The great pandita Naropa received a prophecy from Chakrasamvara and the dakinis that he must go to the eastern part of India and meet Tilopa. Enduring great difficulties he traveled there, met with Tilopa, and studied with him. In the end he received instructions on mahamudra and was able to practice and realize mahamudra and became a siddha. Then he began to gather students, including Maitripa, who was said to be a student equal to Naropa. These are the origins of the close, or proximate, lineage of mahamudra. In India these students were for the most part the eighty-four mahasiddhas.

From the time the Buddha appeared in India until the time his doctrine disappeared from there, it spread widely and vastly. From among the many teachings that were given and the many people who accomplished great things, the best among them were those who achieved realization because of mahamudra: Saraha, Nagarjuna, Shavari, Maitripa, Tilopa, Naropa, Marpa, and many others. The instructions that they gave to their students were these instructions on mahamudra. Thus, from among the many oral instructions, teachings, and doctrines that spread throughout

India under the banner of the Buddha, the highest among them was mahamudra.

The Lineage in Tibet

[119] Through the Vajrayana teachings and the oral instructions of mahamudra, the teaching of mahamudra then spread in Tibet. Marpa the translator was the first Tibetan to receive the mahamudra teachings. In the twelfth century C.E., Marpa went to India and took Naropa and Maitripa as his principal gurus. He remained in India for a long time, receiving the teachings of the Vajrayana and of mahamudra, practiced them, and achieved realization. He gave these teachings to Milarepa, who then gave them to Gampopa.

Marpa, Milarepa, and Gampopa illustrate three different ways to practice mahamudra and achieve realization, and show that a person of any station in life is able to practice and achieve realization. Marpa was married, owned a house and many possessions, and had a circle of students. In these circumstances, Marpa achieved great realization. Milarepa practiced the simple lifestyle of a yogi—he had neither wealth nor home and practiced in solitary places. Milarepa achieved complete enlightenment in one lifetime. Gampopa practiced mahamudra as a monk. He achieved realization and was able to greatly enhance the welfare of sentient beings through establishing a monastic system.

While the teaching of mahamudra as it was practiced in India was a very profound Dharma, it was practiced in a superior way in Tibet. We might believe that in this degenerate time the teaching of mahamudra has declined and has been corrupted and consequently, even if we were to practice, we would not be able to achieve the result. However, the Buddha indicated that there is no reason to have such doubt.

While teaching the *King of Meditation Sutra*, which is about mahamudra, the Buddha said that in the future the teachings would decline and be corrupted. He asked, "Who among you will preserve this teaching, propagate it, and cause it to flourish?" A young monk named Chandraprabha said, "I will. In the future I will propagate this teaching." The Buddha replied, "It is just as you say. In the future you will take birth in a northern land as a monk named Vimalaprabha. You will propagate the *King of Meditation Sutra* and will cause it to flourish."

In the *White Lotus of Compassion Sutra*, the Buddha said that in the future a monk named Jivaka would ensure that the practice of meditation survived in an unbroken and unstained way. In accordance with that prediction, it came to pass that a boy named Jivaka was born in Tibet. He became known as Gampopa, and he gathered around him many students and gave these central teachings. Since that time the lineage has continued with gurus transmitting it from one generation to the next. Students have continued to meditate and achieve realization, and so the teaching of the mahamudra has not declined or degenerated.

With great exertion, great devotion, and great confidence, we can achieve the same realization that Marpa, Milarepa, and Gampopa achieved.

The Lineage Holders of Mahamudra

The lineage of mahamudra has been passed down from teacher to student very carefully. Gampopa spread these teachings widely, with his activity being extraordinary, far-reaching, and of great benefit to sentient beings. This was foreseen by Milarepa, who said to Gampopa, "You should go to the mountain at Dagla Gampo, because I feel that if you go there, it will bring about a great benefit for sentient beings and the Buddhist teaching." After Gampopa departed for that mountain, Milarepa said to his other students, "I had a dream, and in this dream, a wild vulture flew into the sky and landed upon the peak of a mountain.[11] The vulture was surrounded by beautiful white swans so numerous that they completely filled the sky." Milarepa explained that Gampopa was the vulture, and that the white swans were the hundreds of students who would gather around him and benefit from him. Milarepa concluded by saying, "Although I myself am very poor, I see a great wealth of benefit for sentient beings coming about through the activity of my student Gampopa."

Following the instructions of his guru, Gampopa went to Dagla Gampo and began to teach the Dharma there. He began in a desolate place and thought there was no one to teach. But he attracted a huge flock of great meditators, said to number about eight hundred, who came to hear him teach the Dharma and to practice in accordance with his instructions.

The Kagyu teachings are said to comprise four greater and eight lesser lineages. The four "greater" schools refer to those who were the direct disciples of Gampopa, including the great master Pagmodrupa. The eight "lesser" schools refer to the lineages that came from the eight students of Pagmodrupa. Some say that the greater schools were better than the lesser schools, but that is incorrect.

Gampopa's great accomplishment is rooted in the promise that he made many lifetimes previously at the time of the Buddha, when he took a vow to propagate the teaching of mahamudra in the future. Because of the profundity of the meditation teaching and the accomplishment of Gampopa, those students who have followed in his lineage have been able to generate very powerful, stable, and truly extraordinary meditation.

Gampopa taught the Dharma at Dagla Gampo and eventually passed into nirvana. His principal student was a nephew, Gom Tsultrim Nyingpo, Gomtsul for short, who spent much time with Gampopa and received his teachings completely. Gomtsul possessed a large treasury of quintessential instructions, and he wrote many of these down and became an important teacher. Thus in *Moonlight of Mahamudra* you will see many citations from the teacher Gomtsul.

When Gomtsul passed into nirvana, the succession of this lineage passed to a cousin who held the seat of Dagla Gampo. He had met Gampopa and studied for many years with Gomtsul, and thus was the direct student of both of them. He too came to possess a great treasury of quintessential instructions, which he passed on to future generations. He is referred to in this text by the name Gomchung.

The three men from Kham, as they are known, were the other principal students of Gampopa. The one whose enlightened activity was most prolific was the teacher known as Pagmodrupa. He had eight accomplished students, each of whom became the founders of a lineage in their own right. Those lineages became known as the eight lesser lineages of the Dagpo Kagyu. Pagmodrupa is also known Dorje Gyalpo, and the text cites his teachings too on many occasions.

Among the eight students of Pagmodrupa, the one whose enlightened activity was the vastest was Lingrepa. He founded one of the four major lineages of the Kagyu known as the Drugpa Kagyu. The text cites his teachings on many occasions, as he was a very powerful propagator of the teachings of mahamudra. Sometimes it refers to him by his full name, Lingrepa Pema Dorje, and sometimes just as Lingre. Lingrepa's principal student, Tsangpa Gyare Yeshe Dorje, was a highly accomplished meditator and supreme teacher of the Drugpa Kagyu. The text refers to him many times as Tsangpa Gyare, and sometimes just Gyare.

All of these teachers studied mahamudra earnestly and listened well. They meditated in accordance with the way they had been instructed—diligently and with exertion and intelligence. Having accomplished these teachings, they then passed them on to their own students. Sometimes in the texts of one teacher a certain instruction might not be very clear, and so the instructions of another teacher are cited. For instance, we might find something that Gampopa said that sounds very intriguing, but it's not clear what he meant, so we have to refer to teachings that were given by one of his students—perhaps Gomtsul or Pagmodrupa—where the

The Close Lineage of Mahamudra

TILOPA (988–1069)

An emanation of Chakrasamvara who received mahamudra teachings from Vajradhara.

NAROPA (1016–1100)

An abbot at Nalanda University who left and became Tilopa's student.

MARPA (1012–97)

A Tibetan who went to India three times and studied under Naropa and Maitripa.

MILAREPA (1040–1123)

A hermit who received teachings from Marpa and thoroughly practiced mahamudra and the six yogas of Naropa.

GAMPOPA (1079–1153)

A master who received mahamudra teachings from Milarepa and combined these with Kadampa teachings of Atisha. Founded first Kagyu monastery.

DUSUM KHYENPA (1110–93)

The First Karmapa, who took Gampopa's teachings of mahamudra and founded the Karma Kagyu lineage.

KARMA PAKSHI (1206–83)

The Second Karmapa, who was known for his practice and ablity to perform miracles.

RANGJUNG DORJE (1284–1339)

The Third Karmapa, who was a great scholar who wrote many treatises on meditation.

Each Karmapa passed down the mahamudra teachings right up to Thrangu Rinpoche, who was asked to set up the monastic college in Rumtek, Sikkim, by the Sixteenth Karmapa to preserve the lineage.

meaning of Gampopa's words is clarified. Or there may be a passage in the teachings of one of these great gurus that is particularly appropriate or practical. Having several authentic sources of the quintessential teachings brings great benefit for students.

Questions

QUESTION: Rinpoche, you talk about how mahamudra cuts the root of disturbing emotions and develops good qualities. Could you speak further about how mahamudra practice develops good qualities? My mind tends to think that those good qualities are imputed as the nature of the mind, that compassion is the nature of mind.

RINPOCHE: We talk about what is to be abandoned and what is to be realized. Disturbing emotions are to be abandoned, and through realization, wisdom increases and expands. Wisdom increases because the capacity for such wisdom is an aspect of the dharmata of mind.

The buddhas' wisdom is described in various ways. Sometimes it is enumerated as five, sometimes as four, and sometimes as two. The two buddha wisdoms are the wisdom of the *nature of phenomena* and the wisdom of the *variety of phenomena*. The first realizes dharmata directly, while the latter understands all conventional appearances. When we see dharmata directly, we see that all conventional appearances exist within dharmata. Seeing dharmata directly leads to having the wisdom of the full extent and variety of phenomena, which causes the good qualities to increase and expand.

In particular, a very special compassion is generated. From our own experience we see that the disturbing emotions can be abandoned and that wisdom can be expanded. We also see clearly that this dharmata, this mind itself, exists without degeneration in all sentient beings, limitless as space. However, through the misfortune of not having realized dharmata, sentient beings continue to suffer in samsara. Sentient beings do not need to suffer. It happens only because they have not been able to realize the way things are. In this way compassion arises effortlessly. We also come to know directly the methods for preventing suffering. Thus we speak of emptiness that has compassion as its essence. If we realize that emptiness, very strong compassion arises.

QUESTION: You said that mahamudra is taking direct perception as the path. Also, you said that mahamudra is the path of the blessing of faith and longing devotion. Could you explain the relationship of devotion to mahamudra practice?

RINPOCHE: I spoke about three different divisions of the path. They were taking inference as the path, taking blessing as the path, and taking direct experience as the path. The second of those, taking of blessing as path, is the meditation upon yidam deities, the practice of guru yoga, and the practices of subtle channels and drops. The third is being introduced directly to the mind as it really is. These latter two are not incompatible with one another. The introduction to mahamudra is the pointing out of your mind. It is not something distant; it is your own mind. You look and realize it, and in that way your mind is pointed out. At the same time, there might be a particular place for blessing. There are some very fortunate people who are able to realize this suddenly and others who do not have such good fortune who are not able to realize it right off. What is the root cause of being able to realize mahamudra in such a manner? We are able to give birth to this realization by having complete faith, confidence, and devotion. With such a faith, mind can be pointed out to us straight off. But if we have a little bit of doubt, that doubt binds our mind. Even though mahamudra is not so subtle that it is very difficult to realize, if we have the misfortune of not having our mind pointed out, realization does not arise. So, realization depends upon receiving blessing from the guru and upon our own faith, confidence, devotion, and exertion.

QUESTION: Were there two Maitripas?
RINPOCHE: Maitripa was involved in two different lineages. In the long lineage, which goes from Saraha to Nagarjuna to Shavari to Maitripa, he received the teachings from Shavari. He was also associated with the close, or near, lineage, which goes from Tilopa to Naropa to Marpa to Maitripa. It is the same person.

QUESTION: It has been said that the dzogchen teachings are the greatest teachings and have the greatest practitioners with the greatest realizations. I am wondering if mahamudra and dzogchen are essentially the same teachings?
RINPOCHE: In terms of realizing the true nature of phenomena, both the dzogchen and mahamudra teachings are said to be the highest practice. There is a slight difference in terms of their methods, and there are dzogchen tantras and mahamudra tantras. But as far as the meditation itself, they are mostly the same. Some people say they have the great fortune of practicing dzogchen teachings, some people say they have the great fortune of practicing mahamudra, and all say their teachings are very special and the highest teachings. Some people like eating rice and some people like eating wheat: it is like that.

QUESTION: What exactly is Vajradhara? Are you saying there are two kinds: dharmakaya Vajradhara and sambhogakaya Vajradhara?
RINPOCHE: A vajra has five points on it. The five points indicate the five wisdoms. It is called *vajra* because it is unchangeable. *Vajradhara* means the one who holds the vajra, that is to say, the one who holds those wisdoms in an unchanging manner. The dharmakaya Vajradhara is the wisdom mind of the Buddha. When we practice the path, the main result of our practice is the dharmakaya. However, this dharmakaya has no form, and an ordinary person is not able to meet with this wisdom, this mind of a

buddha. If there were no other form in which a buddha appeared, there would be no purpose in a buddha having achieved enlightenment, for if you can't communicate with others, then you cannot help them. For ordinary people to meet with a buddha, a buddha must display a form body. So, the dharmakaya emanates two types of form bodies. There is the pure form body and the impure form body. The sambhogakaya is the pure form body, and the great bodhisattvas and adepts are able to meet with it and receive teaching from it. The impure form body is the nirmanakaya, or emanation body. From among many types of emanation bodies, one that shows the way of achieving liberation and enlightenment and gives these teachings is called a supreme nirmanakaya, or supreme emanation body. An example of this is the Buddha Shakyamuni. In former times there were other buddhas who were emanations of the dharmakaya. In the realm of the sambhogakaya there are a great many buddhas, such as Amitabha, Amoghasiddhi, and Vajrapani. The sambhogakaya Vajradhara is one of these sambhogakaya emanations.

QUESTION: How did the teachings of mahamudra come from Gampopa?
RINPOCHE: The transmission is called "the golden rosary of the Kagyu." Gampopa gave the teachings to Dusum Khyenpa, the First Karmapa; Dusum Khyenpa then passed them along the Kagyu lineage. We could list each person in the extended lama lineage, or abbreviate the matter by saying it comes from the Sixteenth Gyalwa Karmapa. Although there have been sixteen Karmapas with a great many manifestations, the mind of the Karmapa has always been the same. So as far as the teachings of mahamudra are concerned, we all depend upon the Sixteenth Gyalwa Karmapa, Rangjung Rigpe Dorje.[12]

THE PREPARATORY PRACTICES FOR MAHAMUDRA

Entering the Path of Mahamudra

[121] In order to enter into the Dharma we must engage in hearing, contemplation, and meditation. Moreover, we need to rely upon a spiritual friend who teaches us meditation and the Dharma. A good spiritual friend should be a person we regard highly and who can teach the authentic path of Dharma. Since we are dealing with human beings, it is difficult to find someone who has eliminated 100 percent of all faults and has developed 100 percent of the good qualities. But we must seek someone capable of teaching the authentic path and teaching it well.

After we find a good spiritual friend, we must engage in ethical discipline (Skt. *shila*, Tib. *tsultrim*), which is the basis of all good qualities. Discipline means that we must engage in the decent and proper ways of doing things and give up the improper ways of doing things. It is very good if we can engage in the discipline of a person who has renounced the world, such as a monk or nun, but this is not absolutely necessary. As we have seen, in the Kagyu tradition there are examples of people from various walks of life who received mahamudra instructions, practiced them, and attained the highest realization.

The Treatises

Within the teachings of the Buddha are the teachings of the Hinayana, Mahayana, and the Vajrayana vehicles. These vast teachings were condensed into the treatises, or shastras, composed by the great Buddhist scholars of India. Tibetans have tended to rely on these treatises more than on the many sutras and tantras spoken by the Buddha himself. Some people consider this rather strange because the scholars of these treatises were not at the same level as the Buddha. Moreover, the scholars didn't always agree with each other. But there is a very good reason for relying mainly on the treatises. The Buddha taught individuals in accordance with their own situation, abilities, and understanding. If someone asked him, "What is this emptiness you are talking about?" the Buddha would answer based on the particular capacity and perspective of the questioner, "Well, emptiness is such and such, and it is like this and like that." Another person might come to him and ask, "Why is it that we should not kill people?" And the Buddha would answer based on that person's situation. This makes it very difficult for us to understand everything the Buddha taught in a single consistent body of teaching.

    The scholars in the Indian Buddhist tradition gathered together all the teachings that the Buddha gave on particular subjects at different times and to different people. They analyzed and organized these teachings so that people like us could study the treatises and see how the Dharma is organized and understand the reasons the Buddha gave one teaching on one occasion and another teaching on another occasion. This allowed for the understanding of the whole range of teachings, which is so vast that one individual could never study it all. By reading the treatises we can understand the meaning of the Buddha's words.

The Quintessential Instructions

Listening to the treatises and developing an extensive knowledge of them is certainly a good thing. However, it is even more important to practice the oral instructions of our guru. What are the oral instructions? They are very brief and direct explanations of what we should give up, how we should proceed, and what practices we ought to do. When it comes to the question of what we ought to practice, the oral instructions are the most significant. Thus the treatises are more important than the words of the Buddha, and the oral instructions are more important than the treatises.

The most important quintessential instructions are the three cycles of spiritual songs of the mahasiddha Saraha and the treasuries of spiritual songs by Tilopa, Naropa, and others. These spiritual songs are expressed in a few easily understood words and contain the essentials of spiritual practice. In Tibet, the most important of these oral instructions are the spiritual songs of Milarepa and the songs of the gurus of the Karma Kagyu lineage, such as those collected in *Rain of Wisdom*. In these spiritual songs we are instructed very directly on how to meditate. These songs are brief, poetic, and easy to understand, so they are not difficult to keep in mind.

It is not sufficient to merely listen to spiritual songs; we must develop certainty of the usefulness of them by contemplating what we have heard. This will lead to knowledge. But knowledge alone is not sufficient; we must also engage in the practice of meditation.

The Four Reminders

We enter into the general Buddhist path by first hearing, then contemplating, and finally practicing the Dharma. In mahamudra practice we begin by doing the preliminary practices, or *ngondro*. The reason for beginning with the preliminary practices is that we become lazy at times, and we don't feel like practicing the Dharma. When this happens, we practice the antidote to laziness, which is thinking about impermanence. We think that we are in a situation that is always changing, and while we are able to practice today, later we won't have the opportunity. By thinking about impermanence, we become determined to engage in practice now.

There are four aspects of impermanence, called the *four reminders*. The first is the difficulty of finding the leisure and fortune of a precious human birth. The second is the transience of life and the immediacy of death. The third is karma, or the relation between actions and their effects. And fourth is the faults or disadvantages of samsara. Contemplating these four reminders helps us turn back laziness.

These four reminders are called the *four common preliminaries*. It is extremely helpful to reflect on them again and again. In the beginning, thinking about these four common preliminaries enables us to enter the path of Dharma. Once we have entered the path, reflecting on them encourages exertion. Toward the end of the path, they enable us to bring the fruition into our own hands.

Ngondro Practice

[125] After contemplating the four reminders, we take up ngondro practice, which consists of the four uncommon preliminary practices: refuge prostration, Vajrasattva mantra recitation, mandala offering, and guru yoga. We engage in these practices because we need faith, devotion, and confidence in the Dharma to do mahamudra practice.

Prostrations help foster faith, confidence, and devotion toward the Dharma through some physical exertion and hardship.

Vajrasattva mantra recitation clears away various obstacles to good meditation and to realization. These obstacles are the strong disturbing emotions, such as desire, hatred, pride, and anger, that come about due to negative deeds that we have performed with body, speech, and mind. The accumulation of such negative actions makes it impossible for us to practice well or achieve any results. We purify these deeds and obscurations through reciting the hundred-syllable mantra of Vajrasattva.

In addition to purifying obstacles and negative deeds, we must also accumulate merit. Normally we do this through practicing the six perfections. However, in the Vajrayana, which works on the inner mind rather than external things, we accumulate merit by making mandala offerings in the third ngondro practice. By gathering all the desirable things of all worldly realms in all possible directions into a single mandala and then offering it, we increase our merit.

Having purified ill deeds and obstructions and accumulated merit, we still need assistance. In particular, we need to receive the blessings of the buddhas and bodhisattvas, which we receive through faith and devotion. The buddhas and bodhisattvas of the past are distant, having lived a long time ago. Nevertheless, the teachings they gave have come to us through the gurus of the lineage and in particular through our root guru. So we engage in the fourth ngondro practice of guru yoga, where we visualize all the buddhas and bodhisattvas and all the teachers in the lineage in order to enter into and receive their blessings.

Formerly people didn't need these ngondro practices because students had extraordinary faith and devotion. For example, even though he was a great pandit, Naropa had exceptional faith in Tilopa. He gave up his position in the monastery and endured tremendous hardship to find Tilopa and study with him. Because of his unwavering faith and devotion, he stayed with it despite many difficulties. Similarly, Marpa traveled to India three times to obtain the very special oral instructions, and endured great hardship out of his faith, conviction, and devotion toward the Dharma and his guru. Later his student, Jetsun Milarepa, having carefully examined his own situation, felt he absolutely had to obtain the instructions to achieve complete enlightenment in one lifetime. He believed without any question that he needed these teachings and that Marpa could bestow them. Therefore, Milarepa went to Marpa and requested the teachings. Marpa put Milarepa through tremendous hardship, such as building a stone tower with his bare hands, tearing them down, building them again, and then tearing them down again. Yet Milarepa was willing. "In this way I can receive the instructions from Marpa," he thought, "and I must do that." In those times it wasn't necessary for people to engage in the ngondro practices of prostrations and the rest.

Ngondro practice came about later for the purpose of increasing faith and devotion. When ngondro practice was instituted, there was no particular convention about how many repetitions of each one a student ought to do. Some students with tremendous exertion did a lot and some who didn't have that kind of exertion did only a few. However, it was noticed that students who only did a few didn't end up with the right kind of realization and experience. So to increase exertion, ngondro became a practice of doing about 100,000 prostrations, reciting 100,000 Vajrasattva mantras, making 100,000 mandala offerings, and performing the guru yoga 100,000 times.

Subsequently, the teacher Shakya Shri came from India to Tibet, and he had an extraordinary ability to bestow the teachings and a great affection for his students. He believed it was absolutely necessary for them to give birth to experience and realization, and he very kindly required them to do 400,000 of each of the uncommon preliminary practices. However, teachers in the present time, such as the Sixteenth Karmapa, Kalu Rinpoche, and Chögyam Trungpa Rinpoche, out of their great affection and love for their students, thought that 400,000 could be too overwhelming and have said that 100,000 is sufficient.

It is very important that our mind does not wander when we do these practices. We may not be able to do them quickly, and it may even be preferable to do them slowly and gradually. The important thing when we do them, however, is that our mind does not wander.

Many students have come to me saying that, when they practiced shamata, they experienced a peaceful and relaxed state of mind and everything went very well. But when they started to do prostrations, they experienced great hatred or great desire during their practice. When I first heard this, I thought it strange. After looking into it, it seems to me that it comes down to a wandering mind. When we do shamata practice we are able to pay attention. We don't have any physical work to do; rather, we just sit and tend our mind. However, when we do prostrations or mantras, there is physical work for both body and speech. There are feelings and sensations that go along with the practice, and the mind tends to become distracted. Once the mind wavers, we begin to think. Then we do the next prostration and think some more. By the time we do the third prostration we are pretty well worked up and become angry or whatever. That is why I think it is important to stay with it and not let the mind wander.

The Vajrayana has very special oral instructions that enable us to achieve complete enlightenment in one lifetime. However, achieving enlightenment in one lifetime requires exertion. We may think, "I must achieve buddhahood in this very lifetime with this very body, and if I don't, all the Dharma practice I have done will have been a total waste of time." This would be a mistake. Making the exertion that leads to achieving complete enlightenment is certainly a wonderful thing. However, if we cannot exert ourselves to that degree but are able to practice well and achieve complete enlightenment over a longer period, it is also very good. To practice even a little bit is extremely fortunate, and we should not consider it a waste of time. Dharma practice is extremely meaningful, and even the tiniest bit is a marvelous thing.

The Buddha said if we are not able to practice very much but have faith, it is beneficial. If our faith is such that we can put our two hands together and feel tremendous devotion, this is wonderful. Someone asked the Buddha, "If the most you can do is just put one hand up in devotion, would there be any benefit to that?" Buddha said yes, there is definitely benefit from that. And even if we have no faith and simply raise our hand in the air, that is also beneficial.

Question

QUESTION: When you were talking about fruition mahamudra, you said that compassion and skillful methods for helping people arise effortlessly out of emptiness. Could you please say more about how those skillful methods arise out of emptiness?

RINPOCHE: Take the example of a person who is dreaming of a tiger and is very frightened. A realized person with clairvoyance sees that the person is dreaming of a tiger. The realized person knows that the method for preventing the person from suffering is simply to shake them until they wake up. It is because of the emptiness of the tiger that the dreamer can be protected from it. If the tiger were not empty it would also eat the person with clairvoyance. Because of emptiness, we see there is no tiger, and so we are able to help others.

MAHAMUDRA SHAMATA MEDITATION

The Tradition of Mahamudra Meditation

[143] The teachings on mahamudra spread widely in Tibet along with the teachings of the word of the Buddha, the commentaries by the successive Indian masters, and the oral instructions of many accomplished people. Many different lineages of mahamudra arose. Some people have argued that, even though these instructions are very profound and were beneficial in the past, they are ineffective in our degenerate times. Tashi Namgyal explains that these people are mistaken and that, on the contrary, if we meditate on the oral instructions, there will be benefit. It is said that the path of mahamudra involves great realization and accomplishment with relatively little difficulty. Many people practiced it in the past and became mahasiddhas. If we practice it in the same way, we too can become accomplished and achieve the final fruition.

Sudden and Gradual Realizers

[144] Gampopa taught two different traditions of meditation in accordance with two different types of people: sudden realizers and gradual realizers. Sudden realizers are able to generate realization all at once, while gradual realizers must proceed gradually, stage by stage. When Gampopa taught sudden realizers he first taught the view and then, from within the view,

proceeded into meditation. When he taught gradual realizers he first had them develop experience with meditation and then led them into the view. Among gradual realizers there are two subtypes: those whose mind is extremely wild and those whose mind is extremely unclear. To those with wild mind he taught vipashyana first. To those with extremely unclear mind he first taught shamata. The procedure in *Moonlight of Mahamudra* begins with shamata and proceeds to vipashyana.

Mastering Shamata Meditation

[146] Previously the text explained shamata in relationship to the sutras and the shastras. Now it discusses shamata from the point of view of mahamudra. It begins with a variety of applications that are appropriate to shamata.

For the beginner, everything that was said previously about shamata is still appropriate and applicable. In particular it is beneficial for the beginner to go to an isolated place and practice there in a relaxed and quiet way. The advice given here is that we should practice in brief sessions and do a great many of these sessions.

The Posture

[147] When practicing, we should employ the posture known as the seven points of Vairocana. We sit on a comfortable cushion and assume the vajra, or full-lotus, posture with both legs crossed and each foot placed on the opposite thigh. If that is uncomfortable, we can cross our legs loosely, with one placed in front of the other. On this particular point it makes no difference. The posture of the mind is more important. Basically the mind is very relaxed. The hands can be placed with the thumbs touching one another below the navel, or we can rest our palms on our thighs in a position called "pressing down the earth." Either position is fine. The most important thing is that the body is straight and the vertebrae are

straightened and lengthened. The neck is slightly curved, and the tongue is placed on the upper palate just behind the front teeth. The eyes are turned down toward the tip of the nose. Finally, the shoulders are straightened and slightly stretched so that the body is upright, and the chest is open and relaxed. If we are able to sit in this way, our body will be very relaxed and, as a result, our mind also will be relaxed.

Objects of Observation

[149] From the beginning of time we have been accustomed to the mind being very unstable and wandering all over the place. To establish stability when we begin to meditate it can be helpful to rest the mind on an external object. There are two kinds of external objects of observation: impure and pure objects. Impure objects are such things as a small stone or a piece of wood. A pure object could be a small statue of the Buddha.

If we hold our mind on the object too tightly the tension will cause a great deal of discursive thought. Thus, the text instructs us simply not to wander and not to forget the object. We do not analyze the object; we simply observe it in a relaxed way, neither wandering to something else nor forgetting it. It is recommended that we do this in sessions that are brief but frequent.

If we use an internal object, we might choose the attractive form of a Buddha ornamented with the thirty-two principal marks. Meditation upon deities, referred to as the *generation stage*, is extremely important in the Vajrayana tradition. We usually visualize the deities within their abode, their mandala. Sometimes we imagine the deities as very large and sometimes as so small they fit within our hearts. Visualizing things in different ways and in great detail trains our awareness, bringing forth agility, dexterity, and the energy of awareness.

Awareness in visualization can change very rapidly. When we rest on an internal object, we gain mastery over this moving awareness. Sometimes we imagine a mantra garland that is spinning—sometimes slowly and sometimes very rapidly. At this point, we are not only concerned with the mind resting but also with how the mind can be still and stable while consciousness is moving. For instance, if we meditate upon a mantra garland, we first concentrate on the different syllables, visualizing them one by one; then we visualize the syllables starting to turn. It is not like watching material things going around in a circle, rather it is something that we do completely with our mind. When we can do this, it brings about great stability and relaxation in the mind. When we get used to it, it is very good shamata.

This foreshadows how meditation upon a deity brings about the blessings of the yidam, the buddhas, and the bodhisattvas, and how those blessings can help achieve the common and supreme siddhis. If we cultivate tranquillity meditation in this way, it brings about a very special sort of shamata.

The Resting Mind

[152] Achieving an excellent shamata is rather difficult for a beginner because the mind tends to wander. For that reason, we need both mindfulness and alertness.

If thoughts arise in our mind, we try to be aware of those thoughts and with mindfulness return our mind to the object of observation in a relaxed way. Mind can be divided into the main mind and mental factors. In this case, *mindfulness* is a mental factor—a perceiving subject that takes the mind as its object. Mindfulness looks at the mind to see whether or not it has wandered.

The Tibetan word for mind is *sem,* and the word for mental factors is *semjung,* which literally means "arising from the mind" or "arising with the mind." Mind, or *sem,* has six consciousnesses: the eye, the ear, the nose, the tongue, the body sensations, and the mental consciousnesses.

These consciousnesses know their objects individually, so the eye consciousness sees visible forms, the ear consciousness hears sounds, the nose consciousness experiences smells, and so on, with the mental consciousness being where many different thoughts appear and are integrated. The mental factors occur with those main consciousnesses.

There are several types of mental factors. Some are always there and accompany every consciousness. Others appear occasionally. Pleasure and pain are mental factors that always accompany the mind. While the feeling of pleasure or pain is sometimes strong and sometimes weak, it accompanies every mental event. Similarly, discrimination, which is the quality of knowing what things are and recognizing the details of things, is a mental factor that always accompanies the six consciousnesses. Some of the mental factors that appear occasionally are mindfulness and faith. When these beneficial mental factors accompany the mind, that mind is a peaceful mind. There are also mental factors that are not beneficial, such as passion, aggression, envy, and ill will. When these negative factors accompany the mind, that mind is disturbed.

The mental factor of mindfulness (Tib. *drenpa*) keeps us from forgetting the object. As long as mindfulness is present, we do not forget the object, and when mindfulness is absent, we forget the object. We might think, "I am not going to let my mind wander again." But if an absence of mindfulness returns, the mind will fall under the influence of other things once again. So it is important that mindfulness is there all the time to keep the mind from wandering.

Mindfulness is a mental factor that looks at the mind itself to see whether or not the mind is staying with the object. It allows the mind to rest within a state of relaxation and serves as a guardian of that state. If the mind wanders, it is alertness (Tib. *shezhin*) that brings it back. Alertness accompanies mindfulness: if mindfulness is present, alertness is also present;

if mindfulness is absent, alertness is also absent. So it is very important to develop both mindfulness and alertness and to not lose them.

Protecting the Mind

Protecting mind from the disturbing emotions and discursive thought can be compared to protecting ourselves from thieves. Thieves know not to attack a strong, powerful, well-disciplined, and attentive person. Instead, they will attack someone who is weak, lazy, and distracted. Mindfulness and alertness make us strong, attentive, and well disciplined so we cannot be robbed by disturbing emotions and discursive thought. With mindfulness and alertness, the disturbing emotions have no hope of being able to rob us and just give up.

Developing Shamata Using Breathing

[154] We can hold our mind to the movement of prana in two ways: by counting the breath, and by a special breathing exercise called the *fullness of prana*. Counting the breath is the ordinary way of meditating in shamata; we simply count our in- and out-breaths. The fullness of the prana can be done in two different ways. One is called vase breathing, which involves extending the abdomen and holding the breath there. The other is called vajra repetition, which involves coordinating the motion of the breathing with the mantra syllables *Om Ah Hum*. As the wind or breath comes in, *Om* is said. As the wind is held briefly inside, *Ah* is said. As the wind exits, *Hum* is said. We divide the cycle of the breath into three parts and correlate each part of it with *Om Ah Hum*.

[155] The practice of vase breathing can help to clear our mind if it is unclear and stabilize it if it is unstable. It should be noted that there is another practice of vase breathing, which is harsher, using a forceful inhalation and exhalation for the purpose of clearing out the subtle channels in the body. In mahamudra practice, vase breathing does not involve

forceful breathing. Its purpose is to allow the mind to rest, and so it is very relaxed and gentle. When the breath comes into the body, it is done gently, and when it leaves the body, it is also done gently.

We begin with three cycles of dispelling stale breath. The breath is brought into the body very quietly. The body is filled with the breath, and then the breath is expelled in a very gentle manner, again not making any noise. Our hands rest on our thighs. As we expel the breath, we extend our fingers and hands. In the first cycle of this practice, we sense that sickness and discomfort of every sort is leaving our body. In the second cycle we sense that harmful spirits are leaving the body. In the third cycle we sense that any other obstructions to our practice are leaving our body and that we become free from them.

After these three cycles, the breath is brought back into the body and down to a point below the navel. There is a sense that the breath is contained below the navel, as if we were closing a jar holding air. The air is somewhat pressed down from above, and somewhat pressed up from below, and then held there very gently without any sense of strain. When it becomes stressful, we allow the air to leave the body very gently, without making any noise. Holding the breath in this way is a means of pacifying or taming the mind and developing mindfulness. This practice is called "shamata of being filled with wind," meaning that we are being filled with prana.

When we practice shamata in this way, the main point is that the wind is held below the navel and the upper part of our body is left more or less as it always is. We don't attend to the upper part of the body, and in particular, we don't constrict it in any way. We just leave it very relaxed, spacious, and clear. If we intensify our experience in the upper part of the body, it might create some discomfort in our lungs, or our heart, or wherever. So in this practice we only attend to the wind below the navel without doing anything in particular about the areas where we ordinarily breathe.

Ordinarily, when we breathe we neither inhale nor exhale fully. So when we begin this practice it is good to exhale completely for the first vase breath. We might do vase breathing five or six times, but we only exhale completely the first time. Between the inhalation and the exhalation, the breath is held. We draw it in below the navel and put a ceiling above it; we then draw in the lower wind, closing it off, like the empowerment vase with a bulging belly. When the mind is sleepy, dark, and dull or when the mind is wild and unstable, we can do vase breathing many times.

In summary, I have explained some of the ways in which the mind can be brought to a state of rest in shamata meditation and the different sorts of objects upon which to focus when we are practicing it. With external objects of observation, we focus on impure and pure objects. With internal objects, we set our mind upon the movement of the breath in a variety of ways. The reason for proceeding from external to internal objects is that from the beginning of time, our mind has been wandering, fixated on external objects. Because of this, it is difficult for us to set our mind in an even and smooth state of rest. Therefore we first use the support of an external object. When we have gotten used to that, we use the breath as an object of observation, turning the mind inward somewhat. This enables the mind to rest.

Meditation without a Reference Point

[159] The next step is to set the mind in a state of rest without using even the breath. When we do this, we assume the same posture but do not focus the mind on anything at all. We do not think about the past or the future or stop to analyze present events. We simply set the mind in a relaxed way. For a beginner this is not easy to do. However, as we grow accustomed to it, the mind is able to rest without resting on any object.

There are two principal points in this practice: first, the way we search for shamata free from faults, and second, the way we sustain the resting of mind. The first is primarily a discussion of tightening and loosening the mind. Earlier, we talked about the mind becoming dull and the mind becoming wild as the two principal kinds of obstacles in the common stages of shamata. In the quintessential instructions on mahamudra, we talk about the mind either being too tight or too loose, too focused or too relaxed. The advice given is that if the mind is not luminous, clear, and vivid, we need to tighten or concentrate more. And if it is too bright, vivid, luminous, and clear, we need to relax it somewhat.

The great master of mahamudra, Saraha, gave an example to explain this. It was the custom of the day, especially for the Brahmin, to wear clothing that was woven out of cotton thread. Saraha said that when we weave this thread, if we make it too tight, it will snap; but if we make it too loose, it won't hold together. Saraha said it is like that when we practice meditation: if we make the mind too tight, it won't be very good, but if we make it too loose, it won't work well either. Rather, we have to set our mind in a way that is a balance between being too focused and too relaxed, making it very even and smooth. That way, our meditation will be very comfortable, delightful, and pleasant.

It is important to know when to tighten the mind and when to loosen it. It is obvious that we need to tighten our mind and focus our concentration when it has become extremely loose, lethargic, and dull. There are also times when our mind stays with the object of meditation, but the meditation is not very clear; rather it is gentle and soft. It is easy to mistake this for good shamata but, in fact, it is not. Such a subtly unclear state of mind needs to be purified by tightening the mind and making our mindfulness strong, clear, and bright. This brings a sense of lifting both body and mind. The problem with a loose and subtly unclear mind is that various appearances begin to dawn. We might then think, "This must be a sign that I am beginning to have a profound experience and that my meditation is going well." But it is not.

Sometimes, however, the factor of clarity becomes excessive, sparking many different discursive thoughts, and we can't get back to shamata. At this point it is necessary to relax. As Saraha said, "When the mind is very active in discursive thought and we try to bind it, it will just scatter to the ten directions." If we continue to try to tighten it, it just explodes. At that point, Saraha said, we need to relax by letting our mind proceed as a camel does, in a very steady and relaxed way. Today we might think of a cat. If we lock a cat in a room and shut the doors and windows, the cat freaks out, running everywhere. But, if we open the doors and the windows, the cat looks around for a while and then falls asleep. In that way our mind too can become very relaxed.

[160] The most important thing in meditation is to understand how to concentrate and how to relax. Tightening or concentrating the mind when it is appropriate and relaxing it when it is appropriate allows us to develop a shamata in which the mind rests comfortably, evenly. At this point, it is very important not to let mindfulness degenerate. It is important that mindfulness be strong so that the mind is relaxed, yet bright and one-pointed.

In the quintessential instructions of mahamudra, there is a great deal of instruction about mindfulness and only a little about alertness. This is because, as I have noted, alertness accompanies mindfulness. If we have mindfulness, then we will also have alertness. If we do not have mindfulness, we will not have alertness. From this point of view the two are very similar, so Tashi Namgyal omits the discussion of alertness but emphasizes repeatedly the importance and necessity of mindfulness.

When practicing meditation, clear mindfulness may arise, but later we find that our mindfulness decreases, and a strong heaviness and dullness overtakes our mind. At this point it is important to heighten the mind's clarity and brilliance. Sitting up straight, raising our gaze somewhat, and expanding the perspective of our mind by making our perception vast and spacious will help the heaviness of mind pass. If we are still unable to clear away this heaviness and dullness, it is necessary to strengthen our mind with real concentration or, in some cases, to leave the session and then come back to it when we are more fresh.

Sometimes we experience great desire or longing in our practice and sometimes we experience regret. Sometimes we feel angry thinking about something someone has done to us, and we wish harm to that person in return. While wildness, desire, regret, and anger are certainly distinct from one another, from this point of view, they are all forms of mental excitement. When we experience them, we need to relax. In terms of our body, we could loosen up our posture somewhat. In terms of our mind, we must drop all thoughts about how well the meditation is going or how it should go. We just let our mind be very spacious, as if we were resting.

Sometimes we encounter discursiveness in our meditation. Two methods for dealing with discursiveness don't work very well. One is to chase after our thoughts and get completely involved in them. One thought comes, then another, another, and another. The other way is to try to stomp on the thoughts—just stop them cold. That doesn't work very well either. What is recommended at this point is a very subtle kind of mindfulness. We bring in our mindfulness, not with forceful concentration, but with a light touch.

We should deal with wildness in the same way. It doesn't help to tie or bind things. The great Saraha said that that is like trying to calm down a camel by tying it to a very short rope. It won't work because the camel will continuously want to get loose. Instead, we should untie the camel and let it be. It will wander around a little and then settle down. It is similar with our mind—if we try to tie it up, it won't work, but if we just relax, stability will come.

Sustaining Resting of Mind

[166] Sustaining the resting of the mind is related to having a great longing for meditation. In the beginning, we tend to have great longing for meditation practice. Then, if we try to practice for lengthy periods, our enthusiasm tends to decrease. When our enthusiasm decreases, our longing and our aspiration declines, reducing our exertion and practice altogether. The antidote to this is to think about the extraordinary qualities of meditation and its benefits. We need to realize that if we develop meditation or samadhi, good qualities will come from it. And if we do not develop meditation, those good qualities will not appear. If we understand that, we will have great aspiration to practice meditation. Such aspiration will lead to exertion. Exertion develops what is known as *shinjang* in Tibetan, meaning "thoroughly processed." This is a state of being supple, flexible, and pliant. When we reach this stage of being thoroughly processed, we are able to enter into meditation easily.

So, it is important to think about the reasons for practicing meditation and to understand its benefits. If we do so, it becomes far easier to meditate, and we meditate with joy and with delight. Without doing so, meditation tends to be rather difficult.

Stages of a Settled Mind

[169] There are three stages that appear after our meditation has developed. In the first stage, our mind is like a stream crashing down a narrow ravine. When we initially begin to practice meditation, we have the sense of having many, many thoughts. We feel that previously our mind was not dull and wild but now it has become extremely wild. Actually that is not so; it is just that we never bothered to look at our mind before. As we begin to take possession of the situation, we begin to recognize what was occurring all along. We sense that sometimes the mind is heavy and dull and

sometimes it is wild with many thoughts. When we are able to see this, it is a good thing—like recognizing an enemy as an enemy.

In the second stage, the mind is like a mountain stream that flows into a great wide river. The river flows along smoothly and gently. In the the third stage, the mind is like a slow river as it merges into the ocean. Things are very smooth, gentle, spacious, and vast, and the mind rests very smoothly without much fluctuation.

The Importance of Developing Shamata

[173] We need to develop shamata that is steady and one-pointed, and that rests very evenly. If we do not, the good qualities that can come about through the full development of the path will never be realized. Even if we have vipashyana, in the absence of shamata it will not have the strength to abandon the disturbing emotions. But if we develop genuine shamata, our vipashyana can become potent. With a potent vipashyana, everything that is to be abandoned can be abandoned and all the good qualities that are to be realized can be realized. If we don't have good shamata and we sit for an hour, our mind will wander, and we won't actually be there for that hour. But if we have well-developed shamata and we sit for an hour, the time will definitely be something of great importance.

I would like to say that I see how all of you place a great value on meditation, you pay attention in general, you regard the Dharma as something important, you have a great longing for it. Also, you put a great deal of energy into listening to the teachings. And the questions that you have asked are questions that arise from the experience of practicing meditation. This makes me extremely happy. When I was on my way here in the airplane, it was difficult for me because I sat there thinking, "I really don't know whether I am going to be able to help people or not." I was bothered by this. Then when I arrived here and could see that you have a great interest in meditation, that you meditate very well and ask questions that have arisen from genuine experience of meditation, I felt extremely gratified. I want to thank you very much for your kindness and say that now I don't feel there are any problems at all.

Questions

QUESTION: Rinpoche, you pinched your hand and talked about how, if you really look at pain, it was empty. Later you talked about the necessity of looking directly into experience. I am wondering, do we just look at emotions or do we experience them? Western psychology would say that we need to experience the emotion and then we can experience the energy underneath it. If not, Western psychology would say it was suppression or denial. I am wondering how the mahamudra model of working with feelings relates to this Western psychological model?

RINPOCHE: There is much that is similar between meditation and Western psychology and also something that seems to be significantly different. It is certainly true that we need to know what we are experiencing. We need to experience it. But there is a difference between merely experiencing it and looking right at the nature of it, because when we look right at the nature of it, there is nothing that can be found. The thing that was experienced, the experiencing mind, and the whole environment of the experience are ungraspable and cannot be identified as anything whatsoever. This is very different from saying, "I experienced that pain or event."

When we take the experience a step further by examining its nature, this causes us to understand the thing experienced fully and correctly. When we know that it cannot be found, we realize that it cannot actually harm us. Then our mind becomes very peaceful and joyful, and we experience pleasure. Whether we are talking about pain in the mind or in the body, if we look for and try to see its actual nature, we realize that we don't have to get rid of it because its nature is emptiness. In this sense, there is nothing that is unbearable.

QUESTION: Sometimes the word "look" is understood in English as a totally intellectual process, but I have a sense that it is much more an experience in Tibetan.

RINPOCHE: In Tibetan when we say "investigating and analyzing with prajna," we don't mean "looking" with that type of mind; rather, we mean thinking, reflecting, and contemplating. When we say, "look," we mean direct experience without conception—like when you look at something with your eye. So, it may be very similar to what you mean in English when you say "experience."

QUESTION: I lose my mindfulness after I have had it. But I also see that I become more familiar with mindfulness and that is beneficial.

RINPOCHE: Mindfulness doesn't just disappear. Similarly, when you cultivate qualities such as faith, devotion, and prajna, they become more and more stable and clear. They don't just suddenly disappear one day. You can think about it in comparison to the way you go to school and develop knowledge and intelligence year after year. You don't just wake up one day and find theat your knowledge and intelligence are gone. When you go to school, you are developing prajna. Likewise, when you practice meditation you are developing mindfulness and alertness. When you are trained in meditation and develop your mindfulness, you don't just wake up to find that your mindfulness has completely disappeared. If you have been in some real hardship and are quite tired, it is sometimes difficult to maintain mindfulness. But as you meditate more and become more familiar with the good qualities and benefits of meditation, it becomes easier for that mindfulness to remain. If you remember the discussion of the nine stages of resting the mind, particularly what was presented in terms of pacifying and taming the mind in the fifth and sixth stages, you will find explanations about how mindfulness becomes very stable.

QUESTION: On the one hand, I have heard that one must complete ngondro practice before going into a three-year retreat; on the other hand, I have heard that it is not necessary. Which is correct?
RINPOCHE: Generally, the ngondro practice is done within the three-year retreat. If you have completed it beforehand that is very good. If you haven't, then you will do it in retreat.

QUESTION: I was wondering, is it the alaya consciousness that is reborn from one lifetime to the next?
RINPOCHE: Where would one look for this alaya consciousness? *Alaya consciousness* is a name that is designated to the factor of mind's clarity. It is not a coarse type of knowing. I would not say that it is what is going from one lifetime to another. What goes from one lifetime to another is the continuum of the six collections of the six consciousnesses.

QUESTION: Would that continuum be the seventh consciousness?
RINPOCHE: No. The seventh consciousness is the seventh consciousness. The six consciousnesses are the continuum of the six consciousnesses. The seventh consciousness refers to this conception of self, which is unbroken, uninterrupted. This seventh afflicted consciousness pervades all the consciousnesses and is always there. But the six consciousnesses and the continuum of the six consciousnesses are not the seventh consciousness nor are they the eighth consciousness.

QUESTION: What does it mean when we say "perception of self"?
RINPOCHE: There are two different types of self-conception—one that relates to the sixth consciousness and one that relates to the seventh consciousness. With the sixth consciousness, thinking "I" comes and goes because the sixth consciousness is involved with the other five sensory consciousnesses. Sometimes we are thinking "I" and sometimes we are

not. But whether or not we are thinking "I" at the level of the sixth consciousness, there is always the notion of "I" at the seventh consciousness. The conception of self in the seventh consciousness is very subtle and continuous. Whether you are going somewhere, sitting down, or asleep, the continuum of that I is not severed.

QUESTION: Many people endure some deep psychological wounds at some point in their lives and approach the Dharma in the hope that it will clear such things up. When we talk about clearing away the predispositions lying deep within the alaya consciousness perhaps, is that a case of doing something about these deep scars in the mind from traumatic experiences of one sort or another?

TRANSLATOR: I think that traumatic experience is what we call *khongdzin*. *Khongdzin* literally means holding onto anger.

RINPOCHE: The remedy for traumatic experiences is to develop a lot of compassion, which is to say, when another person has harmed us, the person that did so has done this out of ignorance. It is simply a mistake that ordinary people make. If it were some highly accomplished person who inflicted such a wound upon us, that would really be a deplorable thing. But it isn't, it is an ordinary person, someone who is confused. This is just the way things are with ordinary people. As Shantideva said, "If you stick your hand in the fire and get burned, you can't really complain about the fire that burned you, for the nature of fire is to burn things." So it is with ordinary people—they make mistakes and hurt others out of confusion. The best thing to do is to develop love and compassion for these people.

QUESTION: Could Rinpoche give an example of a secret obstacle as opposed to an ordinary obstacle?

RINPOCHE: "External obstacles" refers to obstacles we encounter in daily life. "Internal obstacles" refers to disturbing emotions in our own mind.

But "secret obstacles" refers to obstacles that prevent us from doing the practice of getting into the true nature of mind. They prevent us from doing practices of the subtle channels, the subtle energies or winds, and the subtle drops.

9

MAHAMUDRA VIPASHYANA MEDITATION

Reasons for Practicing Vipashyana

[175] When we practice shamata our mind becomes relaxed and peaceful, and delusion lessens. However, it is necessary to go further and do vipashyana, or "insight" meditation. In Tibetan the word for vipashyana is *lhagtong*, with *lhag* meaning "intense," "superior," or "extra," and *tong* meaning "to see."

The difference between shamata and vipashyana is not great; it is only a slight shift. When we practice shamata, our mind rests naturally in a state that is free from a great deal of thought and conceptuality. We are able to reduce disturbing emotions through shamata, but we are not able to eradicate them. With vipashyana, the quality of luminosity is enhanced, and we realize the mind's lack of any inherent nature. Through the realization of this state of luminosity and emptiness, we are able to abandon delusion at the root.

As you know, the Buddha wanted to emerge from the ocean of misery known as samsara. Having aroused this renunciation he left his kingdom and went to the forest to learn meditation and achieve liberation. Two Brahmin sages taught him the practice of shamata. The Buddha practiced and his mind became quite peaceful. After a while, however, he realized that this peaceful state was not enlightenment and that he would have to go further. The Buddha then found a way to achieve what is called "knowledge that realizes selflessness" in the sutra tradition and "the wisdom of vipashyana" in the mantra (Vajrayana) tradition. Achieving vipashyana, he was able to reach buddhahood.

How One Begins Vipashyana Practice

[176] How do we actually achieve vipashana? First of all, we must listen to the instructions on mahamudra many times. Then, we must think about what we have heard until we have understood it properly. Through listening to and contemplating the instructions, we give rise to "the pure view," which is the initial stage of entering into the vipashyana aspect of mahamudra. This is common to the sutra and the mantra traditions.

Listening to the teachings and contemplating what we have heard leads to conceptual understanding. To realize the nature of mind completely, however, we also have to meditate on what we have learned. To learn how to meditate directly on mind, we rely on the guru's blessings. These blessings, which have come down through the lineage gurus to our own root guru, are a kind of potency or power. Through them we can definitely develop the view of mahamudra. To develop these blessings we practice guru yoga.

The Hevajra tantra says, "No one else can explain this," meaning that only a lama who has experienced mahamudra can explain mahamudra. We must rely on someone who has deep experience and real skill in mahamudra—an extraordinary being who is a truly experienced guru—and when we do, the blessings of the lineage can enter us and help us meditate on mahamudra. With this person's instructions and our own merit we can give rise to the realization of mahamudra. That is why we listen to teachings, supplicate the guru, and practice the meditation of guru yoga.

Types of Vipashyana Meditation

[178] We begin by studying vipashyana as it is described in the sutras. There are many different ways of categorizing the practice of vipashyana; however, it can be boiled down to relating vipashyana to the two aspects of selflessness: the selflessness of persons and the selflessness of phenomena. The great Indian masters Nagarjuna and Asanga described these two selflessnesses clearly and precisely in their texts on the Middle Way, using an analytical approach to demonstrate that phenomena lack inherent existence. The teachings of the Middle Way were studied extensively in Tibet.

Relying on the analytic approach is a good way to begin to understand the emptiness of phenomena. To generate real experience of emptiness, however, it is necessary to go beyond analysis. So the Tibetan tradition follows the instructions handed down through the lineage that begins with the great Saraha. In these instructions we do not look at external things to try to discover whether or not they exist; rather, we look directly at the mind and meditate upon its true nature. It is not a conceptual approach; it is taking direct perception as the path.

When we practice the meditation of mahamudra, we look at our own mind, cut through all of our hesitations and misconceptions about the mind, and decisively understand the mind's nature. We discover that emptiness is the mind's way of being. When we understand the lack of inherent existence of our mind, we can easily understand the lack of inherent existence of external phenomena. This approach makes it quite easy to give rise to genuine experience and realization and therefore is a superior way of proceeding.

The Main Meditation of Vipashyana

WHY WE ACHIEVE INSIGHT

[179] By looking at the mind itself we can realize the mind's true nature.

When we have realized this, all delusion can be abandoned, and wisdom and the other good qualities of mind will arise. This is indicated in the spiritual songs and advice given by the siddhas of the mahamudra tradition. For instance, Saraha said, "When mind has been bound, one is bound; when just that is released, there is no doubt." Saraha was saying that both bondage and freedom come about by way of the mind. Tilopa said, "When the branches and leaves of a tree spread, if the single root is cut, ten thousand or even one hundred thousand leaves will dry up. Cutting the root of mind—samsara—is like that too." In other words, if you cut the root of a tree, all of the many leaves and branches will dry up. Likewise, if the single root of suffering is cut, all of the innumerable kinds of suffering in samsara will be pacified. And the great Shantideva said, "If you do not know the mind, this will become the cause of all suffering. If you know the mind and protect the mind, this is the supreme of uncontrived action." If we do not understand the mind's nature, we will not be able to abandon suffering. If we understand the mind's nature, we can abandon suffering and achieve happiness. That is why it is vital to know the mind's nature and protect it. "Uncontrived action" refers to conduct for the purpose of becoming familiar with and guarding our mind. It involves recognizing mind's nature and then acting on the basis of that nature.

Some people criticize this practice. They say that the essence of the Dharma is meditation upon emptiness, not meditation upon the mind's nature. They also say that if the mind were primordially pure, sentient beings would already be buddhas and no effort would be required to achieve enlightenment. But these people are mistaken. They think that emptiness is something good and the mind is something bad. This is because they have not understood the mind's nature. Actually, the nature of phenomena and the nature of mind are exactly the same. Hence, if we meditate upon the mind's nature, we naturally realize emptiness.

Emptiness is discussed widely in the sutras of the Buddha and the treatises composed by his followers. When it comes to meditation, however, it's not possible to meditate directly upon the emptiness of external phenomena. Therefore, we have to look at mind and cut through its confusion. Having seen the nature of the mind, we can meditate upon that. Thus, in the tradition of mahamudra, we talk about *semtri*, or "pointing out the mind."

THE SUTRAS ON THE MIND'S TRUE NATURE

[183] In the sutras the Buddha said many times that it is important to meditate upon the mind's true nature. Thus, this notion of meditating upon the mind's true nature was not invented later on by those involved in the Kagyu lineage. Also, in treatises and commentaries, scholars and sages from across the ages made it clear that we must meditate on the mind's true nature. Finally, sayings and spiritual songs of the siddhas of the mahamudra tradition in India emphasize the importance of meditating upon the mind's true nature. *Moonlight of Mahamudra* cites from all of these sources.

THE STAGES OF VIPASHYANA MEDITATION

[184] Of the two types of meditation, analytical meditation and placement meditation, vipashyana meditation is predominantly a type of analytical meditation. In a session of vipashyana meditation, we begin by resting briefly in the meditative equipoise of shamata. We then give rise to what in Tibetan is called *salngar*. The first syllable means "clear" or "luminous" and "brilliant," and the second, "a tightening of the mind," or "strength." Together these syllables give the sense of mind that is brilliantly sharp and not relaxed. It is the sharpness of the mind, mind's cutting quality, that gives rise to insight and leads to *the wisdom of discriminating awareness*. This awareness, which arises in the process of looking directly at the mind, is brilliantly clear and taut.

We begin to look for the nature of the mind in the same way that we discover the selflessness of the person as taught in the sutra tradition. When we look for the personal self—the "I" or "me"—we don't find anything. And so we discover the nonexistence of the self. In the same way, we look for the mind by asking, "Is it in the head? Is it in the body? Is it outside the body?" We do not find it anywhere.

When we do this practice, we keep our eyes open. The great master Saraha says the yogin does not close his eyes, which means that the yogin stares wide-eyed, without even blinking, and meditates. Some people have difficulty meditating with their eyes open; in that case, it doesn't make much difference. However in the tradition of mahamudra practice it is said that we keep our eyes open, and that it is a better way to meditate.

According to Saraha, "The Brahmins look up; the peaceful hearers look down; the vajra eyes look directly." In many non-Buddhist traditions of contemplative practice, practioners raise their gaze and look up when they meditate. They are contemplating a deity and feel that this deity lives somewhere in the sky. The shravakas look down so as not to give rise to thought, particularly disturbing emotions; they feel that if they were to look up, they would see many things and start thinking about them, which would then arouse passion, aggression, envy, and so forth. Similarly, in places where the Theravada tradition of Buddhism is practiced, monks keep their eyes on the ground in front of them when they go on their rounds of begging for food from the laity. "Vajra eyes" refers to the practitioners of mahamudra in the Vajrayana tradition. "The vajra eyes look directly," means that these practitioners look neither up nor down; they simply look straight ahead. What exactly are they looking at? They are looking at their own mind.

How We Look at Mind

We begin with the practice of shamata, and as the session continues, we look for the mind while in shamata. Do we look out for our mind, or do we look in for our mind? The text answers this by saying that we look whichever way we feel comfortable. We may have the sense that we're in here somewhere and our mind is over there, so it feels like we are looking over there for our mind. Or we might have the sense that we are on the outside and our mind is on the inside, so we feel we are looking in at our mind. Either way is fine. But when we look, we look nakedly. "Nakedly" means we do not look in the manner of reasoned investigation, but we look directly.

If mind exists, we ought to be able to find it and say, "This is what it is." So we start to look for it. One of the ways we look for our mind is to try and discern whether it has a shape. Is it round? Is it square? Is it in the shape of a mountain? Does it have the shape of a human being? If we can't come up with a shape for it but we still feel that our mind is something, then we ask whether or not it has a color. Is it white? Is it red? Is it black? External things have colors and shapes, but does our mind have a color and a shape?

If mind exists, it ought to be somewhere. Where does it dwell? We probably think that our mind dwells within our body, so we look through our body starting at the top of our head and scan down to the soles of our feet. Is mind in my head? Is it in my arms? Is it in my heart? We look through all the parts of our body but do not find mind in any of the parts. We might then think that it pervades the entire body, and so we look at the body as a whole.

What exactly do we mean when we talk about mind? What do we think mind is? Mind sees and hears and knows and remembers. After we've begun to do some investigation, we might ask, "Don't we think about things? Don't we remember things?" Of course we do. The question is: Where is the mind that is remembering things and thinking about them? That's what we are looking for. We are looking for that mind that knows. Doesn't the mind see colors and shapes and so on? Of course, but where is that mind that is seeing colors and shapes? What about hearing sounds? Of course we hear sounds; but where is the mind that is hearing those sounds? We're looking for the mind that sees and hears and knows and remembers, but we don't find it. This nonfinding of the mind is called emptiness. The nonfinding of the mind is the mind's lack of inherent existence, its lack of any nature of its own.

We think that our mind exists yet we cannot find it. This is why, in the *Heart Sutra*, the Buddha said, "Form is empty, emptiness is form; form is not other than emptiness, emptiness is not other than form." We go through the five aggregates in which all the different elements of body and mind can be grouped, and we cannot find our mind. In the *Heart Sutra*, the Buddha said, "Form does not exist, feeling does not exist, discrimination does not exist, mental formations do not exist, and consciousnesses do not exist." Through our analysis we are discovering that, just as the Buddha said, the body and the mind do not truly exist. We do not find mind anywhere. Is this because mind is too small? Is it because the mind is too brilliant, too clear, or too radiant to see? No. Is it because the mind is hidden behind something else? Of course not, it's our own mind. The reason we don't find our mind is because the mind is empty.

What is the nature of our mind's emptiness? Is this emptiness like the blankness of space? No. We remember things and know things, yet we cannot find the mind that knows and remembers and sees. The mind knows, but the knower is not to be found. "Form is empty, emptiness is form." Likewise, each of the five aggregates that make up a person is empty, and emptiness is each of the five aggregates. Therefore, we can say, "Consciousness is empty, emptiness is consciousness." Form and emptiness happen simultaneously. We speak about the union of appearance and emptiness in regard to visual forms and the union of luminosity and emptiness in regard to consciousnesses or mind. The inseparability of appearance and emptiness means that appearing forms are empty; yet while empty, they appear. Similarly, consciousness is empty and, at the same time, it is luminous. This union of luminosity and emptiness is exactly what we discover when we look for the mind.

After saying, "form is empty, emptiness also is form," the *Heart Sutra* then continues, "emptiness is not other than form, form is not other than emptiness." Likewise, mind is emptiness, emptiness is also mind; emptiness is not other than mind, mind is not other than emptiness. "Not other than" means we won't find them in separate places. It's not possible to put the form over here and its emptiness somewhere else. The emptiness of the mind and the mind itself are one. There is no mind that is not emptiness in terms of its very nature.

Rather than merely understanding this intellectually, we must actually experience it. It is not good enough to say, "Well, I think it's like this." We have to be certain. The text says that the mind analyzes itself in the manner of "rock meeting bone." When we look at mind with this directness and intensity, we find the luminous empty nature of mind, the nonfinding of mind within awareness, and we rest within that. At that point we know the mind is empty. It is no longer a mere theory. We abide smoothly and evenly (Tib. *chammeba*) within that luminosity and emptiness. We don't waver but rest fully, steadily, smoothly, and comfortably within that luminosity and emptiness.

Sutra Tradition of Meditating on the Mind

[186] In the next section, the text cites many more passages from the Buddha's teachings showing the importance of meditating upon the nature of mind, the way to meditate upon the nature of mind, and what is seen and not seen when we meditate upon the nature of mind. It is an exhortation to actually experience the nature of mind rather than settling for a vague understanding of it.

In the sutra tradition, it takes eon upon eon of accumulating merit in order to strengthen and empower the mind to the point that it can actually realize emptiness. In the tradition of quintessential instructions, however, the nature of mind is introduced directly. Recognizing this, it becomes clear that we are incredibly fortunate to have encountered the tradition of quintessential instructions.

How to Determine the Nature of Mind

[190] What kind of experience arises when we look at mind properly, relying upon the quintessential instructions that have been passed down through the Kagyu lineage? When we investigate, we find that the mind has no shape and no color. All matter has shape and color. So, once we've determined that the mind has no shape or color, we can determine that the mind is not a material form.

Does the mind dwell somewhere? When we look, we see that the mind does not dwell outside the body, inside the body, or somewhere in between these two. It doesn't dwell anywhere because there is nothing to dwell. The mind cannot be identified as any thing. It cannot be said to exist in a certain way, nor can it be said to be nonexistent. If it were an existent phenomenon, we would be able discern the way it exists. If we could identify the mind as something that does not exist, then we would also be able say precisely how it does not exist. But in fact the mind cannot be identified even in that simple way, nor can the mind be identified as something that takes a certain aspect or expression and then changes into something else. We cannot conclusively identify the the mind as the changing expressions or moods of the mind. In this way, the mind is found to be free from all elaboration or complexity.

In texts such as the *Sutra of Great Compassion* and the *Manifest Purification of Vairochana Tantra*, mind is said to be like space. We might think that this means it is vast like space or blue like the sky. But these are not the characteristics these texts are talking about when they say that mind is like space. These texts are saying is that the mind, like space, is nothing whatsoever. Mind has no nature of its own. It does not exist by way of its own inherent essence.

The same thing was expressed in the sutras and the tantras and discovered by the great siddhas of the mahamudra tradition. There are many ways to express it. We can say it is the lack of inherent existence. We can say it is the lack of any nature that truly characterizes phenomena. We can say it is emptiness. We can talk about the mind's way of being. In the end, it comes down to the fact that when we look for the mind itself, we don't find anything.

The Mind's Nature
When we look for the nature of the mind, the distinction between the object that is looked at and the thing that is looking is a false distinction. Nevertheless, when we sit down to practice meditation, it seems that there is something that is looked at and something that is looking. Since we are working with our experience, we investigate the way these seem to be. We settle in the meditative stabilization called shamata and look. Who, or what, is looking? Who is it that does not find anything and knows that not finding is the mind's nature? The looker is *the wisdom of discriminating awareness*. It is the wisdom of discriminating awareness that looks for the mind's nature. We cannot stop there, however. We have to look for the looker, asking: Where is it? What is it? and so forth. When we have found that the looker does not exist as this or that shape or nature, we have arrived at what is called *thoroughly nonconceptual wisdom*. At that point, we find the mind to be like space.

When we say that the mind is like space, we do not mean that it is identical to space. Space has no awareness of itself. The emptiness of space is characterized as a lifeless emptiness, a corpse, lacking the quality of luminosity. The mind's emptiness is not like that. The mind is empty, but that emptiness knows. The mind does not exist; nevertheless, it sees, it knows, it understands. In particular, it knows, understands, and illuminates itself. Hence, it is called "the wisdom that is aware of itself." It does not exist, yet it knows and understands that nonexistence.

The great siddha Tilopa explained this in a passage cited by Tashi Namgyal. "Kye ho!" exclaims Tilopa, expressing pleasure, for the mind's nature is a luminosity free from all pain, free from suffering. "This is the wisdom that is aware of itself," Tilopa continues, "It is beyond speech. It is not to be found within the sphere of the mind." "Beyond speech" means we cannot say that the mind exists and we cannot say that the mind does not exist. It is beyond the paths on which speech travels. This echoes a well-known passage in praise of the prajnaparamita, which says that mind's nature is *masam jöme,* which means it cannot be expressed by speech or thought. Mind's nature is not an object that falls within the sphere of ordinary intellect. Therefore, Tilopa says, "I have nothing whatsoever to teach," meaning that since the mind cannot be said to exist or not to exist, he cannot say that it is this or that it is that. So what can we do if we cannot say anything about it? Tilopa explains, "The mind is nearby. It is within you. You can look yourself. You can discover it yourself, identify it yourself, point to it yourself, and know it. And that's what you should do."

Mistakes in Perceiving Mind's Nature

There are three kinds of mistakes that might be made at this point. One of these is to think that shamata—the simple peaceful state of the mind at rest—is the mind's way of being. When the mind looks at the mind, and the samadhi of shamata arises, we might think that we have seen the mind's true nature. But this is a mistake. We have not really seen the luminosity that is the mind's nature, nor have we gained genuine knowledge and conviction of the mind's lack of inherent existence.

A second mistake is to consider the various appearances that sometimes arise in meditation to be the mind's actual way of being. Due to the force of latent dispositions and habitual tendencies (Tib. *bagchag*), various things appear when we sit down to meditate. We might think that we have seen the mind's nature, but this is a mistake, for the same reasons.

A third mistake would be to think that different temporary experiences (Tib. *nyam*) that arise in meditation are the mind's way of being. There are three kinds of such temporary experiences: temporary experiences of luminosity, temporary experiences of nonthought, and temporary experiences of bliss. These experiences, however, are merely superficial. They are not actually the mind's way of being because we have not truly recognized the mind's lack of inherent existence. We have not ascertained the mind's lack of inherent existence with sufficient certainty to have great conviction about it. It is extremely important to have this certainty and conviction.

The Mind's Expressive Power

The mind's expressive power is its ability to move and change extremely rapidly. When the mind moves quickly, it appears externally as appearances and internally as thought. When the mind appears externally, it appears as visible forms, sounds, smells, tastes, and tangible phenomena. The mind is empty, yet things appear. When it appears internally, the mind appears as thoughts, such as liking or not liking something. The mind is empty, yet it prefers this to that. If we understand that external appearances and internal thoughts are the mind's expressive power, we will have understood the essential point of meditation. If we do not understand this, sometimes our meditation will go well, and sometimes it will seem as though we've lost it. So it's important to understand that appearance and thought are the mind's expressive power.

External appearances in the mind—visible forms, sounds, smells, and so forth—are not other than the mind. How is it this so? They certainly seem to be external, apart from mind. Moreover, external things are often hard and solid. How can they be said to be mind? Actually, these appearances are caused mainly by the energy of latent predispositions or habitual tendencies. Sometimes this energy manifests as things that are quite hard when in fact they are not. An analogy is a dream. During a dream, various things appear to us. These appearances look like real, solid things, but they are created by our mind and are not separate from our mind. The things in the dream are created by the mind, yet they appear to be external to it. It's the same with the appearances of waking life. They are not truly other than the mind. They are not solid, independent, but they certainly do appear that way.

Realizing the Nature of Appearances

[196] We may not be able to realize the nature of external appearances right off; however we can look at the mind and experience its emptiness directly. When we do this, we can by extension understand the nature of apparently external appearances as well. Why is this? It is because the nature of the mind and the nature of appearances are identical. The nature of the mind is the same as the nature of all phenomena. Saraha said, "Since the mind alone is the seed of all, it is this that unfolds samsara and nirvana." This means that all the phenomena of samsara and all the phenomena of nirvana arise from the mind. For that reason, when we realize the mind's nature, we will naturally understand the nature of all that appears.

Thoughts and appearances are merely expressions of the mind. Their nature is the same as the mind's nature. We might then think that it's not necessary to pursue any further techniques for understanding their nature. However, there are the instructions on how to recognize the nature of thought and of appearances. We must follow certain stages of meditation to arrive at the realization. The way we do this is quite similar to the way we understand the selflessness of phenomena as taught in the sutras. Because it is easier to investigate the nature of thoughts than the nature of appearances, we start with investigating the nature of thoughts.

We begin by resting briefly in the nature of mind, in the luminosity and emptiness that cannot be identified as anything at all. From within that meditative stabilization, we give rise to a strong thought, such as a thought of hatred or pride. Then we look at it and ask: Where is it? Is it inside? Is it outside? What is its nature? We don't follow after it. We don't brood about a past event, or become seduced by the thought. Rather, we look nakedly and directly at the thought and analyze: Where is it? Where does it dwell? Upon what does it depend? What is its shape? What is its color? When we look, we see that this thought of hatred or pride does not really exist. When we recognize it as not truly real, it is pacified, which is to say, it dissolves into nonconceptuality.

We repeat this process again and again. We let our mind wander a little from the state of merely resting in peace and think of someone who has harmed us. We think of the harm that this person did to us in the past and we arouse anger. Then we look at that anger. Where is it? What is it? Where did it come from? Where is it going? What is it actually? As we look and investigate, the lack of establishment of the anger will dawn for us. When that appears and we understand it, we can then say that we have realized the nature of hatred, the nature of thought, or the nature of mind, because these three are the same.

We can do the same with attachment or desire. From within the state of meditative stability, we think about something or someone we desire. When desire arises, we look at its nature. What is it? Where does it rest? Where does it go? As we examine it in this way, the thought becomes nonthought—it becomes the union of luminosity and emptiness. When we understand this luminosity-emptiness, we have understood the mind's nature and the nature of thought; we have cut through projections and resolved all questions about what the mind's nature actually is. We have found mind's nature to be the absence of inherent existence or any characteristic or quality that defines or belongs to the mind. We do this again and again and again until we have real understanding. When we have some experience recognizing mind's lack of inherent existence, then thoughts that arise in meditation, though they may seem to be obstructions at first, become part of the meditation.

Once we realize that the nature of individual thought, the nature of the mind, and the nature of dharmata are all the same, we then turn to the appearances of visible forms, sounds, smells, tastes, and so forth and determine what their nature is. These appearances seem to be things having particular shapes and colors. For instance, the mind begins to appear as as mountains, houses, and rivers. From the point of view of mahamudra, we say that these appearances arise through the force of latent predispositions.

In the sutra tradition, as we have seen, there is a process of reasoned analysis for determining that the apparent objects do not really exist. We begin this analysis with a large external phenomenon, such as a mountain. As we analyze the mountain we begin to understand that the mountain is composed of particles, which are composed of even smaller particles, and so on, until we arrive at something that is irreducible. Finally we realize that the irreducible particle itself does not exist. Through analyzing very minutely, we discover that the apparent object is not really there.

In the tradition of practicing the quintessential instructions we do not look at and analyze external objects; rather, we look at the mind that apprehends these appearances, analyzing and determining the nature of that mind. We recognize the emptiness that is the nature of that mind. We understand too that emptiness is the nature of the object apprehended by that mind. When a visual form with color and shape appears to an eye consciousness, rather than analyzing that form, we look at the mind seeing it. We ask: What is the mind to which form appears? Does it have a color or a shape? What sort of thing is it? Where is it? We discover that the seeing mind cannot be found. We then realize that if the seeing mind does not exist, the external object does not exist either. This method also applies with sounds, smells, and so forth.

We have described how we work with the appearances of the five sensory consciousnesses. What about the sensation that things are pleasant or painful? Sometimes things seem to be very delightful, and other times things seem miserable. We investigate the mind that experiences pleasure or pain in the same way. We look for the mind that feels pleasure or suffers pain. We find nothing. Rather, the pleasant or painful experience is resolved into the union of luminosity and emptiness. If we do this again and again, we realize that the nature of thought and appearance is the dharmata, reality. It is the nature of mind itself.

Eliminating Doubts about the Root of Samsara and Nirvana

[200] It is helpful if we know how to meditate on the nature of the mind itself, but if we have not learned to recognize the luminosity-emptiness that is the nature of thought and appearance, then thoughts and appearances will seem to be obstacles to our practice of meditation. As long as we can focus upon mind itself, we will be able to meditate smoothly. But if we haven't learned how to meditate with the appearances that dawn from any of the consciousnesses or with thoughts and emotions that arise, the process will be rough, difficult, and tumultuous when we have to work with them. There will be internal conflict. That is why it is extremely beneficial to meditate on the nature of thought and appearance and discover that it is luminosity-emptiness.

10

ELIMINATING DOUBTS ABOUT VIPASHYANA

[200] It is important to know the mistakes that might be made in meditation so we can recognize them in our experience and steer clear of them. Otherwise, we might think we have arrived at at state when we really haven't. For example, we might experience the mind as very relaxed and at ease and interpret this as vipashyana. Having relaxed, we might then experience unusual appearances and forms, such as flowers, different colors, or bright lights, and mistake these appearances for the nature of mind. Or we might experience a sense of vivid emptiness—a huge, open, clear, empty space—and think that this is vipashyana. In fact, none of these experiences is vipashyana.

What then is vipashyana? Vipashyana is not the creation of something new and sensational, nor it is the finding of something that was hidden. Rather, it is a matter of understanding what our mind has always been, naturally, from the beginning. The only problem we have is that we've never looked directly at our mind and therefore haven't experienced our mind as it is.

This chapter of Tashi Namgyal's text, "Severing Projections with Regard to the Basis and the Expressive Power," discusses the process of cutting through doubts, or projections, about the ground and expressive power. In the previous chapter we talked about three phases of looking at the mind—looking at the mind itself, looking at thoughts, and looking at external appearances. These three also apply to the process of abandoning doubts.

Doubts That Appearances Are Created by Mind
[200] The first section explains how to cut through our doubts about thoughts and appearances and resolve definitively that thoughts and appearances are nothing more than mind itself. This means that the movement of thoughts and the appearances of phenomena are not to be found anywhere other than the mind.

What is the difference between looking at the nature of mind on the one hand and decisively cutting through all hesitation and mistaken ideas about thoughts and appearances as mind itself on the other? To settle decisively the nature of thought, the nature of appearance, and the nature of mind itself, we investigate the shape and the color of mind, thought, appearance, and so forth, and see that thoughts and appearances do not exist in their own nature. When we cut through doubts and discover that thought and appearance are mind itself, we look to see the source of these thoughts and appearances. Where do they come from? Where do they rest? Where do they go? When we investigate in this way, we discover that mind is inseparable from thoughts and appearances.

The Technique of Strong Thought
Ratna Lingpa suggested a method for cutting through doubts that we might call "the method of strong thought." We begin by resting in meditation upon emptiness. We then induce a strong thought, such as anger. When this thought arises, we look at it and ask: Where did the thought come from? In response, we might say, "Well, I started thinking about someone I hate and the terrible things that this person did to me, and from this a thought of hatred arose." Roughly speaking, that does seem to

be so, but this reply doesn't answer the question of what the origin of this thought, of this hatred, really is. So we look for the specific point where the thought arises. We look and look, but we do not find any such place.

We might then think that the thought arises from the mind. If so, we ask, what is the manner of its arising from the mind? Does a thought arise from the mind in the way that a child is born from its mother, so that they become distinct and individual entities that can each exist on their own? If not, does a thought arise from the mind in the way that light radiates from the sun or the moon, so that each has its own power and dawning? Or does the mind itself become the thought, so that first it is mind, and then it transforms and becomes thought? If we look carefully, we see that none of these three processes describe it. We see that, in fact, thought is unborn.

We then look to see where the thought abides and how it abides. We tend to regard hatred as very strong and forceful. It seems to be quite real, and we cling to it as real. When we begin to look into it, however, we find that even this powerful thought, with so much energy, cannot be identified as anything at all. There is no way to grab hold of it or identify exactly what it is.

When a strong thought arises we also look to see where it goes when it departs. We look and look for its point of disappearance, and we do not find it. That leaves two possibilities: the thought ceased and became a nonthing, or the thought was naturally cleansed, pacified, and purified.

We do this investigation with powerful thoughts and with subtle thoughts. From where do they arise? Where do they abide? Where do they go?

We might also bring to mind contradictory thoughts, such as the sense that one thing is pleasant and that some other thing is painful. We look at these thoughts, one after the other. What actually is the difference between them? They seem to be different, but when we look, we can't find a place where a sense of pleasantness arises or where a sense of pain arises. Likewise, we cannot find where they abide or where they go.

We might wonder: What is the point of doing all this looking if we can't find anything? The point is that we tend to have very fixed ideas about these things, especially about what we think of as pleasant and what we think of as painful. We think of them as quite distinct from one another. We might also think of mind as being on the inside and thoughts that appear as being on the outside. But when we carefully investigate our experience, such conceptions fall to pieces. We see that mind and thoughts are of the same nature and cannot be separated. We recognize and experience them as such. Experiencing mind and thought as inseparable is the point of all this looking.

If we do not meditate in this way and so discover that thought is inseparable from mind itself, then thought will be a hindrance to meditation. We would be content to meditate upon mind itself, but when thoughts arose, they would tend to destroy our meditation. On the other hand, if we have investigated the nature of thought and found that it arises out of nowhere, rests nowhere, and disappears to nowhere, we will have understood that the mind experienced in meditation and thought are identical. Then, we experience thought as simply another expression of the mind's true nature, and thoughts no longer pose an obstacle to our meditation.

Doubts about Resting and Moving Mind

[203] The next section explains how to cut through our doubts with regard to appearances and resolve decisively that appearances are mind.

As before, we rest in meditation. Appearances, such as visual images, will arise. We look for the point of arisal, the point of abiding, and the eventual point of dissolution of these images. When a visual form appears, a mind apprehends it. We investigate the mind that apprehends appearance. From where does that mind arise? Where does it dwell? Where does it go? What is the relationship between the visual image perceived and the mind that sees it? When we look, we find that we cannot separate appearance and mind and that they are, in fact, not different.

When we do this investigation, it is helpful to look in particular at the mind that perceives beautiful forms and the mind that perceives ugly forms, or the mind that perceives pleasant sounds and the mind that perceives unpleasant sounds. What is the difference between the mind that sees the beautiful image and the mind that sees the ugly image? Again, we look to see where the mind begins, where it rests, and where it goes.

In terms of the mind itself, it is helpful to identify two different phases: the mind at rest and the mind moving. When the mind is at rest there is not much thought—it is peaceful, smooth, and even. When the mind is moving, many different thoughts naturally arise. We investigate the difference between mind at rest and mind that moves. When the mind is at rest, where does that mind come from? Where does it abide? Where does it go? When the mind is moving, where does that mind come from? Where does it abide? Where does it go? What really is the difference between the mind that is still and the mind that is moving? At first it may seem that they have different natures: it seems that the mind that is still is peaceful, free from thought, smooth, even, and the mind that is moving is different.

To investigate this, we rest within a deep meditative state. From within this state, look at the mind that is still. We see that it is empty of any nature of its own, it is nothing other than luminosity and emptiness. We then look at the mind that is moving. Thoughts arise and are released on their own. When we look at the still mind and the moving mind with this technique, we discover that they do not have different natures; they are both empty of any nature that is truly their own. From that point of view, the still mind and the moving mind cannot be differentiated. Their nature is emptiness.

It's quite easy to think that the resting mind and the moving mind have completely different natures and that when the mind is moving, the stillness has been lost. Some students think that they must clear away the motion before the mind can be at rest. They believe that there is a contradiction between the mind at rest and the moving mind. In fact, both the resting mind and the moving mind are the union of luminosity and emptiness. We perceive differences due to our confusion. Stillness does not obstruct motion and motion does not obstruct stillness; they are simply one inseparable entity.

Doubts about Appearances as Unborn

[205] The third section is called "Cutting Through and Resolving Decisively That Everything That Appears Is Unborn." Once again we rest within the unity of luminosity and emptiness. From within that state, the mind looks at itself. We look to see from where the mind arises, what causes it to arise, where it abides, and where it goes when it leaves. We cannot find any point of origin of the mind, any place where it dwells, and any point at which it ceases. When we realize this, we have understood that the mind is not established by way of its own nature. We finally settle that everything that appears is unborn and that mind is just a name. We have identified this mind without identity.

Characteristics of Emerging Insight

[208] This section concerns the measure of whether or not we have given rise to vipashyana. In fact, the strength of mind at rest, or shamata, prevents us from realizing mind's nature, or vipashyana. Due to the strength of mind at rest, we cannot give rise to the certainty, conviction, and realization of vipashyana.

From within shamata, dramatic and persuasive experiences arise. When this happens, we might think that we have experienced something truly and profoundly. We might think we've experienced the mind's emptiness when we have not. The shamata itself obstructs our realization. To achieve the actual realization of the mind's true nature, we need to relax further, separate from the transient experiences, and meditate upon insight.

There are other kinds of problems students might experience. Some with obscured minds are obstructed by karma, or the imprint of past actions. No matter how much they analyze, they are not able to see mind itself. It is necessary for these students to work at other practices for a while, particularly practices for accumulating the collections of wisdom and merit and purifying obstructions that have been accumulated in the past. When they have done this, they are able to give rise to shamata with a crisp and keen edge to it. Through sustaining that shamata, they are eventually able to give rise to the insight of vipashyana, the realization of mind's true nature.

The problem for other students is that they are too intellectual. Their reasoned way has become so strong that it is getting in the way of actually giving rise to real experience. These students need to apply themselves more to the actual practice of meditation, set aside intellectualization, and just look very simply at the mind's point of origin, place of rest, and point of disappearance until their meditation bears some fruit.

This Vipashyana and Other Kinds of Vipashyana

[209] In this section, Tashi Namgyal analyzes forms of vipashyana mentioned in other Buddhist texts to see if they are different from the vipashyana of mahamudra. He shows that the practice of mahamudra vipashyana, which investigates the mind's way of being, is essentially the same as all the other kinds of vipashyana.

Questions

QUESTION: Is it correct to say that, from the point of view of vipashyana, delusion is suppressed in shamata?

RINPOCHE: Delusion is like a dream and an illusion, but we have not realized this when we are resting in the state of peace known as shamata. There's less delusion in the state of shamata, but the nature of the mind and the nature of that delusion have not been realized. For that reason shamata does not serve as an antidote to delusion. It's a temporary solution, although a stepping-stone on the way to a permanent understanding. The mind becomes very relaxed in shamata, and the delusion relaxes too, but the nature of that delusion has not been realized. In vipashyana, the mind and delusion are realized to be empty—like a dream and like an illusion. In that sense, we say that shamata suppresses delusion and that vipashyana cuts it from the root.

QUESTION: Is there is a relationship between the increase of virtue and auspicious coincidence?

RINPOCHE: The connection between the increase of virtue and the gathering together of auspicious coincidences for the practice and realization of mahamudra is principally through the practice of virtue. If we practice virtue, conditions harmonious with the practice of mahamudra can come about. It may come to pass that we meet with a guru who holds the lineage of mahamudra and who can teach it, that we actually hear these teachings, that we feel faith and devotion when we hear these teachings, and that we have the necessary resources and suitable conditions to allow us to pursue mahamudra practice. An increase of virtue brings about the auspicious coincidences that allow us to arrive at realization. If we have not accumulated virtue, auspicious coincidences don't come about.

QUESTION: My understanding is that mahamudra can be applied not just on the cushion but when we're at work and in other situations. My own experience with work is that it's really a time for awareness to go to sleep. When I go to work, I feel like I've been slammed into a mental dungeon. Then I get used to it and I become kind of numb. I cannot think of how to combine awareness with that. I think it's partially because I'm not grinding sesame seeds, which doesn't require that much concentration. I write code for computers, and it takes 100 percent of my mind staring at this code.

RINPOCHE: When we're talking about these investigations, such as looking to see where the mind arises, where it rests, and where it goes, we're talking about the work that we do within the formal session of meditation, the period of sitting on the cushion. When we do that, particularly if we have the opportunity to do it in a retreat session, some experience does arise, and we get some sense of what it's about. The point is that when we get up off the cushion or leave the retreat, we do not forget about that experience completely but sustain it by maintaining mindfulness, or recollection, and awareness of that. Of course, that's not the easiest thing to do, particularly for a beginner. But it's crucial that we not become discouraged and just cast the whole thing away when it becomes difficult. That's really the critical point, to not give up.

It might be a little bit easier were we pounding sesame seeds like Tilopa. But, if you think about it, there are certainly examples of people like Nagarjuna who had extremely complex intellectual work to do and managed to conjoin that with the practice of mahamudra. Nagarjuna achieved supreme enlightenment. That should give us some hope and inspiration that, indeed, it is possible to do truly serious intellectual work and at the same time mix it with our experience of mahamudra, with the practice we've done, and with our sustaining that awareness in the rest of our life. When Nagarjuna was composing the books on Madhyamaka, he really had to tighten his awareness and focus and concentrate. That's similar to the situation in which many of us find ourselves now and certainly to the situation you're describing. But, just as he was able to find a way to conjoin that kind of study and intellectual complexity with the practice of mahamudra, it is possible for us, too. It's not easy in the beginning, but it's important to not become discouraged by that difficulty and to continue. Stage by stage, it will get better.

QUESTION: You were speaking about looking at the looker. When I look into the face of the looker, it ceases, and then a cognizance of looking arises. Is that cognizance another looker, or is it "prajna" or "discriminating intelligence?"

RINPOCHE: What does it mean to talk about prajna or the intelligence of discriminating awareness? Calling it prajna or intelligence is to say that it is not stupid, not obscure, not dull, and not deluded. It understands things as they are. When it sees something, it sees it accurately. It knows that certain things are of good quality, poor quality, or whatever. Think about it this way: if we take two sticks and rub them together, eventually that creates fire, which then burns up the two sticks. In a similar way, if we look at mind, we see that mind is an emptiness that is unidentifiable as anything at all, and we then experience the union of luminosity and emptiness. That prajna, that intelligence of discriminating awareness experiences and knows the union of luminosity and emptiness that pervades all of the mind and all of one's experience. Because it knows this, the prajna itself does not become solidified. We don't hang onto it. We don't experience it as some kind of real thing that we can fixate on.

QUESTION: If we're looking at the mind, we're looking at the looker, and when we look at the looker, that brings a second looker, and then if we look at that one, there's a third looker. This could go on endlessly.

RINPOCHE: Logically speaking, that is so. If we're just thinking about what might happen, then it could happen that way. But if we actually do the practice, it doesn't. It's not like an eye consciousness looking at a visual form. It is the mind looking at itself. And since we have a mind that is of the nature of emptiness looking at its own nature, the object and the apprehending subject are not two things to begin with. Being of the nature of emptiness, the object and the apprehending subject dissolve into that emptiness. So there's a slight fluttering, but it doesn't really go on that way. It quickly resolves itself if we actually get in touch with the emptiness.

QUESTION: Would it be correct to say that the insight known as vipashyana has to be induced? Does the practitioner have to ask the questions and look at the mind in the way that you just spoke about?

RINPOCHE: No matter how long we persist exclusively in practicing shamata, it will not become vipashyana. No matter how much we develop the principal shamata qualities of stability and clarity, it will not bring about vipashyana. Shamata is very good, important, beneficial, and necessary to do. But techniques of shamata will not bring about vipashyana.

Vipashyana means "the prajna that realizes in a very precise way." In shamata we look at mind, but not at what mind is. Looking at our mind, we assess the mind's stability, clarity, wildness, and so forth. But we don't examine what mind is. What is its shape? What is its color? Does it have any of those qualities? That kind of investigation isn't part of the practice of shamata.

In the *Prajnaparamita Sutras*, the Buddha said, "Form does not exist, feelings do not exist, discriminations do not exist," and so forth. In this list of things, starting with the second one, feelings, we are talking about mind. When we look for the mind, we find that these things—feelings, discriminations, and so forth—are nearby, and we can look at them. But when we look, we find nothing there. If there is nothing there, does that mean mind is nothing more that a corpse? No, because the mind's emptiness is suffused by luminosity. Sometimes we talk about this as the "union of space and wisdom," with space referring to emptiness and wisdom referring to luminosity. That experience is vipashyana.

11

MIND AS IT IS AND COEMERGENCE

[213] This section of the root text, "The Stages of Virtuous Practice," consists of two sections: the first discusses the mind as it is and the second discusses coemergence. The explanation given is not from the point of view of meditative experience; therefore, we must study it with our prajna.

The True Nature of Mind

[213] The section on the mind as it is explains the essence of mind, the nature of mind, and the definitive characteristics of mind. The essence of mind is luminosity, or *salwa*. We might interpret this to mean that mind is like light; however the Tibetan word has the meaning of "knowing" rather than light. The essence of mind is also peacefulness, which is to say that it is without discursive thought and conception.

[216] The nature of mind is that it is not produced, it does not abide, and it does not cease. If the mind were an actual thing, it would be produced, it would eventually cease, and in between these two moments, it would abide. But when we examine carefully we find this is not so. Therefore we can say that the mind is not truly existent, the mind is empty.

The nature of mind is also dharmadhatu, the sphere of reality. *Dhatu* means "that which offers no obstruction." If we were talking about space, we would say space is everywhere—there is no place we do not find space. Anything can come into and pass through space, but nothing will ever be limited by space. "No obstruction" indicates that there is an opportunity for anything to appear without being obstructed, as if by a mountain that stands in the way of something else. *Dharmadhatu* indicates that place where it is completely suitable for faults to be abandoned and for all the good qualities to increase. To say mind is both empty and dharmadhatu means that it is not inherently established and is free from creation, abiding, and cessation.

[218] The characteristic of the mind is that it appears as samsara and nirvana. Because it is not a solid entity, the mind can appear as samsara and as nirvana. To ordinary persons such as ourselves, appearing as samsara and as nirvana may seem contradictory, but they are not.

A discussion of the view of the Madhyamaka school may help us to understand this point. There are two divisions of the Madhyamaka school: the Svatantrika and the Prasangika. In the Svatantrika school, appearances are considered relative (or conventional) reality while emptiness is considered absolute (or ultimate) reality. On the relative level, appearances appear, but on the absolute level, they are empty. While there are some contradictions in the Svatantrika presentation, nevertheless the explanations are helpful when we are beginning to understand emptiness.

The Prasangika view is a higher one than the Svatantrika school's. For Prasangikas, emptiness and appearance are not contradictory. Thus the *Heart Sutra* says, "Form is empty, emptiness is form. Form is not other than emptiness, emptiness is not other than form." In this view, form and emptiness exist together. They have the same nature. It is like the appearance of an elephant in a dream. While the elephant appears in our dream, no elephant is actually there. The nonexistence of the elephant and the appearance of the elephant seem contradictory, but in fact they occur together.

When we are on the path of inference, we consider form and emptiness to be like the elephant that appears in a dream. In this way, we come to understand the lack of inherent existence of various phenomena. When we are on the path of direct perception, however, we look straight into our mind and see it as emptiness, as lacking inherent existence. Mind lacks inherent existence whether or not we are looking at it. The mind has been there from the beginning of time, and from the beginning of time it has been without inherent existence. It is primordially free of production, cessation, and abiding.

Coemergence

[220] The Tibetan *lhenchig kyepa* is translated as "coemergence" or "coming together," as with two rivers merging. It could also be translated as "innate," because it quite literally means, "born together." *Coemergence* refers to the fact that the wisdom that realizes the true nature of phenomena is already present within us. It is not something that needs to be newly generated. We have this wisdom, but we have not realized it. Because we have not realized things as they are, or mahamudra, we suffer. Through coemergent wisdom we connect with the reality of things that are already present within us.

THE TERMINOLOGY OF COEMERGENCE

[221] When we speak about coemergence, we are talking about nothing other than the mind's true nature. Thus, coemergence means the clear light that is like space and that is the sovereign of all of samsara and nirvana. When we speak about coemergence, we are also talking about the inseparability of emptiness and luminosity. When ordinary people such as ourselves understand something about the mind's emptiness, we do not understand its luminosity, and when we understand something about the luminosity of the mind, we don't get at its emptiness. But, in fact,

the emptiness and luminosity of the mind are fully integrated. The emptiness of the mind is not an emptiness that negates luminosity—it is the utter groundlessness of the mind. And the luminosity of the mind does not solidify its ability to know. Emptiness and luminosity are not contradictory in any way. They are coemergent.

What is it that emerges together? It is phenomena (Skt. *dharma*) and their essence, or reality (Skt. *dharmata*). We might explain this by saying that there are phenomena, which includes things that are stable and things that move, and at the same time, there is reality. That is how we experience things. Another way to describe this is to say that there is the appearance of phenomena, and at the same time, there is their true nature, which is emptiness. We tend to treat appearances or phenomena as being external to us, as having inherent nature, and as being real things. But the appearance of things and their suchness—their reality, their emptiness—are not sequential such that first one of them occurs and then the other. It is not the case, for instance, that things first exist and later become empty. Rather, the appearance of things and their emptiness are simultaneous. Nor is it the case that we somehow bring that coemergence and that emptiness into being when we meditate. It is just that we normally do not recognize the coemergence that is the nature of the mind and the nature of phenomena. Through meditating, we begin to understand it.

TYPES OF COEMERGENCE

[222] There are several types of coemergent wisdom. In the teachings of the Buddha in the sutras and the teachings of the siddhas in the treatises, coemergent wisdom is divided into ground, path, and fruition coemergent wisdom.

Ground coemergent wisdom is the reality of luminosity and emptiness; it is the mind in its basic nature. This wisdom has existed within us since the beginning of time, but we have not realized it. Therefore, we need to listen to a guru's teaching, reflect on what we have heard, and meditate on what we have understood.

Path coemergent wisdom is when coemergent wisdom is born within us. We become accustomed to coemergent wisdom, and our familiarity with it increases further and further. Eventually all of the adventitious stains, that is elements not inherent to the mind, are cleared away, and all good qualities blossom fully. At that point we achieve supreme siddhi, or enlightenment, which is *fruition coemergent wisdom*.

Two additional types of coemergent wisdom are described in the Vajrayana tantras: The fourth type arises through contemplative practices that involve manipulating the subtle winds and working with the subtle channels and the subtle drops. The union of bliss and emptiness is the fifth type of coemergent wisdom.

Further, the great teachers of the Kagyu lineage have given explanations of coemergence based on their own experience.

The Instructions of Gampopa

[222] While the presentations of coemergent wisdom in the tantras and the treatises are very clear, they are not joined with the quintessential instructions. So it is helpful to look at the quintessential instructions given by Gampopa, which describe coemergence and the practice of meditation.

Gampopa described two types of coemergence: coemergent mind and coemergent appearances. *Coemergent mind* refers to the point of realization when shamata and vipashyana have been integrated and we realize mind as it is—empty, luminous, and free from complexity. We then rest in this true essence of mind. The mind, however, has a resourcefulness, or power, that does not cease. That resourcefulness dawns as various appearances. Because these appearances have not passed beyond the nature of mind, they are called *coemergent appearances*. In this way, we join the instructions on coemergence with the practice of meditation.

Gomchung's Three Types of Coemergence

[223] To help students understand their experience, Gampopa's student Gomchung furthered Gampopa's terminology. Gomchung pointed out that we have many different types of thoughts and emotions, such as joy and passion. We might think of these as good or bad, but they are all nothing other than mind itself. They are nothing other than luminosity and have no independent nature of their own.

Gomchung described three types of coemergence: *coemergent mind itself*, which could be regarded as the dharmakaya; *coemergent appearance*, which could be regarded metaphorically as the light of the dharmakaya; and *coemergent thought*, which could be considered as the waves of the dharmakaya—just as the ocean's waves are not separate from the ocean itself, so thoughts are not separate from mind itself. So while the tantras and the shastras speak of coemergence as ground, path, and fruition, the quintessential instructions speak of coemergence as mind itself, appearance, and thought.

Then, in the instruction on mahamudra, coemergence is called *unified coemergence*. What does that mean? There are three elements: mind (which simply means our mind), thought (mind that has become confused, agitated, and coarse), and dharmakaya (the wisdom that realizes things as they are ultimately). Originally these three were together; subsequently they appeared to us as separate; finally, through relying on the oral instructions on mahamudra given by a teacher, they are unified—just mind—once again. Mahamudra is the method that enables us to realize them as existing together, as coemergent. Thus the instruction of mahamudra is referred to as "the instruction that unites these three coemergent elements."

Gomchung further stated that the coemergent mind is the actual dharmakaya. This means that the mind's way of being—as the union of luminosity and emptiness—is not established from the very first. The *actual dharmakaya* is the mind's integration of luminosity-emptiness when realized in the yogin's or yogini's experience.

Once this dharmakaya has been recognized, then something further can be understood. Gomchung stated, "The coemergence of appearance is the light of dharmakaya." In other words, various things appear, but because we now understand them to be an integration or union of luminosity and emptiness, we do not believe them to be real. Rather, we understand that they have no nature of their own, and on that basis develop the wisdom of dharmakaya. When thoughts are not misconceived to have a nature of their own, they are found to be like waves of the dharmakaya. The inseparability of mind, appearance, and thoughts is both the actual dharmakaya as well as the meaning of dharmakaya. In other words, there is the dharmakaya, which is the undifferentiability of coemergent mind, coemergent appearance, and coemergent thought, and, at the same time, there is the meaning of dharmakaya, which is the undifferentiable coemergence of those three. One aspect cannot be privileged over the others, for all three are inseparable, undifferentiable.

Pagmodrupa's Coemergence

When Gampopa spoke about "the joining of coemergence," he meant looking at thought from different points of view and seeing in it the four bodies of enlightenment. Gampopa's student, Pagmodrupa, took this a step further. He applied the notion of "the joining of coemergence" to the three elements of mind, thought, and dharmakaya. Mind, thought, and dharmakaya are naturally joined from the very first, but we do not realize this. Through the practice of mahamudra, we can discover the undifferentiability of these three. And when we do, that is "the joining of coemergence."

Three Aspects of Coemergence

[225] This section looks at the nature of coemergence by investigating "pointing out coemergent mind," "pointing out coemergent thought," and

"pointing out coemergent appearance." Here we talk about discriminating among the different experiences we might have when we are meditating and identifying what the experience of coemergence actually is.

By looking at it repeatedly and from many points of view, the meaning of coemergence gradually becomes clearer. Gampopa said that mind is coemergent, thoughts are coemergent, and appearances are coemergent.

COEMERGENT MIND

[225] Appearances to mind, mind itself, and mind's lack of inherent existence go together in what we call coemergence. We might think that the existence of something conventionally and the nonexistence of that thing ultimately are different. In fact, they are not, and their being together is coemergence.

To say that the mind is free from production, resting, and cessation does not mean that it is dead like a corpse. The sutras say that mind is the union of luminosity and emptiness. Because that luminosity has an aspect of bliss, in the tantras it is said that there is a union of bliss and emptiness. In the sutra context, we speak about a union of the two truths—relative and ultimate truth. All this is concerned with the way in which mind itself is coemergent.

To approach coemergent mind, we settle into shamata and the mind looks at itself. It does not stop thought but simply purifies itself and becomes peaceful. At that point, mind cannot be identified as anything at all. It rests vividly and clearly in a state of awareness that does not become dull or unclear. Mind doesn't wander, but remains clear and luminous. In *Moonlight of Mahamudra,* Tashi Namgyal says, "The mind itself remains luminous and does not stop understanding." The mind doesn't lose its intelligence but is aware of and illuminates itself. The way it does this cannot fully be explained; it has to be experienced. Even though we cannot express this state in words, we can say that it is an experience of knowing things as they are. This experience gives rise to real certainty. This experience is vipashyana.

We begin this meditation when our mind is free from sinking and wildness. We rest in a very relaxed way. Simply by looking at itself, thought is pacified. This brings forth the experience of shamata in the context of mahamudra. From within shamata, we investigate the qualities of luminosity and emptiness. If our mind appears to be luminous and vivid, we look into that. Just what is that vividness? If our mind seems to be empty, we investigate that emptiness. What is that emptiness? How is it empty? We do not need to put these questions to anyone else; we need to answer them from our own experience.

Within that experience, the stability is called shamata and the intelligence that realizes the nature of things is called vipashyana. Their names are separate but, at this point, shamata and vipashyana are not separate, rather they are different aspects of one thing. They are united and integrated.

When our experience of this settles, that is coemergent mind.

COEMERGENT THOUGHT

[229] Thoughts are also coemergent. At times the mind and its thoughts seem to be different things and at times they seem to be similar. For instance, in Milarepa's song to Bardarbum he says that mind is like an ocean and thoughts are like waves on this ocean. Although waves appear in the ocean, and we see them, they are not different from the ocean itself. Similarly, thoughts appear and are perceived but are not actually different from the mind.

In certain circumstances, however, thoughts seem to be something other than mind. By mind, we mean the aspect of luminosity, and by thoughts we mean the various things that come from the mind, such as joy, suffering, desire, and devotion. These appearances are called discursive thoughts. The nature of these thoughts is mind. Nevertheless, they are experienced as and seen to be something coarse.

In the *Kagyu Lineage Supplication*, Jampal Zangpo says, "The nature of thought is dharmakaya." Some scholars may say this statement doesn't make sense. How, they ask, could confused thoughts and the pure dharmakaya be the same thing? They have a point, for if you look at all the different aspects you would have to say that in some respects thoughts are not dharmakaya. On the conventional level, mind and thoughts appear to be different. But in the context of meditative experience, the nature of thought is the dharmadhatu, and the dharmadhatu is the dharmakaya. Therefore, the nature of thoughts is dharmakaya. From this point of view thoughts are coemergent—there is no difference between thoughts and mind.

Some people misunderstand the teaching "thought is dharmakaya" to mean that when a thought arises, it is pacified or dissolved, and then we are left with dharmakaya. Others misunderstand it to mean that if we realize thought to be dharmakaya, it is dharmakaya. The word dharmakaya, however, is made up of *dharma* meaning "the truth" and *kaya* meaning "embodiment." Thus dharmakaya refers to the ultimate mind of the Buddha. These two ways of misunderstanding the teaching stem from not understanding that, from the very beginning, thought is nothing other than the ultimate reality of the Buddha's omniscient mind. Thought doesn't become dharmakaya at some later time, and it doesn't depend on whether or not we are aware that it is dharmakaya.

The first dharma in the Four Dharmas of Gampopa is, "May the mind be one with the Dharma;" the second is, "May the Dharma go on the path;" the third is, "May the path destroy confusion;" and the fourth is, "May confusion dawn as wisdom." The fourth dharma refers to thoughts. When we look into the nature of the thoughts, we see the union of luminosity and emptiness; in that way, thoughts are seen to be of the very nature of wisdom.

To experience coemergent thought, we begin with meditative equipoise of coemergent mind. Within that state, we deliberately cause a particular thought to arise—it could be a pleasant or an unpleasant thought. We give rise to it so that it is very vivid and sharp and then look right at it nakedly. It's important that it is not an ordinary thought but rather a thought that appears vividly and clearly. In this context, we regard the thought as not truly existent so that when it arises, we don't latch onto it as if it were real.

What is the nature of this thought that arises from within coemergent mind? It is an emptiness that cannot be identified as this or that. Its nature cannot be fixed as this or that. The thought is vivid and clear, and the clarity of that thought is inseparable from its emptiness. The luminous aspect of thought and the emptiness that is its nature are inseparable. When this thought arises without any obstruction and the meditator does not become attached to it, that's shamata. When the meditator sees that this thought has no nature of its own, that's vipashyana. To accomplish the meditation fully, shamata and vipashyana must be completely integrated.

When thoughts appear they have no nature of their own. This is called "the union of appearance and emptiness." Whether or not we realize this union of appearance and emptiness has no effect on the nature of thought. Within the experience of a particular person, however, there is certainly a difference between realizing the union of appearance and emptiness and not realizing it. But emptiness is the nature of things whether we realize it or not. When we understand this in meditation, we realize coemergent thought.

Why do we need to point out coemergence of thought? We generally think that we must meditate with a relaxed, peaceful state of mind, and indeed it is very helpful to do so. But that is not the only way to meditate. In fact, just the opposite is true as well: it is also helpful to meditate with many thoughts. Thus there is the instruction on pointing out coemergence of thought.

Once again, we meditate within samadhi, or stabilized mind, in which the recognition of the mind's nature and the mind resting in peace in shamata are united. Within that, we cause a thought such as joy, passion, or aggression to arise. Such thoughts are described as coarse because they seem very strong and vivid. Whatever thought it is, whether of pleasure or revulsion, we look directly at the thought itself. From where does this thought arise? Where does it dwell? Where does it go? What is it? When we look clearly and precisely, the meaning of coemergent mind and the meaning of coemergent thought are the same. We tend to see the coarse mind and the peaceful mind as different but, in fact, the nature of coarse mind and the nature of peaceful mind are the same. The mind's nature does not change when its state changes. These animated states of mind might appear to be something, but in fact they have never been born. At this point the realization is not just a theory to be deduced; rather it is seen directly. This is why we say in the Kagyu Lineage Prayer, "Whatever thoughts arise, their nature is dharmakaya," which means that the nature of thought is mind itself, dharmakaya.

There is also a very practical use for this realization of coemergent thought. When we experience great joy and pleasure and become strongly attracted to it, or when we experience strong pain and are quite miserable, we give birth to disturbing emotions. These are painful and cause hardship, and our minds become very disturbed. At times like this the teaching on coemergent thought is particularly valuable. If we look directly at the pain that we are experiencing and the disturbing emotions, they will be pacified. And if we look directly at the strong attachment, it will diminish. This is the real purpose of understanding and being able to practice this coemergence of thought.

COEMERGENT APPEARANCE

[233] Gampopa's student Gomchung separated coemergent appearance into coemergent thought and coemergent appearance to make it easier to understand.

In the previous section, we looked at the coemergence of appearances as it pertains to feelings of pleasure and pain. In this section, we will discuss coemergent appearance as it applies to external things such as colors, shapes, and sounds. Here we are investigating the appearance of colors, shapes, sounds, and smells that arise in common because all the people who inhabit the environment performed similar actions to bring those appearances about.

We begin the meditation by resting in the meditative equipoise of coemergent mind that was explained in the previous section and look at mind itself. We then pay attention to what appears as external phenomena, such as a vase, a building, or a mountain. At this point, we might experience some difficulty. This is because, until now, we have established very strong habitual tendencies to see things as external to ourselves. We tend to think that, for example, the mountain that appears is outside and the mind is inside; we think that the mind is looking out at the mountain. Practicing this meditation is a little uncomfortable at first because we are introduced to appearance as an aspect of our mind. It's not that the eye is looking at a mountain; rather, there is an appearance of the luminosity of our own mind as a mountain. The appearance is part of the perceptive fabric of the mind itself. It is nothing other than the mind's innate luminosity. It is not something outside the mind.

When this array of color and shape appears, the meditator does not stop or allow it to become vague. The practice at this point is not a matter of just looking at the mind itself and experiencing luminosity and emptiness, but rather of looking nakedly at whatever aspect appears. The luminosity of that appearance is of a nature that is impossible to identify intellectually. It is an emptiness that cannot be grasped and fixated upon. It is this coemergent luminosity and emptiness, this coemergent appearance, that the meditator is working with in this phase.

Lingrepa said, "The mind itself, which is groundless and rootless, is well understood by thinking about last night's dreams. Last night's dreams are an excellent teacher for pointing out appearance as just mind." When we dream, all kinds of things appear, but when we awaken, we realize that these appearances were nothing other than the mind itself. Dreams are a wonderful teacher, for they help us to understand that the appearances in waking life are also nothing other than mind.

The proponents of the Mind Only school hold that all appearances are just mind. They say that all appearances, including solid external things such as mountains and buildings, are mind. They say apparently solid external phenomena are nothing other than the appearances of internal mind—they are not truly external things. While this is true, it is not what is being pointed out here. Here the term "appearances" does not refer to the external appearances, such as a mountain; rather, it refers to the experiential sense of perceiving something, such as seeing an image or hearing a sound. Some feeling goes with that perceptual experience. We aren't trying to make a point about whether or not apparently external phenomena are external and real. We are simply looking at the experience we have of seeing, hearing, and so forth. We are looking directly at that, and as we do, we see the truth of the matter. That experience becomes inseparable from dharmata. It doesn't go beyond mind itself.

Coemergent thought and coemergent appearance are not different natures, but rather different ways of speaking about one nature.

Questions

QUESTION: Why is it that appearances are not established as what they appear to be? Is it because things do not exist in the way that they appear?

RINPOCHE: This is to be understood in terms of coemergent appearance, which means that whatever appears, we inquire into the way in which it appears. The seeing of it and the hearing of it are not done through inference; rather, they are direct experience, direct perception. When we talk about illusion-like appearance in the context of inferential reasoning, we say things such as, "Because things are empty of inherent existence, they are like illusions." That is not what we are talking about here. What is being discussed here is coemergent appearance. It is looking directly at the experience, or, we could say, the "experiencing."

QUESTION: Rinpoche, I wonder if you could say more about the Tibetan word *salwa*, which is being translated as luminosity?

RINPOCHE: When we describe the mind as luminous and empty the word "luminous" might suggest light, but that is not what it means. Instead it means that the mind knows, that the mind understands. At the same time it is empty because it isn't anything and it cannot be located.

For instance, we speak about an eye consciousness—something that sees physical forms, colors, and shapes. But where is it? If we look, we can never find it. That is emptiness. The eye consciousness isn't anywhere. Nevertheless, it sees colors and shapes, and that seeing is called its luminosity.

Similarly, the ear consciousness hears sounds, yet it can never be found. It doesn't exist anywhere, but it does hear sounds, and that hearing is called its luminosity. This is true for the five sensory consciousnesses—the eye, ear, nose, tongue, and body sensation consciousness—and also the sixth consciousness—the mental consciousness.

Where is the mental consciousness? Is it in the upper or the lower part of the body? Is it in the body at all? Is it outside the body? No matter where we look for it, we never find it. Nevertheless, it remembers, it is attentive. Sometimes the mental consciousness is very coarse and sometimes it is very subtle. The mental consciousness can also realize its own nature. It is the mental consciousness that perceives all appearances of samsara. It understands, and this understanding is described as its luminosity. So we say it is the union of luminosity and emptiness.

QUESTION: I heard that the mind has no inherent nature but it has qualities like luminosity. That means that things can have qualities without existing. Can my personality, my nature, my inherent way of being, exist without my mind?

RINPOCHE: The mind itself is empty and, at the same time, has the aspect of luminosity. People have their own individual characteristics or personalities. We're talking now about the relationship between the ultimate and the conventional. When we say "conventional," there is a sense of something that is covering up and hiding something else. From the conventional perspective, everyone has their own particular qualities: some are proud, others angry, still others kind and compassionate. No question about it. But in reality none of this exists, the mind is empty; there is nothing there. Because it is empty, good qualities and wisdom can develop. Because thoughts and feelings have no real existence, faults can be purified. These qualities are not in the true nature of things, they are just superficial additions and don't need to be there. So we say that because defilements are only add-ons, or adventitious—they can be purified. How can they be purified? By realizing this lack of their real existence, which is the ultimate truth.

QUESTION: I don't understand the difference between coemergent thought and coemergent appearance because I think of thought as no different from your description of appearance or mind; that is to say, there is a mental phenomenon going on.

RINPOCHE: First of all coemergent thought and coemergent appearance are ways of speaking about one nature, not different natures. That is why Gampopa classified the different types of coemergence into only two: coemergent mind itself and coemergent appearance. Later Gomchung subdivided coemergent appearance into two: coemergent thought and coemergent appearance. When that division is made, *coemergent appearance* refers to the different appearances of visible images, sounds, etc., or the appearances of the five sense consciousnesses, and *coemergent thought* refers to the various appearances for the sixth mental consciousness.

QUESTION: Are samsara and nirvana inseparable because thoughts are confusion and thoughts are empty?

RINPOCHE: Yes, basically that is right. We can talk about samsara and nirvana that way. Thoughts are mistaken yet we speak about confusion dawning as wisdom. We are not saying confusion is wisdom. But what we are saying is that confusion is not primordially established, and therefore it can dawn as wisdom.

QUESTION: Does the Tibetan word *sem*, which is translated as mind, include the eight consciousnesses or just the sixth?

RINPOCHE: Generally speaking, *sem* refers to all eight consciousnesses. In this context, however, it is the sixth consciousness, the mental consciousness, that is doing the principal work. This is because the seventh and eighth consciousnesses are somewhat covered over and they do not identify internal or external sensory information very much. Then there are the five sensory consciousnesses, which are nonconceptual. So, at this point what we are principally talking about is the sixth, or mental, consciousness.

QUESTION: When I'm doing sitting practice, there always seems to be an observer. Can you expand a little bit on what the observer is and how to work with it?

RINPOCHE: Yes, we do have the sense of a watcher. That watcher is *namtok*, or discursive thought. And if we look very closely into it, where is it? It isn't really there. But, I don't think that beginners ought to worry about this very much. There is a story in a sutra in which the Buddha explained that we have a sense of a looker and of something looked at, but that it is like rubbing two sticks together to make fire. When fire starts, it burns both of the sticks up. It is like that in your meditation. If you go along in stages, the two of them will become nonexistent, like the sticks burning up.

QUESTION: Rinpoche, I have a problem trying to connect the understanding of emptiness that we arrive at through inference and reasoning with the direct perception of emptiness we have when we look straight into our mind. It seems that both are path. It seems that there should be some nonconceptual aspect of the emptiness by inference that would help us with the discovery of emptiness when we look directly at our minds. Could you discuss that?

RINPOCHE: The Buddha spoke of the sutra path and the tantric, or mantra, path. The sutra path is principally the path of inference. It is a long and protracted path. The sutras say that to reach buddhahood in this way requires three eons, with each eon lasting millions of years. So we need to accumulate merit and wisdom for centuries to develop certainty about the nature of things. The certainty about the nature of things becomes clearer and clearer until we arrive at direct perception, meaning a nonconceptual state. In the sutra path this realization comes about through our own ascertainment; we have not been introduced to the nature of mind by a guru. In this way we achieve first the path of accumulation, then the path of preparation, and then the path of seeing. On the path of seeing we have direct perception of emptiness. Then comes the path of meditation and finally the path of no more learning, which is buddhahood. That is the way we go about it in the sutra path.

In the Vajrayana we take direct perception as the path. In this path, millions of years are not required for achieving enlightenment. Rather, having renounced the world, enlightenment can be achieved in this lifetime. Even if we do not succeed at that, we can achieve complete enlightenment in two or three human lifetimes. In this path the guru introduces us to direct perception, and we simply meditate on the mind to which we have been introduced. Even though we have been introduced to direct perception, sometimes it is not stable. When this happens, it is very good to study the presentations that are made in the path of reasoning and inference. This will help us to develop stability in what we have ascertained and bring about good experience and realization.

Some people, having been introduced to this nature of mind, think, "I can just forget the sutras and shastras because I have the transmission, and I don't need any of that." That is not so. Studying the sutras and shastras will help bring about a very stable, clear meditation in terms of the nature of mind, which the guru has introduced.

QUESTION: Rinpoche, it seems possible to imagine seeing mind and even thoughts as empty and luminous, but I can't imagine seeing the body as empty and luminous.
RINPOCHE: At this point in the presentation of mahamudra we are pointing at the nature of mind. By knowing the nature of mind, we begin to understand the nature of all phenomena. The analysis of external phenomena is extremely important when we proceed by the inferential path. When we proceed by the direct perception path, the mind is already right with us, and we can look directly into it, so it is an easier path. The examination of the nature of mind in the path of direct perception goes

like this: Appearances are mind and mind is empty, and this emptiness is spontaneous.

When we proceed in this way, first we must resolve that external appearances are mind. We do this by using two logical arguments together: the argument of clear and knowing and the argument of the definite observation. We look into all these external appearances and how they appear clearly and vividly to consciousness. They are not existent except from the perspective of consciousness. We determine external phenomena are just appearances for mind. We do this using our body, which is merely an appearance for mind like the elephant in the dream. By examining mental factors, we would say that the body is an appearance for mind, not a mental factor. It is an appearance made by the mind and it is an appearance made for the mind; in short, it is an appearance for mind and it is mind appearing. How this comes about is through predispositions that have been established formerly in the alaya, the eighth consciousness. Lingrepa spoke about this in a spiritual song in which he said that, when we go to sleep and dream, the appearances in dreams are the teacher showing us the way in which all appearances are mind.

12

ELIMINATING FLAWS THAT MAY ARISE IN MAHAMUDRA

[237] We have discussed coemergence of mind, coemergence of thought, and coemergence of appearance, as well as methods for pointing out these three aspects of experience. Once this has been pointed out, we then meditate on mind. Sometimes, however, our meditation goes astray, and at times, even though it goes well, it is incomplete. If we understand meditation's potential flaws we can avoid them in our own practice and, when we teach others, we can help them eliminate faults too. The text goes into these matters in some detail.

Flaws in Incorrect Meditation

QUALITIES OF GOOD SHAMATA MEDITATION

The text begins by discussing the three positive qualities of shamata meditation. The first is samadhi. *Samadhi* includes the experience of pleasant body and mental sensations, extreme lucidity, and nonconceptuality. While the experience of samadhi indicates excellent shamata meditation, to develop complete mahamudra, we must bring the definitive characteristics of excellent meditation to completion.

The second quality of excellent meditation is bodhichitta. *Bodhichitta* is a Sanskrit word that means "mind of enlightenment" or "heart of enlightenment." "Arousing the mind of bodhichitta" means that our meditation must be joined with an extremely pure motivation. The practice of meditation is very pleasant, and we might practice to experience that nice sensation alone. But this happiness is only temporary. A stable meditation does not necessarily eliminate the disturbing emotions or bring about all the good qualities of a fully enlightened person. We must practice in such a way that we eliminate all disturbing emotions and achieve all the good qualities.

More important, to achieve enlightenment for just ourselves would be unacceptable. In this world alone, there are billions and billions of human beings and animals that live scattered all over the earth—on mountains, in forests, on plains, in the ocean. For these beings happiness is extremely rare. They experience great suffering and have no protector. If I were to achieve the complete enlightenment of a buddha, I would have the ability and the courage to free others and to show them the path that leads to freedom from the pain of samsara. This is the attitude that we need when we practice meditation. If we practice with this attitude, it will be a very pure practice that will lead to extensive results; if we don't think in this way, the result will not be very vast.

It is good to have stable meditation and the mind of enlightenment, however we also need a third quality, which is the realization of emptiness and selflessness. If we realize emptiness we will be able to completely abandon all the disturbing emotions and bring forth the wisdom that perfectly and clearly realizes the nature of phenomena. Without the understanding of emptiness, our meditation will weaken the habitual patterns of the disturbing emotions temporarily but it will not eliminate them.

To realize the quintessential instructions of mahamudra and the co-emergence of thought and appearance, we need to recognize not only the resting mind, but also the nature of that mind. We need to understand what resting mind is not only through inference but also through direct observation. And when we realize emptiness directly, we have understood the nature of phenomena. Therefore, in addition to achieving shamata and arousing great bodhichitta, we also need the vipashyana that realizes the nature of phenomena. When we have some experience of these three qualities of samadhi, bodhichitta, and vipashyana we have a fully qualified meditation.

It is quite natural to experience problems and make mistakes in meditation. It could be because we don't understand the Dharma very well, or because we have been with our guru for only a brief period. As a result of problems, we might become less certain about what we are doing, or our meditation might become sloppier. When this happens, the force of our meditation and mindfulness decreases. We may even lose the essential points of meditation to the degree that what we are doing doesn't really deserve the name "meditation." Various kinds of appearances might arise and we might think, "This is fantastic. These are the signs of really superb meditation!" when, in fact, they are not.

If we understand these kinds of mistakes, we can dispel them when they come about. Even if they don't occur in our experience, merely knowing about them can be tremendously helpful.

MISTAKES DUE TO LACK OF VIPASHYANA

Our shamata meditation may be going extremely well—even to the point of achieving some clairvoyance—but if we have not fully realized vipashyana, the true nature of emptiness of self and of phenomena, we will not have achieved mahamudra. In this section we will discuss mistakes or flaws that arise from not having achieved genuine vipashyana.

[238] Some students' meditation may grow lax, but because they have not absorbed the lama's instructions sufficiently they are not be able to recognize the faults in their meditation. Even though they may have had some glimpse of mahamudra, they haven't ascertained it well, and they begin to lose whatever insight they had. Gradually their mindfulness and

alertness become lax, and they think that whatever meditation experience they have is real meditation, when in fact they have wandered into a blind alley and become lost.

Another mistake is to allow dullness and a darkness of mind to arise and increase. Gradually the objects that ordinarily appear to the sense consciousnesses become vague and unclear. The eyes don't see forms properly and the ears don't hear sounds properly. Eventually they don't see forms or hear sounds at all. The consciousnesses become unclear and actually cease to operate. Even if it doesn't go to that extreme, if, through a lack of mindfulness, a student allows the mind to lose its luminosity and sharpness, that person is not meditating properly.

A third mistake occurs when there is genuine clarity and brightness to the mind, but the qualities of mindfulness and alertness have not been properly maintained. There is a vividness, but the mind's awareness of itself is lacking. In this case, the meditation is neither virtuous nor nonvirtuous—it falls into a middle range that is described as neutral, neither particularly beneficial nor particularly harmful.

The mistakes become subtler and subtler. A further mistake is to think that the meditation of mahamudra is simply a state in which thought is absent. The meditator might discover the intermediate space between the dissolution of one thought and the arising of a new thought and think that resting in this space is the meditation of mahamudra. In that state there is no awareness of anything and no real quality of mindfulness or knowledge. That, however, is not genuine meditation. The essential characteristic of vipashyana is clear, definite, certain knowledge of the mind's way of being. If that definite knowledge is lacking, so is vipashyana. In vipashyana we know that the mind is empty and that this emptiness is not a lifeless emptiness. It is an emptiness in which it is suitable to know, to see, to perceive, to feel. If we have not discovered that emptiness, we have not found mahamudra vipashyana.

[240] The text describes three types of temporary experiences that might lead the meditator to think, "I have discovered something truly remarkable and profound. This is genuine meditation," and explains why these experiences are not the actual mahamudra vipashyana. First, there is the temporary experience in which the mind has a very strong sense of bliss and rests in that blissful state. Second, there is the temporary experience of emptiness; the meditator may be free from thoughts of the past, present, and the future and rest in that absence of thought. Third, there is the temporary experience of luminous appearance, in which the mind seems so fully in possession of its extraordinary abilities that the meditator thinks, "I can see everything now. I can see things that are far away, I can see inside completely and clearly. Everything is now vividly clear for my mind." We may have these experiences individually or in some combination. They are very seductive, but something vital is missing. What's missing is the definite knowledge of the mind's way of being, which is the fundamental characteristic of vipashyana. In Tibetan that definitive knowledge is said to be "the mind that has seen its own face," or "the mind that has cut its own root."

MISTAKES DUE TO LACK OF SHAMATA

Our meditation may arrive at some degree of insight but lack shamata. When that is the case, the vipashyana cannot become very strong. In shamata, our thoughts are pacified right on the spot, and our mind rests evenly and peacefully. Without that kind of meditative skill, thoughts that arise will seem to be obstacles—even very subtle thoughts will seem to interrupt and threaten to our meditation. It then becomes very difficult to meditate for even a short period of time. Beginners will experience these kinds of problems of the mind and will not be able to rest easily. So it's important to train in shamata to enhance the mind's stability.

CRITICISMS OF SAKYA PANDITA

[241] *Moonlight of Mahamudra* includes many refutations of the opinions of others that I have not discussed these in detail because they are not pertinent to the practice of meditation. These refutations serve an important purpose, however.

Sakya Pandita, a learned and distinguished scholar with extraordinary good qualities, wrote two special treatises that included refutations of the views of other Tibetan scholars. The first treatise was about valid cognition, *pramana* in Sanskrit, and the second was about the three vows (Tib. *domsum*)—the Hinayana vow of individual liberation, the Mahayana vow of bodhichitta, and the Vajrayana vows. In this second treatise, Sakya Pandita included many refutations of the Kagyu mahamudra. These were refutations of the mistaken practice of mahamudra but not of mahamudra itself. He pointed out problems and mistakes of those who had mistakenly thought that they had realized mahamudra—those who had confused the various levels we were just discussing, those who believed they had discovered the deep nature of things but had not, and those who had received practices that were not the genuine method. Sakya Pandita's book has proven extremely helpful. *Moonlight of Mahamudra* replies to many of those points, illuminating clearly the various faults and good points of the teaching of mahamudra.

In his treatise on the three vows, Sakya Pandita wrote, "If a fool meditates on mahamudra, that person will probably take birth as an animal or end up in the formless realm." This statement does not fault the mahamudra teachings but the person who practices without understanding. In fact this is true of any meditation, not just mahamudra. If we practice ignorantly and don't understand how to practice properly, or if we make mistakes and don't know that they are mistakes, such things come about. So it is important to recognize mistakes as such and not make them.

Flaws of Partial Meditation

Until now we have been discussing faulty states of meditation in which the student makes a mistake, doesn't realize it, and heads off in the wrong direction. Now we will discuss meditation that is incomplete, so that only some of the important factors are experienced.

The first example is meditation in which the samadhi is clear, lucid, and luminous, and we have some sense of things being empty. This subjective sense of emptiness is quite captivating, but it is not the same as true understanding of things as they are. There is a real difference between this passing sensation of emptiness and the utterly certain, penetrating, definitive knowledge that things do not exist as they appear. If this defect occurs, we need to examine our mind and see clearly and directly that things are empty of any inherent existence. We need to understand with complete certainty that our mind lacks existence in its own right.

A second example is meditation in which we have developed a certainty about emptiness but believe incorrectly that it is necessary to stop thought and appearance. At this point we must understand that thoughts and appearances are coemergent wisdom and that the goal is not stillness of mind with no thought or appearance. With the view that thoughts and appearances must be stopped, we begin to feel that they are enemies, and our meditation becomes extremely irritating. To avoid falling into that misunderstanding, we need to understand coemergent thought and coemergent appearance, so that whether thoughts arise or not, we are able to recognize it as coemergent wisdom.

If we believe that thought is contrary to realization, problems may arise in postmeditation as well. For while it may be possible to cancel out thoughts and appearances in meditation, we cannot stop them when we leave our meditation and return to the appearances of our daily life. Integrating our practice into daily life would be impossible if appearance and meditation were incompatible.

Realizing Flawless Meditation

[243] "Things as they are" refers to emptiness and reality. In mahamudra we are referring not to the emptiness of external phenomena but to the mind's emptiness. Understanding the mind's emptiness and reality is slightly different from understanding the emptiness of external phenomena. The emptiness of external phenomena can be understood through inferential cognition but it cannot be realized directly. Understanding emptiness through inference takes a while, so the journey is long. The mind's emptiness is considerably easier to realize than the emptiness of external phenomena. The mind's emptiness is pointed out in what the gurus of the Karma Kagyu lineage call ordinary mind (Tib. *tamal gyi shepa*).

The best way to understand ordinary mind is to think of it as "the mind as it is." Some people might think ordinary mind means a mind that is overcome with disturbing emotions, but that is not what we mean here. By *ordinary mind* we mean that the mind, by itself, is empty and luminous. It is only when we begin to manipulate mind that we become confused and mistaken, and the disturbing emotions arise. So when we refer to ordinary mind, we are talking about a mind uncontrived, unfabricated, and left just as it is.

WHY IT IS CALLED ORDINARY MIND

[244] The term "ordinary mind" was applied to the mind's true nature by Gampopa and by other great and accomplished meditators. Their thought in doing so was that, when we are practicing mahamudra, we are not seeking to recover something far away or concealed, and we are not trying to remove the obstacles that prevent us from acquiring something. Instead we are simply looking for the nature of our own mind, which is right there in our own mind. What could possibly be more accessible than that?

We could easily think that the nature of our mind is extraordinarily fine, extremely pure, and utterly unusual, and so we should discard everything that is old and familiar and arrive at something that has never been experienced before. But that would be to manipulate and contrive; we will never discover the nature of our mind that way. So to dispel such misconceptions, the term *ordinary mind* was used to indicate that it is and has always been just the mind's nature without any manipulation or any contrivance.

THE CHARACTERISTICS OF ORDINARY MIND

[245] In a commentary, Gampopa said, "Ordinary mind is unstained by any perceived forms, unmuddled by any existential projections, and unclouded by dullness, depression, or thought." Ordinary mind, he continued, is not polluted by the Dharma, not stained by worldly consciousness, and not wrapped up in a heavy mind. Not polluted even by any aspect of the Buddhadharma means that our mind is not polluted by philosophical systems of reasoned analysis and inferential conclusions, such as thinking that something exists or that something does not exist. The mind is neither manipulated nor fabricated in that way, nor is it affected by temporary experiences that occur when we practice. So the first characteristic is that the mind is not some new thing that has to be fabricated.

The second characteristic of ordinary mind is that it is not filled with the turbulence of disturbing emotions or the discursiveness of mind. Ordinary mind is uncontrived, free from such preoccupations.

The third characteristic of ordinary mind is luminosity; it is not wrapped up in a dull, obscure state of mind or within conceptuality.

In brief then, we could say that ordinary mind isn't altered by something else—it is just itself. There is no need to try to get rid of what we regard as bad or to turn it into something good. If we realize ordinary mind, this is called "the wisdom that knows itself"; if we do not realize it, even though it has always been there, this is called "coemergent ignorance."

WHAT ONE MEDITATES ON WITH ORDINARY MIND

[247] We meditate on ordinary mind by recognizing it *as* ordinary mind. We know it for what it is—empty and luminous. Through the force of habitual tendencies we lose track of ordinary mind. We sustain recognition of ordinary mind by way of mindfulness and alertness. Thus Gampopa emphasized that the practice of ordinary mind is simply not becoming distracted and wandering from it.

If ordinary mind is so universal and unfabricated, what is there to distinguish a yogin from someone with no awareness of ordinary mind? Gampopa explained that although ordinary mind is the nature of both the yogin and the worldly person, the worldly person does has not received instructions on recognizing and working with ordinary mind, while the yogin has. Not recognizing ordinary mind, the worldly person experiences all sorts of dualistic conceptions; by recognizing ordinary mind, the yogin is liberated from dualistic conceptions, and all experience becomes an experience of great bliss.

Gampopa also discusses the Dharma practitioner who does not have the instructions on ordinary mind, that is, someone who is developing knowledge and good qualities through a more conventional path. When compared to the yogin or yogini who has the instructions and the practice of ordinary mind, we would have to say that the ordinary Dharma practitioner is not very different from the ordinary person in the world.

We should not spend a lot of time noticing what the mind is not. Rather we should see what it is with nothing added or subtracted. Ordinary mind is not polluted. It is not a matter of contriving something regarded by the Dharma as good, such as wisdom or luminosity. Ordinary mind is mind as it is without the interference of passion or aggression. It is just our mind noticing itself. It is not a matter of looking at something else, or trying to fix itself or do anything. It is simply our mind looking at itself and resting in that. And the way that this is sustained and extended is through mindfulness. Mindfulness notices that some thought has boiled up and is about to take us for a ride and just doesn't go with it.

For example, I would say this glass of water sitting on the desk in front of me is a glass. I see that it is a glass. If I were to analyze it conceptually, I would stop and think about it, and then say that this is a glass and that it's filled with water. I could go around and around like that. On the other hand, I could see just a glass and water. If I engaged in hyperbole, I could say it is not just glass, it is diamond, the most magnificent glass; and it's not mere water, it is the healing nectar of the deities. On the other hand, I could think that this doesn't deserve the name glass and that contaminated sand was used to create it, and that this isn't water, it is poison. I could become quite excited about it. But that is not what we are talking about. We are talking about just looking and seeing that it is a glass and that it has water in it.

It is the same with our mind. We don't have to look at it and exaggerate it by saying how wonderful it is or how completely rotten and filthy it is. It is just our mind, and there is no need to think about it as good or bad. It is just what it is, that's all.

13

MAINTAINING MAHAMUDRA IN MEDITATION AND POSTMEDITATION

[251] Devotion and faith are necessary for our experience in meditation to increase. In the Kagyu Lineage Prayer it is said, "Devotion is the head of meditation." If we have a head, then we can see, hear, eat, speak, and so forth. If we do not have a head, we can't do much of anything. Similarly, in meditation if we have devotion, our meditation will improve; it will become clearer and more stable.

Devotion

The power of devotion is illustrated in the story of the old woman who had great faith in the Dharma and the Sangha. The woman's son was a merchant who went back and forth to India. One time, prior to his departure, the woman said to him, "You are going to India, the birthplace of Lord Buddha, and the place where many scholars and siddhas lived, taught, and became realized. I want you to bring back a relic for me that can serve as a basis for faith." Her son then went to India but forgot all about it. He came back with nothing.

When her son was about to go to India again, the old woman said, "This time you just have to bring something for me. Don't forget. I really need this." Her son went to India, conducted his business, and forgot all about it once again. When he was about to leave a third time, his mother begged him, saying, "This time please, please bring something for me. If you don't, I am going to be very sad and will die right in front of your eyes." Again he almost forgot, remembering only on the very day when he was to meet his mother. He thought, "Oh no! Now what am I going to do? If I don't bring her something she will die!" He looked around and saw the remains of a dead dog by the side of the road. It had been there for quite a while, so most of the flesh was gone, leaving just the dried bones. He went over and yanked out a tooth, cleaned it off, and wrapped it up very nicely. "You are extremely fortunate," he told his mother, "I have brought you a tooth of the Buddha himself."

Believing that it was the tooth of the Buddha, the woman supplicated the tooth, made offerings to it, and generated extraordinary faith and devotion. The tooth had no potency or blessing in and of itself. Nevertheless, there appeared in it what is known as *ringsel* (tiny, pearl-like relics) that spontaneously appear in the body of a powerful guru, in a particularly sacred stupa, or in association with a great lama. Due to her confidence and faith alone, the tooth had received the blessings of the Buddha.

This story indicates the great power of faith. Similarly, if we have faith and devotion toward our root guru, the gurus of the lineage, and the great practitioners, when we practice mahamudra, our meditation will progress more and more.

The Reason for Maintaining Mahamudra

[251] How do we sustain the meditation that we have developed through exertion, mindfulness, and alertness? The text doesn't teach the nature of mind but discusses pointing it out, because there is nothing to learn; we simply need to recognize. Pointing out the nature of mind, however, is not enough. We must sustain our meditation on it so that what has not yet

become clear will become clear, what is shaky will become stable, and whatever good qualities are present will develop further.

It is inconceivably fortunate to have the nature of mind pointed out to us. Our practice has led to the birth of a profound opportunity within the stream of our being. If we don't exert ourselves in sustaining this recognition and realization, however, the good qualities we have inherited will decrease and our faults will increase. If we do not sustain the meditative experience, we return to the state of an ordinary person, and realization will have been meaningless. Thus we should feel we have found a precious jewel and take care not to cast it into the mud. This requires exertion.

The great master Tsangpa Gyare said, "Not nurturing the meditation that has arisen in your mental continuum is like a rich man carried away by a wind illness." In the Tibetan medicine there are three different systems that are subject to illness—wind, bile, and phlegm. In one wind illness, the body's wind energy becomes completely imbalanced when we don't get enough to eat. It is ridiculous for a rich person to suffer an illness of malnutrition. Tsangpa Gyare also says that if we have a precious jewel, we ought to care for it by wrapping it in good quality cloth and handling it properly. Not to take care of our meditative realization—our insight into the mind's way of being—is like allowing a precious jewel to fall into the mud.

Sustaining Mahamudra Meditation

This nature of mind has existed within us from the beginning of time, but, until the point of our recognizing it, we were confused. The habits and predispositions established by our confusion are so strong that, even if we recognize the nature of mind, these latencies resurface and our confusion returns. Therefore, we must meditate again and again. The Tibetan word for meditation is *gom*, which means habituation. So we must habituate to, become familiar with, the nature of mind. For our meditation to improve, it is important to hold our mind on the nature of mind.

Shantideva said that those who wish to protect their minds and practice the Dharma must have three things: mindfulness, alertness, and attentiveness. These are largely similar, but when we analyze them in detail, we can distinguish their different natures and characteristics.

Mindfulness, Alertness, and Attentiveness

[253] We could say mindfulness (Tib. *drenpa*) means not forgetting. In this context it means not forgetting mahamudra, not forgetting mind as it is. Alertness (Tib. *shezhin*) is very closely related to mindfulness. The alertness that we are speaking about is in-the-moment alertness, a present, active knowledge that becomes possible by way of mindfulness. If we have mindfulness, alertness can develop; if our mindfulness declines, alertness is not possible. When we talk about attentiveness (Tib. *bagyöpa*), we are evaluating our mind, asking: Are faults of this sort or that sort arising? Is samadhi or the stability of meditation declining? Attentiveness is making sure we don't get on the wrong track in our meditation.

Mindfulness and alertness are important at all times. The reason for this is very simple: If mindfulness and alertness are present, faults will not arise; if they are absent, faults will arise. Shantideva compared disturbing emotions to bandits. Thieves and murderers will not harm us if we are protected by people who are strong. But if our guardians become lazy, stupid, or weak, burglars will be able to sneak in, harm us, and steal whatever they want. Shantideva said that it is similar with thoughts and disturbing emotions. As long as we are protected by mindfulness and alertness, thoughts and disturbing emotions cannot take control. But as soon as mindfulness and alertness slacken or are abandoned, thoughts and disturbing emotions arise and bring trouble by blocking and covering over whatever good qualities there are. Therefore it is important to adhere to mindfulness and alertness at all times.

Attentiveness tames the mind—it subdues the disturbing emotions and keeps us from doing things that cause others to give rise to aggression, envy, pride, and so forth. At the same time attentiveness dispels the joy we take in doing harmful things; in other words, it prevents us from seeing attachment and aggression as good characteristics. Attentiveness lets us see harmful things as faulty so we don't enjoy them. It is attentiveness that understands why Dharma is beneficial. It enables us to take delight in the Dharma and prevents us from disliking the Dharma.

In sum, mindfulness, alertness, and attentiveness enable our meditation practice to develop further and further. Let's look more closely at mindfulness and alertness.

Mindfulness

The text says, "As for mindfulness, it enables one not to forget the meaning that one is seeking to accomplish." Mindfulness keeps our mind on the point we are contemplating in our meditation and maintains clarity within our meditation.

The *Sutra Requested by the Student Who Had a Jewel upon the Crown of His Head* points out the different functions of mindfulness. The first function is that "through mindfulness, delusions do not arise." Because we have become so accustomed to disturbing emotions, and have established such strong predispositions and habits in that direction, disturbing emotions arise quite naturally through the force of these habits. If we can sustain mindfulness, however, disturbing emotions such as desire, hatred, and pride will not have an opportunity to arise. The second function of mindfulness is that "through mindfulness, we do not become involved in harmful activities [Skt. *mara*]." These first two functions are related as root and branch: through mindfulness, we protect our mind so that disturbing emotions do not arise; once disturbing emotions do not arise, the activities of body and speech do not go in the direction of harmful action. Finally, "through mindfulness, we do not stray from the correct path." Mindfulness keeps us on the path that leads to genuine benefit. In this sense, mindfulness can be understood as a doorway. Since mindfulness prevents the mind from going in a nonvirtuous direction, the text says, "We should exert ourselves in genuine mindfulness."

When we talk about mind in the Buddhist tradition, we often talk about mind and mental factors. A mental factor is "that which arises from mind." Mental factors are different types of thoughts, which in Buddhism are subtly distinguished from one another. Mindfulness is one such mental factor. Its particular aspect is continually recollecting whatever we are trying to pay attention to, whether it is remembering our vows, maintaining a beneficial motivation, or avoiding harmful actions. In this context, mindfulness allows us to keep the mind on the point of the meditation. If we guard our mind well with mindfulness, it will not wander from this point; we will not sink into dull mental states or develop wild mental states. When we have understood the dharmata that is the mind's way of being, the power of mindfulness prevents us from straying from that to something else. Thus, mindfulness is critical in guarding the realization that comes about as the insight of vipashyana.

Alertness

Alertness is knowing what's going on in our mind and examining it closely. Alertness arises in dependence upon mindfulness. The text says that first we have to establish mindfulness; then this quality of evaluating what's going on in our mind in the present moment can arise. It monitors the activities of body, speech, and mind, and discerns what to pursue and what to reject. Alertness is critical for nourishing a healthy state of mind.

In *Guide to the Bodhisattva's Way of Life*, Shantideva put it very simply, "When mindfulness guards the door of your mind, then alertness naturally arises."

In mahamudra meditation, it is important to rely upon mindfulness and alertness because they sustain our realization of the mind's way of being and enhance that realization. Since mindfulness and alertness enable us to know precisely what to accept and what to reject, then without them, faults arise. In *Guide to the Bodhisattva's Way of Life* Shantideva said that without alertness, the fruits of listening to the Dharma, reflecting upon its meaning, and meditating upon what we have understood will disappear. Our good qualities will not increase and we will not retain what we have accomplished. It will be a waste of time.

When we have proper mindfulness and alertness, then self-restraint or conscientiousness can arise in the continuum of our mind. What exactly is this self-restraint or conscientiousness? It knows when delusion is arising and sounds the alarm, "Oh, I think there's a delusion coming around here." We can then respond appropriately.

Mindfulness as the Root of the Other Characteristics

If we sustain mindfulness, our meditation, or samadhi, and all good qualities will increase straight away. If mindfulness declines, our meditation and good qualities will also decline. Therefore the siddhas of the Kagyu lineage talk about "holding mindfulness." Mindfulness is like the shepherd who collects the sheep when they have wandered into a place where fierce animals could devour them. If a sheep wanders into a dangerous place, the shepherd brings it back to a place with water and grass, a place where it will be happy and want to stay. In the same way, when the mind strays from meditation, mindfulness brings it back and places it in the relaxation of meditation so that we can enjoy its benefits.

Mindfulness is vital to the practices of listening, contemplating, and meditating on the meaning of the Dharma. Furthermore, mindfulness is important for sustaining meditation because it focuses the mind on a single point and prevents it from becoming distracted. If we do not have mindfulness, we lose sight of the purpose of our meditation; we become confused and get lost. If we have mindfulness, we can maintain our meditative stabilization; if we do not, our meditative stabilization gets lost. For that reason, it's important.

Je Drikungpa said, "The main highway for the buddhas of the three times is mindfulness that is never interrupted." How did the buddhas of the past, the buddhas of the present, and the buddhas of the future progress to enlightenment? In all cases, the great highway on which they travel is the highway of mindfulness. They have a mindfulness that never lapses. Je Drikungpa continued, "If you do not know undistracted mindfulness, then you will fall prey to restive tendencies of body and mind." If we don't have mindfulness, we simply won't attain the fruition that is buddhahood.

The Nature of Meditation and Postmeditation

[261] What do we mean by meditation and postmeditation? Meditation is when faults such as heaviness and wildness of mind have been cleared away and the mind rests within recognition of mind as it is. Postmeditation, or subsequent attainment, is when we have "risen from that." This does not mean that we get up from our cushion, but rather that our mind shifts and then our mindfulness of fundamental nature is restored. It means that we have recovered what we had before.

It is particularly important to consider how we sustain the meditation and how we come to have postmeditation, because once we have risen from the meditation period, we are particularly prone to becoming completely wild in thought. That is the time we need to sustain meditation. If we learn how to do this, then the meditation can be joined with whatever activity we are doing through the power of mindfulness and alertness.

In the tradition of the quintessential instructions it is often said that meditative equipoise, or meditation, is like space. This means that the main practice—when we recognize just what the mind is—is like space. The period of postmeditation is said to be like an illusion. This means that whatever work we do between the sessions of meditation appears to be like an illusion. If worldly activity is joined with the definite knowledge, certainty, and mindfulness of mind as it is that we experienced in meditation, then worldly activity is said to be like an illusion. Saying meditation is like space emphasizes the aspect of emptiness. Saying that postmeditation is like an illusion emphasizes the factor of appearance.

The Beginning Level of Mahamudra

When discussing the practice of mahamudra, we classify the stages of a practitioner's journey somewhat differently than we usually classify these stages. Ordinarily we talk about the student's journey from confusion to liberation in terms of the ten bodhisattva levels. In mahamudra, we speak about the four yogas. Those four yogas are one-pointedness, freedom from complexity, one-taste, and nonmeditation.

The first yoga, the yoga of one-pointedness, is the stage of a beginner. At this stage, the experience that the student has is temporary in nature. While the experience might be quite dramatic, it doesn't last. At the stage of one-pointedness, the student has a temporary experience of insight during meditation rather than genuine realization. Such a student does not experience genuine meditation or postmeditation. The latter three yogas—freedom from complexity, one-taste, and nonmeditation—have actual meditative equipoise and actual postmeditation. In these stages, the practitioner experiences genuine and complete meditation and postmeditation.

The first yoga of one-pointedness is free from the fault of a heavy and wild mind. It is a mind that rests upon the true nature of mind, which is the coemergent mind that was previously pointed out to the student.

Thus, in the first yoga, the meditator comes to rest within luminosity and emptiness. Moreover, the meditative equipoise of one-pointedness is free from other thoughts and mental activity. It does not wander or become involved in thinking about this or that. It does not lose this mindfulness. It is a mind that has come down into its own nature and that rests there, without being distracted by anything else.

In his *Quintessential Instructions on the Middle Way*, Atisha said, "One abandons all mindfulness and mental engagements." This teaching does not mean that we cast aside our mindfulness and intelligence, as it is mindfulness that causes us to remain with the understanding of reality and not to wander from that. Rather it means that we should not take other things to mind when we are resting within meditative equipoise upon the nature of mind. We should give up mindfulness and consideration of anything other than the meditative stabilization within which we are resting. As long as we remain mindful and do not wander, thoughts of other things will not arise. But when we do lose our mindfulness and begin to wander from that, other things come to mind. If we gave up mindfulness altogether, it simply would not be possible for meditative experience and realization to come about.

As long as mindfulness remains steadfast, mind remains focused on understanding reality, and distracting thoughts do not arise. When mindfulness wanders just slightly, very subtle thoughts arise; when mindfulness wanders greatly, gross thoughts arise, thoughts apprehending and assenting to the appearance of things as if they were inherently established. The arising of these thoughts and appearances means we are no longer within meditative equipoise; rather, we have passed to "ordinary subsequent knowledge and appearance." *Subsequent* here means we've gone back to being an ordinary person with a very ordinary mind, as if we'd never experienced meditation. Later, when we rediscover mindfulness, we can again rest within he mind's true nature without having to avoid thought and appearance. Our awareness will be permeated by the mindfulness that is aware of and rests right on the mind's way of being. When we have rediscovered mindfulness in this way, we have found "the union, or integration, of appearance and emptiness." Thought and appearance do not become obstacles in any way; rather, they are understood as merely inseparable appearance and emptiness, the nature of which cannot be identified as anything at all.

To summarize, we begin with the meditative stabilization of meditation on the mind's way of being. That state is then lost. Mindfulness returns, and we achieve meditative stabilization on the nature of mind once again. For that reason, it's called subsequent attainment. Meditation is spoken of as being like space, meaning it is free from dullness, heaviness, sinking mind. Postmeditation is said to be like an illusion, meaning that appearance is illusory in the sense that although it appears, we know that it is really nothing.

Further Skills for Sustaining Meditation

[263] Gampopa discussed three skills in sustaining meditation: skill in the beginning; skill in adhering to experience; and skill in cutting through elaboration.

Skill in the beginning is mainly a matter of understanding that meditation is valuable and that it brings with it good qualities. This causes us to delight in meditation and aspire toward it. We understand that if we have meditation, good qualities come about, and if we do not have meditation, whatever good qualities we have will disintegrate. And so we have great confidence in meditation and feel strongly inspired. At the same time we do not feel aversion toward it or take delight in what undermines meditation; in other words, we are not overwhelmed in a flurry of thoughts and disturbing emotions.

The second skill is being skilled in recognizing the two basic faults in meditation—heaviness and wildness—and knowing how to repair them. In addition, we learn not to become attached to temporary experiences (Tib. *nyam*) that arise in meditation. There are three types of temporary experiences: experiences of great clarity or luminosity, experiences of nonconceptuality, and experiences of bliss. We must learn not to become attached to these temporary experiences of pleasure, clarity, and nonthought, which can be rather seductive and deceitful. These experiences seem to be real but in fact they are false. They are like the husk around something. We have to strip them away to get down to the mind as it is—naked, unfabricated, and uncontrived. So the second skill is "the skill in how to avoid becoming attached to such experiences."

The third skill of cutting through elaboration occurs when we have developed our meditation to the point where we are not easily seduced by these false experiences. Nevertheless we are not able to sustain our meditation for any length of time, so we begin to resent meditation and find it to be irritating. When we begin to feel this way, it is very difficult to continue meditating. We must become skilled in seeing this totally unelaborated meditation as delightful. When we see our meditation as good and delightful, we want to practice. The name of this stage is "eliminating our resentment and irritation with regard to the practice of meditation." It has the sense of getting rid of what is left over after the main part of the meal.

Methods for Maintaining Mahamudra within Meditation

[264] We will first look more closely at how mahamudra is sustained within periods of meditation. There are six basic methods for doing this.

THE SIX POINTS OF TILOPA

We will first consider Tilopa's famous six points for sustaining meditation, also known as Tilopa's six ways of resting. The verse from Tilopa says:

> Do not recall,
> Do not think,
> Do not anticipate,
> Do not meditate,
> Do not analyze,
> Do rest naturally.

The words all mean more or less the same thing, however we can observe some distinctions. The first three points are concerned with how to sustain meditation within a formal session of meditation by working with thoughts of the past, the present, and the future. "Do not recall" means do not follow after thoughts that are concerned with the past. "Do not think" means don't fabricate or ponder in the present moment. "Do not anticipate" means do not invite thoughts that are concerned with the future, that is, don't make arrangements and plans for what to do later.

The fourth point, "Do not meditate," means that you simply sustain the awareness of mind without trying to manufacture something else. For example, do not meditate upon emptiness because, by doing so, you will manufacture emptiness upon which to meditate. Similarly, do not meditate upon luminosity and thereby fabricate some luminosity upon which to meditate.

"Do not analyze," means that you do not become involved in speculation about or analysis of the quality of your meditation. For example, do not think that the meditation is good or bad. Do not investigate using theoretical speculation or inferential realization. Rather, place your mind directly, without any intermediary, upon your own mind.

Finally, "Do rest naturally," means that the mind rests with mind as it is in an unfabricated way. Mind is placed in ordinary mind; it rests in the mind's own nature. These are six methods taught by Tilopa for sustaining a session of meditation.

THE FOUR POINTS OF GAMPOPA

[267] Another set of instructions includes the four ways to sustain meditation that are renowned in the Kagyu tradition. These were first explained by Gampopa. The meanings of these four instructions are similar, but the words and perspective are slightly different.

The first instruction for the meditator is not to tighten, constrict, or concentrate, but to relax.

The second instruction is to experience freshness and newness; that is, mind as it is without theories, classifications, or fabrications of emptiness or luminosity.

The third instruction is to let the mind be. "Let the mind be" means do not dress mind up, fabricate or manipulate the mind, or look for something special or unusual. Instead, just sustain the awareness of that which was previously pointed out.

The fourth instruction is to realize that the nature of mind already exists within your mind. There is no need to dress it up as something else, or to think, "I'm not sure I'm doing this right." There is no need to get involved in pride, thinking, "I've figured it out." Understand that the recognition of the mind comes through the blessing of our guru, and simply relax.

THREE OTHER METHODS OF MAINTAINING MAHAMUDRA

[270] Three more main points for maintaining meditation are discussed. The main point of Tilopa's six points is the one that says, "Do not meditate." This means simply rest in ordinary mind without fabricating anything. From that point of view, meditation is not a mental activity. This is illustrated by the advice given by the great master Saraha in which he likens the practitioner's mind to the red thread worn by a Brahmin—the thread must be neither too tight nor too loose. If our mind is too tight, we will have problems in our meditation. The antidote to this is, "Do

not meditate." This advice allows us to relax. If we relax too much, however, pretty soon we won't be meditating on the mind's true nature. The antidote to excessive relaxation is, "Do not be distracted." These two antidotes contain within them the advice we need for training and extending our meditation on the mind's true nature.

The second point applies when the mind begins to scatter and all sorts of thoughts begin to arise. The mind wanders here and there, and we fall under the sway of the different patterns that arise. At this point what is helpful is mindfulness and alertness, and of these two, mindfulness is especially helpful. The essential point is not to wander. Thus all the instructions on how to sustain meditation could be summed up in these two points: "Do not meditate" and "Do not wander."

The third point considers how "Do not meditate" and "Do not wander" include within them the essential points of meditation. "Do not meditate" is principally connected with shamata in that the instruction is for mind to relax, and "Do not wander" is principally concerned with vipashyana in that it instructs the meditator to tighten or to focus appropriately.

For a beginner it is easy to fall into a state in which the mind sinks and becomes dark and heavy, or becomes wild. As the antidote to the sinking and heaviness of mind, the instruction is not to meditate. As the antidote to wildness of mind, the instruction is not to wander.

Maintaining Mahamudra in Postmeditation

[279] Between sustaining mahamudra in meditation and sustaining it in postmeditation, sustaining it in postmeditation is more important. The reason is that, in any twenty-four-hour day, we can spend only a small amount of time in formal meditation; the rest of the time we are doing something else. It will be extremely beneficial if we can sustain our experience of mahamudra in the times of postmeditation. It will enable

our experience to develop further and further while also reducing stressfulness and hardship in our work and our life. Therefore the methods for sustaining our meditation experience in the periods of postmeditation should be regarded as extremely important. This aspect of mahamudra practice is what makes it particularly useful for the Western world and for the twentieth century.

MINDFULNESS IN POSTMEDITATION

Maintaining unbroken mindfulness in postmeditation requires some exertion. The aspect of mindfulness that is required is not forgetting coemergent mind. If we were to maintain mindfulness completely and never wander from our experience of coemergent mind, we would still be in the period of meditation. What then is the difference between actual meditation upon the nature of the mind and the periods that follow? In the periods of postmeditation, resting in the mind's true nature is maintained slightly. The text suggests, "It is not lost." We just don't stray from it. There's still a bit of mindfulness of the mind's true nature.

As long as we maintain that little bit of mindfulness of the mind's way of being, then when different kinds of thoughts or appearances arise, we don't fixate upon them as some real and true thing that must either be rejected or affirmed. Rather, we remain right with that thought or that appearance, experience it and experience the luminosity of it. Because we have that kind of mindfulness and are able to refrain from clamping down on things as real and true, we don't get involved in attachment and aggression. We don't have to form opinions—evaluating thoughts or appearances as good, bad, and so forth.

The example for this is a young child in a Vajrayana shrine room. When a young child sees depictions of the peaceful and wrathful deities, the child just looks at them, without having to decide whether they are good or bad. In the same way, mindfulness allows us to experience thoughts or appearances that present themselves in all their vividness and brilliance without fixating upon them, without giving rise to various views and conceptions of them. And so we are able to remain in a state that is not only spacious but also pure and unadulterated because it is not harmed by thinking of things as being either good or bad, attractive or unattractive.

Sustaining Mindfulness in Postmeditation

The method for sustaining meditative experience in postmeditation is mindfulness. We spoke earlier of the three types of coemergence: coemergent mind, coemergent thought, and coemergent appearance. In the meditative session we are concerned with coemergent mind; we are recognizing and studying the coemergent mind and its nature.

When we rise from a meditation session, we must make some effort at mindfulness while we go about our business, engage in conversation with others, and do other activities. This mindfulness doesn't come about naturally. At times we have mindfulness and at other times we do not, but as we exert ourselves, mindfulness becomes steadier; as we become more familiar with mindfulness, it becomes more continuous.

In the meditation session we are mindful of the mind's nature. The mindfulness of postmeditation is to not separate from that. In postmeditation we have the mindfulness of reflecting, thinking, and remembering the nature of the mind. Our mind is affected by the force of that mindfulness. Thoughts arise, various appearances arise, and we don't attempt to stop them. At the same time we don't become attached to them. As different thoughts and appearances arise, we do not become afraid of them or uncomfortable in the face of them, nor do we give rise to the disturbing emotions. Rather we feel peaceful, free from attachment, and free from fear. In the example of the young child who has wandered into a shrine room and is looking at various objects, the child sees everything, but doesn't stop to think, This is white, This is red, This is a deity, This is the

Buddha, and so forth. If we have that attitude and mindfulness in postmeditation, our mind will become very relaxed, spacious, and vast.

What exactly do we do with thoughts and appearances as they arise? The text approaches this by setting out two kinds of mistakes that we could make, and then explaining the proper way to go about it.

The first mistake is to obstruct or dam up thought and appearance so that it is either halted or it doesn't appear clearly. The other mistake is to follow after or be led along by thoughts and appearances so that we become completely distracted and lose our mindfulness. We get involved in very ordinary thoughts as though we'd never practiced meditation at all. We then become like ordinary people, harshly rejecting some things and affirming others. Instead, we must work with the thoughts and appearances that arise for the six consciousnesses. No matter what their objects are or how they appear, we maintain the understanding of them as being of a nature that defies any of our efforts to categorize, grasp, or define them.

The fruition of the meditative experience of coemergent mind is that all thoughts appear as emptiness. They appear but we do not grasp at them. We do not contrive, fabricate, or manufacture anything. Rather, we sustain the meditative awareness in which the mind has settled into its own way of being. That's the kind of mindful understanding we require to maintain our meditation as postmeditation.

We need to keep this kind of mindfulness active in whatever we do. As beginners, we are distracted most of the time. There are two things we can do about that distraction—one in meditation and one in postmeditation. The most helpful thing to do in meditation is to give rise to a very strong mindfulness of the mind's coemergent nature. In postmeditation we must exert ourselves in applying our mindfulness. Once we have done that, we will be able to stay in luminosity and emptiness, without applying much exertion when thoughts and appearances arise.

If this mindfulness and the experience of thoughts and appearances as luminosity-emptiness do not arise, this is a sign that we have not related sufficiently with meditation. It is an indication that when we practice formal meditation, we need to make an effort to experience coemergent thought and coemergent appearance, examining them in terms of where they arise, where they abide, and where they go.

Bringing Everything to the Path

The third section on postmeditation is concerned with how we bring thought onto the path. Gampopa suggested that we do this in three ways. The first is "destroying whatever is met with." If we have some familiarity with the experience of postmeditation, it is like meeting an old friend. When thoughts arise, we immediately give rise to mindfulness and alertness that understands their nature. We recognize the nature of thought very soon after thought arises, without getting involved in analysis. When we can do that, we are able to enter into the unborn mind when thoughts and appearances dawn without having to first analyze. We naturally recognize the nonarising of mind, its birthlessness.

The second way is "reviving awareness." This is like noticing that a friend who has been visiting us has left something behind. We have to run after and try to catch up with our friend to return what he or she left behind. That's the way we are practicing at this point. We've really fallen under the spell of thoughts and appearances, we've been somewhat overwhelmed by them, and we have to put our whole meditative process back together from scratch. We have to look at things carefully and revive our mindfulness of what's going on.

The third way is translated literally as "emanation of nonexistence." In this situation we are thoroughly familiar with the practice of mindfulness in postmeditation. It is like a great fire blazing in a forest. Whatever we throw at the fire is consumed right on the spot. If the fire is in its early stages, then damp wood or a gust of wind tend to threaten the fire. But once the fire is blazing, whatever it comes upon becomes more fuel for it. At this point we have become so familiar with the practice of mindfulness in postmeditation that any kind of thought or appearance, even one that would ordinarily be quite difficult, is just the spontaneous expression of reality, dharmata.

These three ways of working with thought and appearance in postmeditation come down to how familiar we are with this practice. If we are very familiar with it, we can practice in the third way described; if we're somewhat less familiar, we practice in the first way described; and if we're still less familiar than that, we practice in the second way described.

SEEING EVERYTHING AS A MAGICAL DISPLAY

The fourth topic in this section is a discussion of what it means to say that appearances are like illusions. We said earlier that meditative equipoise is like space and postmeditation is like an illusion. When we say "like an illusion" we mean that the things of the world—colors and shapes, sounds, smells, tastes, tangible objects—are not established as what they seem to be. They appear to be a certain way for a consciousness that does not see things as they are.

Two things need to be present if we are going to truly realize reality as an illusion: the realizations that phenomena are empty and that appearances are illusory. When the mind understands this definitely and clearly, we have "illusion-like appearance." An example is when a magician creates the appearance of things—such as horses and elephants—that others actually see with their eye consciousnesses. Of course, the magician who creates these appearances is not fooled by them; he or she knows that the appearances are not what they seem to be from the perspective of the eye consciousness. In illusion-like appearance, things appear to the sense consciousnesses, but the mental consciousness knows, without hesitation, that these appearances are not what they seem.

Illusion-like appearance occurs when the appearance and the definite understanding that the appearance is false occur together.

What does *illusion* mean in "whatever appears is like an illusion"? A passage in the *King of Meditation Sutra* says:

> Meditation on characteristics
> Is empty of an unborn essence,
> Like a mirage, a phantom city of gandharvas,
> Like an illusion or a dream,
> Understand all phenomena in this way.

Tashi Namgyal suggests that illusion could mean, one, that dharmata and complete realization are illusion and, two, that phenomena such as the five aggregates are illusion. Illusion-like appearance refers to the meditator's knowledge that things do not exist in the ways that they appear.

Having identified the mind that understands illusion-like appearance, the text then explains the way in which illusion-like appearance arises. Various things will appear to the sense consciousnesses—the eye, ear, nose, tongue, or body sensation consciousness—but the mental consciousness knows that these phenomena do not intrinsically exist and are mere appearances. That is the dawning of illusion-like appearance in postmeditation.

The text then presents ways in which we could deceive ourselves about illusion-like appearance. In the quintessential instructions on mahamudra, it is frequently said that we should not manipulate our mind in any way; rather, we are to recognize it as it is without fabrication. We let our mind settle into the space that is natural to it. There are a number of ways we might misunderstand these instructions. We might, for instance, be experiencing many disturbing emotions based on external objects and be quite confused and then think, "I will just relax within this without trying to alter it or fix it." That would be a big mistake. Or we might experience mistaken appearances that are based on and polluted by ignorance and think that the practice of illusion-like appearance is to relax within that. There is a big difference between relaxing within mind as it is and relaxing within ignorance. It is not correct to relax within ignorance or conceptuality that does not understand things as they are.

Union of Meditation and Postmeditation

[289] The text goes on to discuss the way in which the periods of meditation and postmeditation can be brought together. The mixing of meditation and postmeditation occurs only at a very high level of realization, and it requires tremendous exertion. At the present time, we don't have much control or power over this. Nevertheless, it is set forth here in the text to clarify this point.

When asked by his students about the mixing of meditation and postmeditation, Gampopa replied that it refers to never being separated from clear light. This means that the realization of clear light occurs in anything we do—sleeping, eating, anything.

Questions

QUESTION: When we do not recognize ordinary mind and are in a mess, how do we go about practicing the Dharma and trying to be of use to sentient beings?

RINPOCHE: It's wonderful if we can give birth to the realization of mahamudra in the stream of our being. If we are unable to do so, however, it is not that all of our actions are worthless and futile and that there is nothing we can do to develop the Dharma. We can revitalize our faith and devotion to our root guru, generate love and compassion for sentient beings, practice shamata to pacify our own mind when it is in a worried state, and perform virtuous activities. When we do such things, our understanding increases and we are of more help to others.

QUESTION: You said the three definitive characteristics of ordinary mind are that it is not polluted by the Dharma, not polluted by worldly thoughts of passion and aggression, and not encased within heavy conceptuality. Do we recognize this by noticing the absence of something that's usually present? For a brief period of time do we notice, either on the spot or later, that something wasn't there?

RINPOCHE: It's not necessarily a short period of time. In any case, the main thrust is not noticing what the mind is not, but noticing what it actually is. When we talk about it being unpolluted, it's not a matter of contriving something that is regarded as good, such as wisdom or luminosity, but rather it is the mind without the interference of attachment and aggression, which are not essential to mind's nature. Likewise, it's not the case that the mind's nature is wrapped up in thought or in heaviness due to fabrications on the one hand while ordinary mind is unfabricated and uncontrived on the other. It's not a matter of looking at something different. It's the mind noticing itself, not trying to fix itself or accomplish anything. It is mind just seeing what it actually is and resting within that. Through mindfulness, that is sustained and extended. Mindfulness notices that some thought has boiled up and is about to take us for a ride and just doesn't go with it.

QUESTION: Of mindfulness, alertness, and attentiveness, which is the most important?

RINPOCHE: From among these three, mindfulness is the main thing. Mindfulness keeps us in, or brings us back to, meditation. It may involve some intention and effort, "I am going to meditate," and if we slip and lose the meditation, mindfulness thinks, "Whoa, what happened here?" and restores the meditation. If mindfulness is present, alertness will come about. If mindfulness is not present, there is no possibility of alertness.

Alertess looks to see how well the meditation is going and takes a closer look: "Now that I am meditating I can look and see how well my meditation is going." It is on the lookout for different faults that might arise. It looks to see what the state of the meditation is, whether thoughts have arisen and are taking over.

Attentiveness is a bit different. It is a care, a very definite concern or heedfulness, that we do not allow certain problems to arise. So it is not so much an inquiry into whether or not something is happening as it is a very definite taking care of one's state of mind.

QUESTION: If we are practicing this particular meditation without object and a thought arises, do we simply avoid feeding it and allow the thought to dissipate? How does this relate to not regarding thought as an enemy?

RINPOCHE: Meditating upon the nature of mind is somewhat easier than meditating upon other sorts of things. We are simply recognizing mind's luminous emptiness, which is already there. It is not like meditating upon external phenomena because we can only apprehend the emptiness of external phenomena through meditative and analytical strategies, and that inevitably involves some difficulty, distance, technique, contrivance, and fabrication. Looking at our own mind involves only looking at our own mind with our own mind. We don't have to look somewhere else, and we don't have to concoct an elaborate strategy for how to do it. So it is a good bit easier.

As for how we regard thoughts that arise at that time, we are not looking to negate them; we are simply investigating their nature, recognizing them for what they are. Suppose some very coarse thought arises in our mind. We simply look at the thought to see what it is: from where did it arise, where is it, where does it go? Like bubbles that arise in water, thoughts appear to arise from somewhere, abide somewhere, and disappear somewhere, but in fact they don't. We look at thought in this way not because we want to stop thought but because we are investigating the nature of our mind. We do not want to get rid of thoughts or do anything to them; we simply want to know what they are. So that is how we investigate them.

QUESTION: I was wondering if you could explain how we would remedy dullness by using nondistraction and wildness by using nonmeditation. A passage in the book says, "Beginners should know that nonmeditation connotes tranquillity and relaxation, but that an excess of relaxation will produce dullness; and that nondistraction includes insight and exertion, but an excess of exertion will produce wildness." How do we work with these in our practice?

RINPOCHE: The essentials are nonmeditation and nondistraction. Through nonmeditation the mind rests in peace or shamata, but if that resting becomes too strong, the mind becomes dull. Through nondistraction sharp insight develops, we experience vipashyana; but if that becomes too strong, wildness arises. The essential point is that both need to be present and in balance. What has been described as developing something as an antidote and then falling into the other situation is a matter of the two not being in balance. That is to say, either the factor of nonmeditation becomes too strong or the factor of nondistraction becomes too strong. So what is ultimately required is a union of shamata and vipashyana in which nonmeditation and nondistraction are completely balanced.

QUESTION: Is it spinning our wheels to exert mindfulness with the intent of mixing meditation with postmeditation, since we don't have much experience in this?

RINPOCHE: No, it's not a waste of time for us to exert ourselves at mindfulness during postmeditation. We tend to forget samadhi within postmeditation, and because we forget it, the force of it doesn't come into our experience. But if we were to develop some mindfulness of it, to remember the keenness and the feeling of samadhi, then later when we returned to samadhi it's strength would increase. Therefore the mindfulness of samadhi within postmeditation is very helpful for meditative equipoise.

It also is helpful for the postmeditation period because it tends to weaken the disturbing emotions. It is very helpful given all the difficult experiences we have during postmeditation, for the times in which our body is in pain or our mind is ill at ease, frightened, or undisciplined. If we can bring the sense of samadhi, the memory of it, the mindfulness of samadhi, to bear on the life we live in postmeditation, that will help to pacify our fears, to tame our disturbing emotions, to ease all the physical and mental suffering that we have. So it is a very helpful thing to do; it helps our body, our mind, and it helps everyone else.

QUESTION: In that case is it useful to use reminders, an object of focus in postmeditation, to encourage meditation?

RINPOCHE: Within samadhi we experience our mind as lacking any nature of its own. If we can remember that experience in postmeditation, it helps a great deal with the suffering that we encounter, such as strong passion and attachment, strong aggression and hatred. If we can remember that feeling of samadhi, it helps to increase the stability of our mind. It helps to lessen any pain we are feeling, and it enhances our stability and insight when we practice meditation again.

For instance, if we were to practice meditation and then make no effort to sustain the meditation during postmeditation, when we sat down to meditate again a month later we would feel, "What happened? I meditated last month but there doesn't seem to be anything happening now."

However, if we maintain some awareness during postmeditation, it will help a lot the next time we sit down to meditate.

ELIMINATING OBSTACLES TO MAHAMUDRA

[293] In mahamudra, first the nature of mind is pointed out, and then we train in that, learning to sustain our recognition of the nature of mind in meditation and postmeditation. When we train in meditation on mind itself, different kinds of obstructions and adverse circumstances may arise. These are regarded as errors into which we might fall and mistaken paths we might take. All of these need to be abandoned, cleared away, overcome. From this point of view we must understand the dangers and the faults of meditation. These are known as the four ways of going astray and the three mistaken paths.

Eliminating the Four Ways of Going Astray

Each of the four ways of going astray has two different aspects. The first is to make a mistake in the method of practicing meditation. This is a "temporary straying." The second is to make a mistake in how we develop our understanding and mental image of the nature of things. This is an "original straying." An original straying occurs when we have not given rise to meditation properly in the continuum of our body and mind.

The first of the four ways in which we might go astray is by misunderstanding emptiness. This means we do not understand that emptiness is the nature of all phenomena, of everything that appears to our mind.

Learned persons have identified the emptiness we need to understand as "the emptiness that possesses the supreme of all aspects." This means that despite having no nature of its own, emptiness is what allows everything to appear. Emptiness in no way contradicts dependent arising or the interdependent relationship of phenomena.

A person might infer from the lines of the *Heart Sutra*—"Form is empty, emptiness is form"—that emptiness is dead, or nothing at all, and therefore not worth meditating on. Or they might think that emptiness means our actions have no repercussions, and therefore virtuous actions don't bring happiness and wrongful actions don't bring suffering. These are mistaken views. Thus, the first way we might go astray is to misunderstand the real meaning of "the nature of phenomena is emptiness."

The second way we might go astray is to misunderstand the way to take emptiness as the path. In the practice of mahamudra we meditate on mind's nature in its unfabricated state. If we do not understand that mind in its natural state is already the ground, the path, and the fruition, we might think, "I want to achieve enlightenment, and therefore I will meditate on this emptiness. Later, as a result of this meditation, I will achieve some fruition." That is not the correct path. What we are actually meditating on is dharmata, which already exists within ourselves; in meditation we bring dharmata from an unmanifest state to a manifest state. If we don't understand this, then we have misunderstood the way emptiness is taken as the path.

The third way we might go astray is to regard emptiness as the antidote. If we do not understand that the disturbing emotions lack inherent existence, that they are coemergent thought, and that their nature is coemergent wisdom, we might believe that the disturbing emotions are real things and that emptiness is the proper remedy for them. We would mistakenly think the disturbing emotions are one thing and emptiness is something different; we would not realize that emptiness is the very nature of the disturbing emotions. We would therefore meditate with the wrong point of view, not understanding that the disturbing emotions already lack any true reality.

The fourth way we might go astray is to think that we must realize phenomena with emptiness. This is to misunderstand that things already lack inherent existence and not recognize the actual way our mind already is. Not understanding that the mind is empty, we feel we must fix things up, manipulate things, transform things that aren't empty into things that are empty. That is unnecessary because emptiness is already the nature of things.

Tashi Namgyal discusses two levels of each of the four ways of going astray. The first level is fully misunderstanding the concept, and the second level is occasionally misunderstanding the concept.

Of the four ways of going astray, the first is the most important one to abandon. Misunderstanding the emptiness that is the nature of all things that appear to our mind is the most dangerous mistake. Why is it such a problem? It is a problem because a nihilistic view causes us to think that there is no interdependent relationship among phenomena. We mistakenly think that emptiness is mere voidness or nothingness. Because the word "emptiness" causes us to think of nonexistence, other terms are used for the emptiness of mind in the Kagyu tradition—"mind as it is," "mahamudra," and "ordinary mind." We are less likely to think of mere nothingness when we hear these other terms. If we misconstrue emptiness, we will not travel the genuine path. How can such a misconception be cleared away? It is cleared away by the mind resting in the unfabricated state of equipoise.

An extension of this is to think that because things are nonexistent, it doesn't matter whether we engage in virtuous thoughts and actions. It is thinking that virtue, being empty, doesn't really help, and nonvirtue, being empty, doesn't really harm. The great mahasiddha Saraha said, "To conceive of things as being real is foolish. But to hold on to emptiness is even more foolish." This mistake is extremely dangerous.

The other strayings are not so dangerous, but they do prevent our meditation from going well. In this way they serve as instructions for our meditation to proceed properly.

How do we eliminate these aberrations? By realizing that true nature is not newly constructed but exists in us primordially. The Third Karmapa, Rangjung Dorje, in his *Aspirational Prayer for Mahamudra*, said, "All phenomena are the illusory display of mind. Mind is empty of any entity that is mind." When we say we see our own mind, it is not that we see anything. However, by looking directly into our mind, we see that the true nature of our mind is beyond anything, such as being true or false, existent or nonexistent. We pass beyond doubts of thinking the mind is like this or like that.

Two Additional Strayings

[298] In addition to these four ways of straying due to a misunderstanding of emptiness, Gampopa pointed out two other strayings.

The fifth way of going astray is to confuse experience with realization. This is related to the extraordinary method (Skt. *upaya*) of mahamudra meditation, in which the winds begin to move through the channels in the body, and we experience bliss or luminosity. We might mistake these experiences for genuine realization and become very attached to them. This is to confuse experience with realization.

The sixth way of straying is to confuse realization with experience. With the blessings of the guru we realize the nature of our mind, which is not established in any way and cannot be identified as anything in particular. When we try to continue meditation, however, we might not be able to stay with that, and our meditation begins to degenerate into various temporary experiences, such as bliss and luminosity. If we do not realize that the meditation has degenerated, we might think this is realization. The remedy for this is to meditate with certainty and a definite knowledge of the true nature of mind.

Eliminating the Three Mistaken Paths

[299] There are three kinds of mistakes a student can make that are concerned with the practice of meditative stabilization itself. When a student has been introduced to the mind's true nature and meditates within that, gradually a separation of the purified, brilliant quality of consciousness from literally the "dregs" of consciousness occurs. As a student sustains meditation, and the purified aspect of consciousness begins to be experienced, different kinds of temporary experiences—forms, sounds, smells, and thoughts—appear to the student's mind. These can be summarized as three: bliss, luminosity, and nonthought.

The first is an experience of bliss or pleasure, which can be experienced both in the body and the mind. Physically, we might feel a sense of bliss pervading the body. Mentally we might feel extremely happy and joyful.

The second is the experience of luminosity and clarity. We might have the sense of an extraordinarily brilliant light and experience no difference between night and day.

The third is the experience of nonthought, which is the sense of all things as being empty. The mind feels very steady, free of projection, straightforward, and free from thought.

We may have the experience of bliss, clarity, and nonthought all together or we may have them individually. There is no problem if we have one or all of these temporary experiences and do not become attached to them. If we regard them as wonderful and want to replicate them again and again, however, we imprison ourselves and create an obstacle for further development. The problem is that we take these experiences to be extremely important. When they arise we feel very glad, and when they don't happen, we feel that there is something wrong, and we become discouraged. We have become so caught up in them, thinking they are the true nature of phenomena and that we are having genuine meditation, that we don't understand we've not realized the nature of things. In fact, we have become distracted and have mistaken these three temporary experiences for the nature of reality.

These kinds of experiences will naturally arise when we practice meditation. The important thing is to understand that there is no need to feel particularly happy if they come about or sad if they don't. These things happen. Sometimes we have a good experience in meditation; sometimes our meditation experience is painful. There's no purpose in fearing difficult or painful experiences in meditation or in becoming attached to good experiences. The important thing is to sustain our meditation within the mind's way of being. Whatever comes along, we let it come and go. If we get involved in hope and fear about meditation, our meditation will not progress properly.

The best way to work with these temporary experiences is to recognize the cause of our going astray and to turn it in the other direction. We become attached to these experiences and enter into hope and fear with regard to them because we do not understand that they are empty. Whether it is the experience of bliss, luminosity, or nonthought, it is emptiness that cannot be identified as one thing or another. All these experiences are free from arising, free from abiding, and free from cessation. If we don't realize this, we will regard them as being truly existent. Thus, the antidote for attachment to temporary experiences is to not think of them as real, but to recognize them as the union of luminosity and emptiness.

The temporary experience of bliss, luminosity, and nonthought is the first of the two additional types of mistaken paths discussed by Gampopa. The second type of deviation involves developing realization through the blessings of the guru and then becoming stuck on temporary experiences.

[305] Gampopa said, "You must understand bliss, luminosity, and nonthought as unborn. If you do not understand them to be unborn, then you have not ascertained appearances. If you do not know them to be unborn, then you do not understand the nature of appearances." Gampopa was talking about meditation subsequent to the mind's nature being pointed out to us. First we recognize the mind's nature, but then we experience these kinds of temporary experiences of bliss, clarity, and nonconceptuality and become attached to them. Because of this attachment, these experiences conceal or obscure the mind's nature. Because they conceal the mind's nature, we are unable to ascertain them as the luminosity and emptiness that is the mind's way of being. Gampopa said, "It's necessary to enter into the knowledge of all these as unborn."

So the first type of deviation begins with temporary experiences to which we become attached; this prevents genuine realization. The second begins with genuine realization; then temporary experiences come along and we become stuck on them.

Methods for Removing Obstacles on the Path

[308] How do we clear away obstacles? Obstacles, or hindrances, are divided into two classes: the general hindrances, and the inner and outer hindrances. Previously, we discussed the methods of tightening, or concentrating, the mind as an antidote to heaviness of mind, and loosening, or relaxing, the mind as an antidote to wildness of mind. At this point, however, such methods are not employed. Instead we simply look directly into the nature of the obstacles. These obstacles are, after all, just sensations and feelings that have no inherent existence of their own. We do not need to regard them as false or make an effort to clear them away. Rather, we look directly into them, seeing their true nature as emptiness. Gampopa

said, "At this point, if we were to engage in the methods for clearing away this heaviness and wildness of mind, it would be like lighting a lamp in the daytime to clear away darkness." It is fine to light a lamp at night to clear away darkness, but to do so in the daytime is silly. In other words, once we recognize the nature of mind, there is no need to apply the traditional antidotes to dull and wild mind.

The second class of obstacles or hindrances—the outer and inner hindrances—covers many different things. One hindrance, which was described by a particularly accomplished meditator, involves the *mara,* or demon, of darkness entering into our head, the mara of speech entering our tongue, the mara of scattering entering into our heart, and the mara of motion entering our feet. The mara of darkness entering our head means that no matter how much we try to meditate, our mind remains dull and unclear, and we cannot experience clarity. The mara of speech entering our tongue means we cannot stop talking. The mara of scattering entering into our heart means that we are beset with thoughts; our mind just will not settle down. The mara of motion entering into our feet means we cannot hold still and sit down and meditate; we have to get up and go somewhere immediately. When these hindrances happen, we supplicate our guru. We imagine our guru at our head, at our throat, or at our heart. This has been found to be an effective way to deal with these obstacles.

Other hindrances that can occur include sickness, harm from human beings, harm from nonhuman beings, thoughts that arise, and emotional turmoil. Nonhuman beings are spirits, ghosts, hungry ghosts, and animals such as tigers and poisonous snakes. These are not things that come about because of meditation practice. We don't get sick, harmed by others, or fall into emotional turmoil because we are meditating. These things happen because that is the nature of samsara. Through the power of different kinds of actions and different deluded states of mind we wander from lifetime to lifetime. Sometimes we get sick, sometimes we're having such a good time with our friends and family that we become thoroughly distracted and don't get around to meditation. Sometimes thieves take possessions from us, harm us, and cause all kinds of problems for us. That's just the nature of samsara. What should we do at that point? We should supplicate the guru—we imagine the guru sitting upon the top of our head and pray that our efforts to understand the view and to practice meditation will go well. Later on in the text, we will talk about how to bring sickness to the path, how we can turn the experience of adversity into the path of mahamudra, how we can work with painful, deluded states of mind and bring them to the path of meditating in mahamudra. But at this point, the text advises us to supplicate the guru on the crown of our head when these kinds of obstacles arise.

Question

QUESTION: You said that one of the major obstacles is when you don't recognize that the mind is unborn when you have the experience of luminosity and bliss. Is that because there is still a reference point of someone experiencing that?

RINPOCHE: Yes, the temporary experience of bliss and luminosity is an obstacle to the practice of meditation because it involves the fixation upon the conception of self. The conception of a self is what leads to the attachment. From that point of view, it tends to get in the way of your meditation developing further. So the absence of that attachment is necessary, and the way to bring about the absence of that attachment is to rest in the mind's way of being.

15

THE PRACTICE OF UTTERLY RELEASING

Exceptional Methods for Enhancing One's Meditation

In the last chapter we looked at methods for abandoning various mistakes that arise in meditation. Abandoning the mistakes, however, is not enough. We must also enhance our meditation. In this and subsequent chapters we will discuss methods for developing our meditation, stage by stage, to higher levels. Some people are extremely fortunate, and their meditation develops naturally. But others must exert themselves in exceptional methods to progress.

The Determined Mind

There are two exceptional methods for increasing our meditation. The first is known as *lada*, which means a decisive, doubtless understanding of emptiness. We will discuss lada in this chapter. The second special method involves bringing everything to the path and training in the resourcefulness of this realization. We will discuss this method in the next chapter.

The Practice of Lada

[314] The Tibetan word *lada* is translated as "utterly releasing." Utterly releasing means abandoning all doubt and hesitation in our meditation

and settling decisively what mind is. *Lada* literally means leaping over a pass rather than going over in a step-by-step progression. *Lada* in the mahamudra tradition corresponds to *tögal* in the Nyingma dzogchen tradition, which literally means "leaping over."

The term *lada* conveys the sense of having complete conviction and practicing with total freedom from doubt. It is like going up a mountain in a car: There is one long route that winds up the mountain in a slow careful way and another short, difficult route that goes straight up the mountain and requires great exertion. We are not going to take the long easy route; instead we are going to take the short cut, which is very quick but very difficult.

When is it appropriate to do that? Beginners frequently have temporary experiences; if they continue to meditate stage-by-stage, however, the husk of these experiences is broken and actual realization comes forth. When that happens, it is time to engage in the practice of lada, of going straight up the mountain. It is possible to do lada too soon or too late, and each has its own particular peril. It is too soon to do lada if we have some intellectual understanding but don't yet have the proper experience. For example, a person may be knowledgeable about the Dharma and talk quite eloquently about a high view but in fact not really have an attitude of renunciation or any realization and deep experience. For this type of person it is too soon to do this practice of going straight up the mountain. On the other hand, if we wait too long, there is the danger of becoming strongly attached to the meditative experiences that we have, which then serve as obstacles to further development.

Determining the Nature of Mind

[316] Where are we going with lada? From within the recognition of the nature of mind that was pointed out by the lama we move very strongly and directly to the mountain peak—the nature that is the ground of all

phenomena, wherein birth, production, arising, has never been experienced. It is the emptiness of all phenomena, the true nature. That is where we are going.

Watching Mind to Develop Determined Mind

[318] How do we go directly up the face of the mountain? The third section of *The Moonlight of Mahamudra* explains that we do this by releasing utterly. There are two parts to this. The first is utter release through looking at thought and appearance; the second is utter release through looking at the object of meditation and the meditator. In both cases, we begin by supplicating our root and lineage gurus, because further development of our meditation depends upon faith and devotion.

To begin the practice of looking directly at thoughts and appearance, we give rise to devotion. Guru yoga is particularly appropriate at this point, for it enables us to recognize and meditate within dharmata. Having aroused devotion for the guru, who is understood as the dharmakaya, we make fervent requests for the realization that any appearance is the dharmakaya. Then, we extend one-pointed meditative equipoise by resting in that realization. The mind rests in such a way that insight does not waver and there is not even the slightest flutter of distraction. The mind has no target whatsoever; it rests in an unelaborated manner. Whatever dawns at that time—whether it is a subtle thought, an obvious thought, or no thought at all—is looked at nakedly and directly.

Generally speaking, there is no difference between lada and the introduction to coemergent thought that we discussed previously, but there is a slight difference in the way we meditate. This difference is basically a function of the meditator's capacity; at this point, the meditator has a very powerful capacity for looking directly and nakedly at whatever thoughts arise, including even the subtlest thoughts. The meditator can look within a state that is undistracted and yet not focused on any object. Within that state, which is pure and spacious, the meditator can investigate subtle and obvious thoughts and see if any difference exists between them. The meditator can also investigate the difference between the mind at rest and the moving mind. Whether thoughts are subtle or strong, whether there are many thoughts, few thoughts, or no thoughts, the mind's nature does not change.

Also, the meditator is able to look at whatever pleasure or pain arises, or at any of the eight worldly concerns, and cut through them all, settling decisively what their nature really is. Sometimes thoughts will cease, sometimes thoughts will radiate; the meditator can look at all of them clearly and see exactly what they are. In looking at external phenomena—whether a form that is beautiful or ugly, large or small, or a sound that is pleasant or unpleasant—the meditator is able to look nakedly and see them as they are. Moreover, the meditator is able to study the difference between appearances and mind, and appearances and thought, and by severing all superimpositions, release utterly into the mind's way of being.

The second way we release utterly is described in terms of the object of meditation and the meditator. For the object of meditation, we look at that which is being meditated upon, which is, of course, our own mind. We look at our mind not in terms of intellectual understanding but directly, and therefore we develop genuine experience and great conviction. We look to know what this object is and what its nature is. Ordinary ways of thinking or understanding will not work, for this is the point at which superimpositions (accretions or fabrications) must be cut. The meaning of that which must be cultivated in meditation is looked at again and again—clearly, vividly, and without distraction or fixation.

The second aspect of this has to do with the mind that is meditating upon the mind, that is, the meditator. This is done to understand that the object and the mind that looks at the object are the same thing. The Tibetan words are helpful here: where we say "object" and "subject,"

Tibetans say "object" and "that which has an object." In the same way that we looked at the object of meditation, we must now look again and again at the mind that is meditating. What is the relationship between the object upon which one is meditating and the meditator? Is there a sense of one being outside and the other inside? If there is any sense of dualism, we must look and investigate again. We then come to understand that there is no object and no thing that has an object. In short, this way of looking is a method for abandoning dualistic conceptions.

The Actual Release

[323] Having presented what it means to release utterly into the mind in terms of thought and appearance, the object of meditation and the meditator, the text then describes the actual release into unobstructed clarity (Tib. *zangtal*). This word *zangtal* has the sense of both "utterly penetrating" and "completely penetrated." What's being worked with here is attachment to meditation itself.

When we are beginners, definite knowledge of the mind's way of being, which is the object of our meditation, is absolutely necessary and indispensable. But when we have become accustomed to the mind's way of being, the instruction is to allow that certainty to crumble. There is a sense of something extra, some exceptional certainty, which we allow to dissipate. As important as mindfulness has been, the mindfulness of the meditator is now allowed to relax, and the deep desire for that which is to be experienced is set loose. We cast off the exertion of the experiencer and relax.

This lada practice is called "the actual lada to the unobstructed clarity." We begin by sitting unconditionally in samadhi, resting the mind upon the emptiness that is the unborn, without any hope of anything happening. We don't have thoughts such as, "I have to have a good meditation," because we are trying to recognize our mind as it is. The nature of our mind doesn't change whether our meditation goes well or not. We can do this practice in all different situations, for example, when we are traveling somewhere, eating, or caught up in some passion.

This is a period of practice that requires tremendous exertion. The text says if we find it to be very difficult, we should rest for three or four days and then undertake the practice again. If we do so, it can bring about a very powerful advance in our meditation.

Mixing Day and Night

This section speaks of mixing day and night continuously, in the sense of surrounding all of our experience with meditation. It could also be thought of as the mixing or blending of meditation and postmeditation. This applies not only to our experience in the daytime but also to our experience at night. How do we sustain our meditation through formal meditation and postmeditation? Through the utter release into unborn unimpededness. At this point, the meditator must learn to relax mindfulness, because mindfulness involves a certain intention. The force of mindfulness at this point tends to give rise to a kind of holding and attachment. This conceptual and emotional attachment is released through the relaxation of mindfulness.

It's important to keep in mind that, at this point, we are talking about the meditation of someone who has traveled a long, long way along the path, given birth to excellent experience of the mind's way of being, and learned to sustain that experience. For that person, the way to progress further is to relax even the subtlest desire to maintain mindfulness and to identify things.

We might think, "If I were to practice in that way, wouldn't that mean that I was falling into a completely unmindful state? How could that be beneficial?" That's not what's going to happen. What is being pointed out is that the mindfulness that we have had up to this point still involves some kind of emotional and conceptual fixation. In this relentless journey toward discovering the mind's genuine way of being, we have arrived at the point where we can allow even that slight conceptual and emotional fixation that is a component of mindfulness to dissipate. We rest within a state that is free from any mental work, any deliberate bringing to mind of anything at all. Within such a state, we are mindful of things as they are, the mind as it is. Thus this kind of mindfulness is greatly superior to the mindfulness we have been able to develop previously, which is either too tight or too loose.

What does it mean to suffuse our experience with this meditative realization? Ideally, of course, we would extend this even into our sleep. In just the way we learned to meditate within the mind's way of being without deliberately taking anything to mind, so we would be able to continue this into sleep and bring sleep and dream to the path. That would be ideal, but for the most part, that is not possible even for a yogin or yogini at this level. It does happen, but not that much. What is more common, even for those who are at this high level, is that, when we go to sleep, we lose our mindfulness of the mind's way of being, and dreams dawn in a confusing way. When we wake from sleep, however, we almost immediately recognize what happened and have insight into the way of being of that sleep and that dream. Then our insight into the mind's way of being resumes in an uninterrupted way, and our daytime experience is again saturated with this meditative realization.

The Heart of Enlightenment

[330] When we meditate upon mahamudra, the most important thing is to meditate on the mind's nature. Upon realizing the emptiness of the mind, we progress gradually over the stages of the paths.

Students sometimes wonder what the relationship is between mahamudra on the one hand and compassion for other sentient beings and bodhichitta on the other. Actually, there is a close connection. In his *Aspirational Prayer for Mahamudra*, the Third Karmapa, Rangjung Dorje, said, "The nature of migrators is always the Buddha." "Migrators" here means sentient beings, who travel from lifetime to lifetime without having any fixed home. The Karmapa's teaching means that buddhahood is not something foreign to sentient beings. Rather, it has always been and will always be the very nature of sentient beings. The second line says, "Not realizing this, they wander endlessly in samsara." "Not realizing," means not realizing our own nature. Sentient beings wander in samsara, never coming to the end of that wandering; one lifetime follows another endlessly. And in those various lifetimes, sentient beings experience many hardships, delusions, obstructions, and different kinds of pain. The third and fourth lines say, "For sentient beings who have suffering without end, arouse compassion. We should give birth to compassion." The point is that seeing that the suffering of sentient beings is never exhausted, compassion arises naturally.

If we have had the good fortune to give birth to profound and extraordinary realization of mahamudra, that's very good. If we have understood mahamudra just a little bit, that's also very good. We remember that we have achieved a human body, we have been able to enter into the door of the Dharma and hear these extraordinary instructions, and we have had the opportunity to practice these quintessential instructions. That, in and of itself, is inconceivable, incomprehensible, good fortune. It is so rare as to be incalculable. For those who have not had such an opportunity, we give rise to compassion and think about how to help them. This is how we cultivate compassion in the practice of mahamudra. You bear in mind that you have had the opportunity to receive the instructions on mahamudra and to meditate upon them, and you resolve that you will do whatever you can to further the welfare of sentient beings and to make it possible for others to have this opportunity. In that way, you arouse bodhichitta, the heart of enlightenment. Please do that all the time, and listen to the teachings in this way.

Questions

QUESTION: Rinpoche, you mentioned looking into our dreams to help us see the illusion of our daily life. Can you give us any further indication on how to wake up in the dream, or become aware in the dream?

RINPOCHE: If you maintain mindfulness and alertness of what's going on in your mind during the day, that mindfulness and alertness will carry on into the night. If, during the day, you are mindful of what you're doing with your body, speech, and mind, this will establish a predisposition for mindfulness, and as you become accustomed to that, these predispositions will help you to recognize your dreams as dreams. The most important thing is the practice of mindfulness. If you become habituated to it during the day, it will carry on into your dreams. If you don't carry out your activity mindfully in the daytime, then you will become confused when you are asleep.

QUESTION: How do we relate to temporary experiences while they are happening? Are we to enjoy them or to avoid them?

RINPOCHE: Temporary experiences, or *nyam*, tend to come in two flavors. Either we think our meditation is going very well or we think our meditation is going very poorly. So we can say there are good nyam and bad ones. But the point is, when we are having a good one, we should not take too much delight in it, and when we are having a bad one, we should not be too discouraged by it. If we exert ourselves in meditation, the intensity of these experiences will diminish little by little until we separate from them. Gradually the nyam lessen and meditation and realization become clearer. When we talk about the husk with something inside, it is like the nyam is covering over something, enclosing it, and gradually, as the husk falls away, the inside becomes manifest.

Whether or not we are able to realize things as they are, separate from the misery of samsara, and achieve enlightenment, depends upon the kindness of the guru. Also, if we have confidence in our guru, then we will have confidence in the instructions of the guru. If we have confidence in those instructions, we will practice them. If we practice them, we will achieve results. Without confidence in our guru, we will not have the confidence in the guru's instructions and we will not practice. If our confidence is 100 percent, our practice will be 100 percent, and we will get 100 percent of the result. If our confidence is 50 percent then our practice will be 50 percent, and so on. So conviction, faith, and devotion are extremely important. If we understand this properly, then faith and devotion are not attachment.

QUESTION: How do we understand this properly so that our faith and devotion are not attachment?

RINPOCHE: The reason faith and devotion to our guru does not become negative attachment is similar to how a mechanic relates to his tools. The hammer, wrenches, and so on are quite valuable to a mechanic for fixing a car, but the tools are nothing more. Similarly, the realization of mahamudra is born in our being dependent upon the guru's kindness. Because it is very important to realize mahamudra, the guru is very important. But the guru isn't a relative or a husband or a wife. It's a different kind of relationship.

16

BRINGING OBSTACLES TO THE PATH

[330] To enhance our meditation, we train the mind's expressive power through what is known as "bringing to the path," which means making various difficult situations, such as strong thoughts, strong emotions, or difficult physical circumstances part of our practice. It is important that we do not fall under the influence of such situations, but rather use them to fuel our meditation. If we do not learn to bring the whole range of our experience onto the path, it will be difficult to enhance our practice further. This practice begins after we have gained sound experience of the coemergent mind, thought, and appearance.

What exactly is brought to the path? Very ordinary thoughts that involve the sense of something apprehended and something apprehending it—these are brought to the path. Such thoughts involve an obscuration by fundamental ignorance. We must bring them to the path because they are what cause us to remain mired in samsara.

When to Bring Obstacles to the Path

[331] There are three sections in the discussion of bringing obstacles to the path. The first concerns when it is appropriate to bring obstacles to the path and what this activity actually is.

We do these practices when we have become attached to the appearances in our life such that they have become very strong, or when we have a strong passion or aggression we cannot overcome. We also do them when we encounter extraordinary circumstances that hinder our meditation, such as becoming very ill. So that we do not fall under the influence of such adversity, through the force of our stable meditation we actually use these adverse circumstances, making them part of our path. It is appropriate to engage in such action when our meditation shows signs of development and we have gained some confidence. If we undertake these actions prematurely, we run the risk of falling under the power of the eight worldly concerns.

What is the purpose of such action? We engage in such action to further stabilize and clarify our practice of samadhi.

What kinds of actions are there? There are those of the father tantras and those of the mother tantras. There is also a particular way described by the practice (Kagyu) lineage: If we go to a place that is very pleasant and solitary, we will not know whether our samadhi has any real strength and endurance, any integrity. However, if we seek out adverse circumstances, it will be very apparent whether our meditation has truly become steady and clear. So in the practice lineage, the instruction is to seek out an undesirable place, such as a charnel ground, or a very crowded place, where disturbing emotions can easily arise.

Generally speaking there is not much difference between people of the East and people of the West in terms of the practice of Dharma. But in this particular practice, in which we seek out unusual situations that bring adverse conditions to the path, there is a difference. In the East there is a great deal of fear of evil spirits and powerful deities. In Tibet people have lived in a certain place for many generations. People believe quite strongly that there are powerful deities and harmful spirits in certain locations and are afraid to go there. So in Tibet if yogis or yoginis want to discover whether their practice is going well, they go to a place that is said to have demons. This practice is particularly specified for ordained monks and nuns. The situation is different in America; many people have not lived here that long and don't believe that spirits and deities inhabit certain places.

We do this practice of bringing strong emotional experience to the path when we experience great happiness or great pain. For instance in America if we are married and our spouse runs off with another person, we may feel great pain—hatred and envy; or if we lose our job or cannot make an adequate living, we may feel hardship and pain. This is truly the time to practice to see whether or not we can bring feelings of pain and hardship or emotions of envy and jealousy to the path.

How to Bring Obstacles to the Path

[335] There may be times when we want to test our ability to work with the emotions that arise during difficult situations. Perhaps we have been meditating in a pleasant, isolated place, and no disturbing emotions have arisen. Generally that is quite good. But meditating in such a place doesn't allow us to discover whether we can overcome the disturbing emotions that arise in adverse situations. Therefore we deliberately go to a crowded place and mix our realization with our experiences there to see whether our realization is sufficient to pacify our disturbing emotions. We go to a place where there are lots of people, lots of distractions, and all kinds of obstacles, and there we develop our realization further.

Six Practices for Bringing Obstacles to the Path

[337] The text describes six different kinds of situations that are to be brought to the path. From some points of view, these conditions would be regarded as adverse. There are three important instructions that apply to all six of these practices. First we recognize what's going on at the outset: we identify dualistic thoughts or appearances arising from either good

or bad circumstances but do not come under their influence. We identify pleasure but do not become attached, and we identify discomfort or pain but do not give rise to aversion or the wish to harm. The point is simply to identify whether the circumstance is pleasant or unpleasant and not come under its influence.

The second instruction concerns how to work these situations in the intermediate period. The instruction is to cast away the idea of self, to let go of both the conceptual and the emotional clinging onto self. Whatever has arisen in our mind, we neither become attached nor develop aversion—thinking of it as either faulty or good. Instead, we simply rest in meditation.

The third instruction concerns how to proceed in the conclusion. The instruction is to avoid the narrow straits of hope and fear. This means, very simply, that we do not hope that some good thing will come about or fear that some terrible thing will happen. Such hopes and fears are confining. The way to work with hopes and fears is to let go of them and just relax. These three ways of working with whatever situations arise are the root for any practice of bringing seemingly adverse situations to the path and turning them into friends that help us.

The first of the six specific practices is bringing thoughts to the path. The first step is to recognize thought as thought. Different thoughts arise, and we sometimes consider them obstructions to our meditation. They may appear powerful and vivid. When they do, we apply mindfulness. We may also have thoughts we're only faintly aware of, and we go along with them without even realizing what's happening. The text instructs us not to allow ourselves to be carried away by our thoughts but to "squeeze them with mindfulness." It's not necessary to overdo this. We simply apply mindfulness and hold our seat instead of being taken for a ride by our thoughts.

When we have identified thoughts as thoughts, we cast away the idea of self. How do we do this? The text approaches this by laying out three mistaken ways to proceed. The first mistake is trying to avoid thinking rather than applying our mind to the problem. We draw our mind in and pursue nonconceptuality as an antidote to thought; we try to meditate upon nonconceptual wisdom. But that's not the way to work with thought in this scenario. The second mistaken way is to analyze where thought arises, where it dwells, and where it goes, and through doing so, to try to settle decisively that it has no nature of its own. That's not how we work with thought here either. The third is to just give thought its own head and let it go. We follow along with it, somehow trying to be mindful while it's going on. But that's not it either. Instead, the instruction given here is, having identified the thought, without nibbling away at a little piece of it, to apply our mind right there. We don't think of thought as faulty or good, try to stop it, pursue it, or do anything to it with our mind. Thought is colorful, pure, relaxed, spacious, and brilliant. We simply sustain it just as it is, without fixating in any way. We sustain it without any ideas or any attitudes about it, without hanging onto it. If we practice in that way, it will dawn vividly as meditation. That is called "raising thought to the path."

Sometimes we will be able to raise thought to the path and sometimes we will not. Whether or not we are successful, be careful not to tumble into the narrow straits of hoping that we will be able to do so or fearing that we won't. Without worry or hesitation, we don't calculate, figure, or fixate. Once the whole thing is over, we just let it be over and forget about it. We don't think about whether we did it well or badly; rather, we let the whole thing dissolve without a trace, and then go about our business.

This example demonstrates the basic procedure for bringing adverse situations to the path. As we look at the other five situations, we'll see slight variations in the procedure, but what has just been said is, in essence, the way we work with all of them.

The second practice focuses on bringing disturbing emotions to the path. Usually this is said to be "transforming poison into healing nectar." In this practice, we turn something that kills into something that gives life. We are talking about transforming the five major disturbing emotions of attachment, aggression, ignorance, pride, and envy into the five wisdoms: mirrorlike wisdom, the wisdom of equality, the wisdom of discriminating awareness, all-accomplishing wisdom, and dharmadhatu wisdom. How do we bring these disturbing emotions to the path? The first disturbing emotion is desire or attachment. It might be desire for a person or a thing. When the mind is attached and stuck, we must recognize that the desire has arisen. The second disturbing emotion is anger or aggression. This may involve an uncomfortable feeling inside when we regard someone or something. The third disturbing emotion is ignorance or bewilderment. This bewilderment is when the mind has sunken into some kind of darkness and dullness. Basically, our mind has become vague and unclear. It's important to recognize bewilderment when it arises. The fourth is pride. Pride is a matter of becoming attached to oneself, thinking, "me, me, me." We think that "I" am superior to others, and we become quite arrogant and haughty. The fifth is envy or jealousy—discomfort with others' prosperity or well-being. We experience some sort of harsh, obstinate feeling and cannot be content with the good fortune of others. We need to recognize envy or jealousy when it arises.

Usually we don't recognize disturbing emotions when they arise. When they appear, we don't follow after them, try to stop them, or analyze them in terms of where they arise, where they abide, or where they go. We just look right at them. In the terms of coemergent mind, we look and rest in the mind's luminosity and emptiness. The mind is clear, knowing, and luminous, yet it cannot be identified as this or that. Whether or not we are successful at bringing delusion to the path—transforming the disturbing emotions into healing nectar—we let it go. We don't hope for something or fear something else but rest in a very relaxed way. You can see that the way to practice with the mental afflictions is the same method that we practiced in terms of thought.

[337] The third practice focuses on bringing gods and demons to the path. In Asia many people hold beliefs about gods and spirits. Here in America, it's not quite the same. For people in the West, it may be relevant to think about this third situation in this way: Whether or not the magical activity of gods and demons actually arises, we may well have this sense of our mind going in a particular direction that is very hard to explain. For example, we might feel sad for no reason at all. Or we might feel fear, or anxiety, when there's no apparent basis. That kind of thing could be regarded as the magical tricks of gods and demons. If we can identify that kind of thing in our experience, the advice given here will be quite helpful.

The first step is to recognize that we have become sad, depressed, frightened, anxious, whatever. The next step is to entrust ourselves to the practice that has been described. Whatever sort of magical trick seems to be going on, such as the feeling of fear without any apparent cause, we look into its nature, which is luminous emptiness, and then let go of the whole situation. First we recognize what's going on; second we work with it properly, and third we let it go without a trace, and relax.

The practice of bringing gods and evil spirits to the path works best of course if we believe in gods and evil spirits. This belief causes fear to arise. We pacify this fear by engaging it directly. As a result, our meditation practice is enhanced considerably.

How we dispose of the dead is different in the East and the West. In the East the body is tossed in the charnel ground. Sometimes it is chopped up, and the bleeding limbs are scattered around. It can be frightening for people to go into the charnel ground. In the West dead bodies are put away very neatly, so no one knows what is there; and then of course nobody is afraid.

In the East, people might also believe that a certain rock or tree is the abode of a particular evil spirit. Everyone says, "Don't go there!" and so no one goes there. The yogins, however, deliberately go to these spots to test the power of their realization. If we don't think there is something there, however, we won't feel afraid, and if we don't feel afraid, there is nothing to bring to the path. Similarly, if we go to the charnel ground where there are pieces of bodies scattered about, we might feel horrified, but if all we see is a bunch of gravestones, we won't feel afraid, and there won't be anything to bring to the path.

The fourth practice is bringing pain to the path. This refers to the mental pain of feeling sad and poverty-stricken. We tend to feel that such pain is doing us considerable damage, that the situation is unbearable. The practice here is not to fall under the sway of such an impoverished mental state. Here we mix our mind with the self-pity and look directly at this disheartened state. When we do, we see its actual nature, which is emptiness. If we do this considering the pain of others, the meditation is a gateway to developing love and compassion. If we do it with our own pain, the meditation enables us to recognize the nature of our mind.

The fifth practice is bringing illness to the path. When illness arises, we look directly at it. This includes both physical illness and the mental suffering that accompanies it. Generally when we feel well we are able to practice meditation, and when we are sick we are not able. But it is possible to bring even sickness to the path and, in so doing, increase the strength of our meditation. Usually when we are sick, we become quite concerned about our body and think about it a great deal; at the same time, we experience illness as something very harmful. But by meditating on the true nature of our mind, we can look directly into the very nature of the illness. "What sort of thing is it?" We will see that the nature of the illness is just the way we see the nature of our mind. This meditation doesn't make the illness go away, but it renders the illness into something that doesn't harm us in quite the same way. We diminish its capacity to strike us, and so it is not as destructive and harmful.

We may wonder why lamas of extraordinary realization, such as Gyalwa Karmapa and Dudjom Rinpoche, get sick. How could this happen when they are so highly accomplished? While these people have very deep realization, they also have bodies of flesh and blood. People with bodies, which are composites of flesh and blood, inevitably get sick. However, people with profound realization don't experience the illness as painful. For instance, in the film *The Lion's Roar*, His Holiness Karmapa was shown to be quite sick from terminal cancer, yet he was smiling, laughing, and talking with people. People asked him how he was doing, and he replied that he was fine. How could that be? The illness affected his body, but he brought it to the path. He looked directly into it and saw its true nature. Therefore he did not experience it as suffering the way ordinary people would.

It is very important for us to bring suffering and illness to the path; however, it is very difficult to bring a serious illness to the path at the beginning. When talking about bringing illness to the path, my own guru says to pinch yourself hard and ask, "Does it hurt?" "Yes," he then says, "It hurts. Look right into that painful feeling. How is it? It's not so bad. It diminishes. You can actually look right into it." The point is that we should start with something small rather than with extreme suffering.

The sixth practice is to bring death to the path. We are usually very afraid of death; our mind is very shaky when it faces the fact of death. Here we look at death itself and discover that it is nothing other than dharmata, nothing other than reality itself, and that in that reality there is no change. There is nothing that exists in and of its own nature, and therefore there is nothing that could serve as a basis for pain. From this viewpoint we overcome our fear.

This last practice also involves bringing the intermediate state, or *bardo*, to the path. *Bardo* is a Tibetan word that means "in-between state." There are many intermediate states, but here we are talking about the intermediate state of dharmata, which is the intermediate state between death and rebirth. In both the sutras and the tantras, this intermediate state is said to last seven days, or sometimes up to forty-nine days. It is the time between leaving the old body and taking up a new body. During this time all sorts of confusion and false appearances occur. What we mean by bringing the bardo to the path is that we recognize the various appearances in the intermediate state as dharmata's own light and sound. At this point, the practice is to begin to familiarize ourselves with dharmata's own light and sound so that we will be able to practice when we enter into the intermediate state.

To illustrate this light, we can close our eyes very tightly and press slightly on the side of our eyes. At first we see only black, but then a bit of light begins to dawn, even though our eyes are still closed. Various forms and colors appear in this light. Little drops might also appear. This is actually dharmata's own light. Similarly, if we grind our teeth a little and then stop, we hear silence, and then a purring sound: "drrrrr." After a while the sound becomes very loud, but there is no source from which it is emanating. This is the sound of dharmata. We must look right at the very nature of this light and sound, and then they will decrease. Such experiences of light and sound come about in the intermediate state. The important point is to become familiar with them now, so that when we die we will be able to do this practice in the bardo, bringing this intermediate state to the path.

HOW REALIZATION DAWNS

As we understand quite well by now, it is necessary to sustain our meditation experience and not wander off into distractions and false paths. Not only must we remain on a genuine path, but our meditation must also develop to ever-higher levels. To enhance our meditation, we must engage in the practices of deliberately entering adverse situations that provoke obstructing conceptions. When we have learned to sustain realization through all sorts of situations, realization then dawns in stages. As we progress along the path, realization becomes clearer and more profound. In this chapter we will discuss how realization arises.

The Need for Pure Motivation

Whether we are practicing meditation, studying the quintessential instructions, listening to instructions, or giving teachings ourselves, it is extremely important to have a pure motivation at all times. At first, this pure motivation is a seed. We think, "I'm going to practice the Dharma, not to subdue my enemies or to accumulate wealth, but so that I'll be able to achieve liberation from samsara and achieve the omniscient state of complete enlightenment." With that motivation, we listen to instructions, meditate, practice, and so accomplish our own welfare. Furthermore we earnestly try to advance the welfare of others. "As I listen to these instructions and practice them, I do it not for my sake but for the sake of the many, many sentient beings, so that later I will be able to teach the Dharma to them properly and protect them from the suffering of samsara. I will be able to help them find liberation and complete enlightenment by showing them the paths that lead to such a state." Therefore the intention to achieve supreme enlightenment for the sake of all sentient beings is vital when we listen to instructions, and it is vital when we teach the Dharma to others. It is absolutely necessary that whatever activity we are engaged in be directed by this aspiration to complete enlightenment for the sake of all sentient beings.

The Need for Devotion toward the Guru

To develop our practice further, we need to generate devotion. The object of our devotion may be our root guru, or it may extend to the gurus of the lineage, such as Milarepa, Marpa, Naropa, or Tilopa. By reading the spiritual biographies of the gurus of the lineage, we may begin to feel great faith and devotion toward them, offer supplication to them, and receive their blessings.

How is this possible? It is possible because the nature of our mind is emptiness; our mind is undifferentiated from the vast space that is inseparably united with insight. Likewise, the great gurus of the lineage have mixed their minds undifferentiably with this union of space and insight. Since our mind is undifferentiated from the union of space and insight, and the minds of the gurus of the lineage have mixed with and manifested this realm of space and insight, the gurus of the lineage are not so distant from us. If we feel and ascertain the mixing and inseparability of the minds of the gurus with our own mind, then we receive their blessings, and the great potency of the minds of the gurus enters into us.

We may meet face-to-face with accomplished teachers. If we supplicate to them by visualizing light pouring from the three centers of their bodies and dissolving into the three centers of our own body, the exalted body, speech, and mind of the guru mixes undifferentiably with our own ordinary body, speech, and mind, and we generate confidence and an unusual sensation that the blessings enter into us. When our meditation has poor clarity or stability, we can supplicate the gurus with devotion. Their blessings will enter into our continuum and benefit our practice, making our meditation clearer and more stable.

The Three Levels of Practice

[350] There are three families of practitioners; which family we find ourselves in depends on how much and how well we trained in former lifetimes. The first family of practitioners consists of those who have extremely sharp faculties and for whom the levels of realization dawn all at once (Tib. *chigcharwa*). The second group consists of those who "bypass stages" (Tib. *tögalwa*). Although these practitioners may practice a lower level, they realize a higher level. This higher realization, however, is not stable; sometimes it is clear and sometimes it is vague, sometimes it is present and sometimes it is absent. The third group consists of those who proceed gradually, step-by-step, stage-by-stage (Tib. *rimgyipa*).

There are also three levels of knowing the nature of dharmata, which are called understanding (Tib. *go*), experiencing (Tib. *nyong*), and realization (Tib. *tog*). The first level—understanding dharmata—uses the mental consciousness to investigate, study, and think about how phenomena are empty and how mind has the nature of clarity. Through valid cognition, the meaning of emptiness or the nature of dharmata is known by way of words.

As our understanding of dharmata becomes clearer, we arrive at the second level, which is experiencing dharmata. At this level we do not just put words together but actually experience the concept in our meditation. Events arise and we experience the deep nature of mind. We do not yet have great familiarity with the nature of mind, and so sometimes it appears clearly and other times not very clearly.

At the third level—direct realization—we experience the deep nature of mind clearly and directly. We know the meaning of all dharmas, or phenomena, without any intermediary, and as a result, our knowledge of dharmata is decisive and does not waver.

When looking into the nature of mind, it is possible to mistake one level of knowing dharmata for another. For example, we might think that mere understanding is realization, or that realization is mere understanding of dharmata. In fact, mere understanding can obstruct realization. Therefore we must recognize that understanding is not realization and move further to the point of actual realization. We realize the deep nature not through mere understanding, but by seeing it nakedly and directly.

The first way to comprehend dharmata is through reasoned understanding. The second way is through experience. Gampopa explained that to experience dharmata is still not to transcend mind. Rather, it is like experiencing the sun on a day of occasional clouds—at times the sun is bright and clear, while at other times the sun is hazy and obscured by clouds. This is similar to the temporary experiences of bliss, clarity, and nonthought, which are sometimes present and sometimes not. If we persist in these passing experiences without becoming attached to them, we can transcend all doubt about the way in which the mind exists and develop a definitive conviction. And that is realization.

The Validity of the Four Yogas

[354] A number of authors have said that the four yogas (first introduced in chapter 13) are not part of the Buddhist Dharma but were made up by Kagyu scholars. They point out that many Buddhist texts discuss the five paths and the ten bodhisattva levels but do not mention the four yogas. Tashi Namgyal, however, shows that the four yogas were mentioned in the *Lankavatara Sutra*, and cites passages from various tantras to illustrate that the four yogas were not invented by Kagyu scholars.

The Meaning of the Four Yogas

[358] The four yogas are one-pointedness, freedom from elaboration, one taste, and nonmeditation. Each of these has three internal divisions: lower, middling, and great. Thus there is the lower one-pointed yoga, the middle one-pointed yoga, and the great one-pointed yoga, making a total of twelve internal divisions for the four yogas. Moving through these twelve yogas, we arrive at the fruition of complete enlightenment.

To arrive at one-pointed yoga, first we accomplish shamata and then we join this with vipashyana. Initially, our shamata is not very stable and the mind will not rest. *One-pointedness* indicates that shamata has become stable—our mind has been brought to rest. Then through this resting, we see mind clearly; any superimpositions are cut through, and complexities are resolved into simplicity.

At the lower level of one-pointedness, we see the nature of mind; however, we see it in a somewhat coarse manner. Having seen mind's nature, we become mostly free from anxiety and pain. At the middle level of one-pointedness, we achieve power over this meditative stability and begin to have some independence such that meditation is not difficult or hard work. At the great level of one-pointedness, it is said that the experience of meditation surrounds us in every way—meditation is continuous.

When we develop a genuine, definite conviction and become free from elaboration and complexities, we arrive at the second yoga, freedom from elaboration. This yoga involves recognizing luminosity and emptiness, and generating conviction about emptiness.

At the lower level of freedom from elaboration, we realize the unborn nature of phenomena. At the middle level we understand that phenomena are not only unborn, but actually rootless. At the great level the meditator understands that external appearances are not separate from reality, or dharmata, so all projections of external phenomena are completely severed.

As the experience of the second yoga intensifies, we arrive at the yoga of one taste. Our meditation becomes clearer, and we understand that samsara and nirvana are one taste. We understand that which is to be abandoned and that which is to be adopted as one taste.

Because our realization of things as they are has become manifest, at the lower level of one taste we see that there is no difference between samsara and nirvana. At the middle level we cut through the root of seeing a difference between the apprehended object and the apprehending subject, so that they no longer appear to be separate. At the great level we see that all phenomena are truly of one taste. We no longer regard anything as dangerous and thus feel tremendous fearlessness.

By becoming ever more familiar with the realization of one taste, the meditator arrives at the point at which she or he does not need to engage in a formal structure of meditation. This is the level of nonmeditation. The nature of mind has been resolved, and the meditator does not need to practice any particular meditation to experience this.

At the lower level of nonmeditation, because mind itself and reality have become manifest, we no longer need to meditate. There is no longer the sense of something meditated upon and someone meditating upon it. Striving and effort are required to some extent at the lower level of nonmeditation, but at the middle level we achieve spontaneous presence such that striving and effort are no longer necessary. It is said that at the great level, we have arrived at the bodhisattva level where we meet the dharmakaya, which is to say, the dharmakaya has become fully manifest. At this point, the clear light of ground and the clear light of the path mix.

Postmeditation and the Four Yogas

[364] A different postmeditation experience corresponds to each of the four yogas. Following the first yoga of one-pointedness, we are not very familiar with the deep nature of mind. At this stage in postmeditation

we experience various appearances and believe them to be real, but we have few thoughts or perceptions, and little discursiveness.

In the postmeditation experience subsequent to the second yoga, freedom from elaboration, the factor of clarity has gone further, and our understanding of the deep nature of mind has deepened. As various phenomena appear, we understand them and regard them as being like illusions. In this yoga we do not have much conceptuality.

The postmeditation experience subsequent to the third yoga, one taste, involves understanding the union of appearance and emptiness. We do not yet fully apprehend this union, although our experience of emptiness is stronger.

The fourth yoga of nonmeditation is distinguished by the mixing of meditation and postmeditation. Due to this mixing our compassion for all sentient beings becomes stronger. Because we now have a great capacity for realizing the deep nature within meditative equipoise, there is a much greater force to our compassion for sentient beings.

Instructions for the First Yoga

[373] One-pointed yoga refers to a single-pointedness of mind within which we gradually and clearly understand the nature of mind. Developing this requires some exertion. It is helpful to do a silent retreat for perhaps one or two days, since a lot of conversation tends to create confusion. When we are practicing this yoga of one-pointedness, we might experience dullness or wildness. It is important to clear away and abandon such states of mind. We might do this by applying concentration for the sinking state and relaxing for the wildness of mind. Or we might use the special mahamudra method of looking directly into the nature of mind and dispelling any obstacles in that way.

If we experience what is called a "real darkness of stupidity," it is necessary to use methods for purifying ill deeds and obstructions, such as guru yoga. We receive various empowerments for meditative stabilization, make offerings of various sorts, and confess our ill deeds. Engaging in such methods reduces the severity of the obstacles we are experiencing. We could also speak with our guru or fellow meditators, asking them what they did when this obstacle came up and what would help in this particular case.

When we learn that we have wrong views about points of Dharma and meditation, we strive for the correct view. Sometimes we take refuge and recite the liturgy for receiving refuge. We reflect on the ways in which samsara has no essence and samsaric pursuits are entirely futile. This generates a genuine wish to become free from samsara, furthers our devotion to the Dharma and the guru, and helps generate compassion for sentient beings.

We may find that, after practicing for a long time, we are tired. In that case it is appropriate to rest and allow our mind to become spacious. At all times, however, mindfulness is important. There are two kinds of mindfulness at this point: an extremely concentrated, focused mindfulness and a somewhat looser mindfulness.

Sometimes when we are practicing, we may suddenly have an extraordinarily good understanding of something and experience genuine insight. In postmeditation whatever appearance takes place, the instruction is to not become involved with it but simply to let it go. Sometimes we may feel that a meditation experience was good, and sometimes we feel that a meditation experience was bad. Whichever experience we have, it does not matter. The important point is not to evaluate them in this manner, but just exert ourselves at the practice. These are the instructions for the one-pointed yoga.

Instructions for the Second Yoga

The instructions for the second yoga of freedom from complexity are to go to an isolated place, remain alone, and practice meditation. Mainly we meditate by relying upon the more relaxed type of mindfulness previously discussed. When it seems beneficial for our meditation, we make offerings, supplicate the gurus of the lineage, and engage in methods for increasing devotion, pure appearances, and compassion for others.

When we are practicing this yoga, it is helpful to talk occasionally about our meditation experience with our guru or with companions who have had similar experiences. This helps the experience to progress further. It also helps to arouse more longing. In addition, we might read the spiritual songs of the siddhas—such as those of Marpa and Milarepa or those in *Rain of Wisdom*—think about the essential points in these songs, or sing them to ourselves.

When our meditation is not progressing, we might practice the meditation on our own yidam. We imagine this deity vividly and clearly. This will help our meditation practice considerably.

Instructions for the Third Yoga

[374] To develop the third yoga, one taste, sometimes we practice alone and sometimes we go to a place with many people. By doing this we see just how our mind and meditation are going. Is the meditation increasing or is it declining? Are disturbing emotions being generated or not? Sometimes when we practice we rely upon strong mindfulness; sometimes we leave the mindfulness very loose and just observe.

In the yoga of one taste the factor of realizing and ascertaining emptiness may become very strong. Because of this we might mistakenly minimize the relation between actions and their effects and thereby ignore the practice of cultivating virtue and eliminating nonvirtue. That is a serious mistake. If we begin to think that way, it is very important to understand why it is incorrect.

Instructions for the Fourth Yoga

In the yoga of nonmeditation we experience more relaxation and spontaneity and fewer disturbing emotions. At the fullest development of this stage we reach buddhahood, realizing the nature of our mind directly in all moments. We see that there is no need to abandon things because we experience their natural state, purified of all projections and delusions. We realize that there is nothing that needs to be realized, because we understand that the nature of our mind is always there.

The Four Yogas and the Five Paths

[402] The four yogas of mahamudra can be correlated to the five paths of the sutra vehicle. The yoga of one-pointedness corresponds to the first two paths of accumulation and preparation. We do not have direct realization of emptiness on these paths; nevertheless insight has been generated to some extent within our continuum. The yoga of freedom from complexity corresponds to the third path of seeing. Emptiness is now realized directly, unmediated by conceptuality. The yoga of one taste corresponds to the fourth path of meditation, and the yoga of nonmeditation corresponds to the fifth path of no more learning.

The text and treatises speak extensively of extraordinary qualities—emanations, powers and clairvoyances, the thirty-two marks and the eighty signs of a buddha, and so forth—that we develop on the paths and that are complete on the final path. When we have progressed through the four yogas and arrived at the final yoga, we do not have the qualities of emanation and clairvoyance or the physical signs of the Shakyamuni Buddha. Why is that? There is really no difference in terms of the qualities of mind—in terms of what needs to be abandoned and what needs to be realized. Buddha Shakyamuni, however, spent incalculable lifetimes accumulating merit and wisdom, so that when he took birth in India, he took birth not through the force of ordinary karma but through the force of having accumulated vast collections of merit and wisdom. Milarepa, on the other hand, was born a very ordinary person. Through the ripening of actions and afflictions that were accumulated on the basis of confusion, he was extremely fortunate to be able to meet with a fully qualified guru and receive profound instructions from that guru. He was able to exert himself ferociously at his practice so that he achieved enlightenment in one lifetime. The mind of Milarepa was no different from the mind of Shakyamuni Buddha in what it abandoned and what it realized; however, not having progressed over the path in the same way by accumulating such vast merits, Milarepa did not have the qualities of body and speech that Buddha Shakyamuni had.

Questions

QUESTION: When I am sitting, bubbly little feelings go through me. I'm having a hard time knowing what to look at and what not to look at.

RINPOCHE: There are two different issues there. One is the tightness in the body that can develop when we practice meditation. It can be as if the flesh in our body intensifies, and the channels or nadis are very focused and intense. That can easily lead to all sorts of uncomfortable physical sensations. The point is to relax our mind and body completely when we practice meditation. The other issue is that perhaps there are some problems with the body that a doctor might be able to help with.

When you are meditating, it is good to check in with your body from time to time to see if you are getting too tight. As the awareness becomes concentrated, the body can easily become concentrated too. This concentration in the body is not helpful. So you check the feeling throughout the body and relax the whole body.

QUESTION: Trungpa Rinpoche once said that there is still pain after enlightenment. He added that it was no big deal, and of course neither was pleasure. I wonder if you might comment on this in the light of the teaching on one-pointedness.

RINPOCHE: I don't know that I understand precisely the measure of Trungpa Rinpoche's thought, but it strikes me that it was said from an extremely vast point of view. If one were to say that even a completely enlightened being still has pain, one might mean that a buddha sees the pain and the frustration that all sentient beings throughout space are experiencing and feels tremendous compassion for them, wishing to do something that would actually help. This buddha would also feel a sense of a great responsibility in that he or she has vowed to relieve all sentient beings of suffering and to establish them in a state of happiness, and is now at the point where he or she has the capacity to help all sentient beings. Because this pain can be dispelled there is no great danger. A buddha has cleared away every last trace of samsara and is now completely free from its pain. For that reason a buddha is happy. At the same time that pleasure is empty of any nature of its own. The pleasure is experienced directly and clearly and from that point of view, it is no big deal.

18

HOW WE SHOULD PRACTICE

I am delighted we have had this opportunity to study *Moonlight of Mahamudra*. Among the many oral instructions concerning mahamudra, this text is very special. As I explained at the beginning, when he was asked which book would be of the greatest benefit if it were to be translated into English, Gyalwa Karmapa chose *Moonlight of Mahamudra*. The text, however, is very long, and many students who have been instructed to study it have been somewhat overwhelmed by its length. So I am glad that, in a concentrated period of time, we have had a chance to look at it together, to study what it has to say, and to think about it in an environment of practice. I am extremely happy about that.

There are many books that we might study that are concerned principally with knowledge. When we try to join them to experience, however, we find that it is not so easy to do. Other books focus on internal experience but are difficult to understand. As Tashi Namgyal said at the beginning, there are many laypeople who study a lot but don't go on to practice and to gain experience of the meaning of what they have studied. And there are others who practice a lot, but because they are not skillful with words, they aren't able to explain things clearly. So Tashi Namgyal composed this text combining the words, the meaning, and the experience; it is useful for both study and practice.

When we read *Moonlight of Mahamudra* for the first time, it is not that easy to understand. Who would expect it to be? If we reread it carefully, however, we will begin to understand why it is important and meaningful, and we will develop some interest and enthusiasm for it. By repeatedly looking at the text and practicing the instructions given there, the meaning will become clearer and clearer. In this way, tremendous benefit will occur.

The most important thing is to bring this experience and realization into greater clarity and stability. If we study and practice gradually, our understanding of the meaning and the character of the teachings on selflessness and so forth will increase. The meaning presented in this text is profound, vivid, clear, practical, delightful, and not all that difficult. Please do not stop at understanding. Go further to the point of experience, and further to realization, until you have reached a complete perfect buddhahood.

Some students have a lama who knows exactly what is going on in the student's mind. I have neither the compassion nor the blessings to impart this. I don't have that kind of clairvoyance. Nevertheless, I have given instructions on the practice of mahamudra. They are not my own instructions but the instructions that have been passed down through the Kagyu lineage. I have been extremely fortunate in my life in that I have been able to receive many special and blessed oral instructions from many great teachers. I offer these to you who wish to practice the Dharma, with my genuine confidence that if you practice these instructions they will unerringly lead to complete liberation. Some of you might think, "Well, if he has no blessings or clairvoyance then probably he is on the wrong path." But you do not need to have any hesitation of that sort—these instructions are genuine. If you practice them, you will find that your practice will become perfected and you will achieve the result that was intended.

To arrive at realization in the tradition of the sutras we must practice and accumulate merit and wisdom for an incalculable number of eons. But if we have been introduced to the oral instructions of mahamudra, we might have the experience of prajna when we hear that all phenomena are emptiness. Those who are fortunate will then have the experience directly. Others won't have this experience right away but will understand the meaning, and gradually this understanding will become experience. We are in a fortunate situation and should not waste it. We should practice and meditate well.

When some begin to practice, they feel a very strong wish to renounce the world altogether. They think, "I am just going to practice the Dharma. I don't need a place to live. I don't need to worry about my husband or my wife. I will forget my children. I don't need to be concerned about food. I don't need to be concerned about clothing." They believe they can throw everything else away. But that sort of renunciation does not tend be very stable or enduring. Moreover, our family and parents are very important, and it is important not to just throw them away. Instead we should continue with our work in the world and with our practice of the Dharma. Because we are practitioners of the Dharma, we should not be people who have no love or compassion, with our heads spinning all the time.

Because we have been fortunate enough to experience the Dharma, we tend to be people who have love and compassion and the wish to help others. Our mind does not continue to be distracted and dragged along by everything that comes by. When there is not much time to practice meditation, it is the time to practice mindfulness and alertness. When there is time to take a long or short retreat, it is beneficial to do so. What is crucial is that we maintain mindfulness in all our activities and at all times. That will help our mind tremendously.

We should recognize how extremely fortunate we are to have the opportunity to practice meditation. We should also recognize that there are a great many people who have no faith in the Dharma. They are not terrible or bad people, so there is no reason for us to become proud of our Dharma accomplishments; it is just that they are temporarily unable to have an interest or confidence in the Dharma and so enter into it. These people should be recipients of our love and compassion. To urge people to enter the Dharma by saying the Dharma is wonderful just pushes them away. It is a fruitless enterprise and not very skillful. Some people simply have not yet generated faith in the Dharma, but it is always possible for them to do so. If at the appropriate time we are able to help them find the path, that is very good, but it is important to lead people to the path of Dharma in a skillful way.

Some students are ready and others are not. Those who are not ready will gradually become ready. When the time is ripe the Buddha's activity will arise spontaneously, and there will be an opportunity for them to enter into the door of the Dharma. For those that are not ready to enter into the Dharma, we must not push and urge them but wait until they are ready and able. Therefore, looking to see whether or not the person is ready is important.

If we have the good fortune to enter into practice and interest in doing so, but contrary conditions come about, that is the time for patience. Patience will facilitate the clearing away of such difficult and contrary conditions. When the opportunity for practice arises again, we should not waste it.

The Buddha said that taming one's mind is the very essence of the Dharma. Taming our mind involves abandoning what is bad and cultivating what is good. We need to abandon or pacify the afflictions such as desire, aggression, ignorance, pride, and jealousy. We need to cultivate wisdom, which leads to the good qualities and extraordinary attributes of a realized person. The principal method for abandoning what needs to be abandoned and developing what needs to be cultivated is meditation. Having mindfulness and alertness is the proof of realization.

When practicing meditation there is both the meditation session and the postmeditation session, which arises from the meditation session. We maintain the continuum of mindfulness and alertness through both. In that way the meditation session and the postmeditation session will benefit each other mutually. The important point is the continuity of mindfulness and the nonwandering of mind. That is what the Buddha meant when he said that the very essence of the Dharma is taming one's mind.

NOTES

1. Buddhists say that ordinary beings suffer because they do not see the true nature (Tib. *nelug*) of phenomena or the true nature of their mind. Rather they see and become attached to outward appearances, which are in reality empty of any inherent essence, or nature.
2. Buddhism distinguishes primary (Tib. *gyu*) and secondary (Tib. *kyen*) causes. The primary cause of a plant, for example, is a seed, while secondary causes are things such as sunlight, water, and manure. The seed is a primary cause because without it there is no possibility of there ever being a plant. Saying discipline, listening, and reflecting are primary causes means these are absolutely essential, while devotion is very important but can wax and wane.
3. Emptiness (Tib. *tongpanyi*), the ultimate nature of all phenomena, has the quality of luminosity (Tib. *salwa*). In the outside world this luminosity is what allows everything to appear. If everything were instead real and permanent, then nothing new could appear. Due to its luminosity, emptiness provides the ground for every manifestation.

    In relation to mind, *luminosity* refers not to light but to the mind's intelligence and capacity to know. The instruction to increase luminosity within meditation means figuratively to escape the dark fog of our dull mind and bring brilliance, or clarity, to our awareness.

4. Conventional truth (Tib. *kundzob denpa*), also called relative truth, is the world as it appears to us unenlightened beings who see the world in terms of duality. Ultimate truth (Tib. *dondam denpa*), also called absolute truth, is the world as it really is, that is, as seen by an enlightened being.

5. Tibetan anatomy identifies a vast network of subtle channels (Skt. *nadi*) in the body through which drops (Skt. *bindu*) and energy winds (Skt. *prana*) flow. These channels are not visible to the eye but are analogous to meridians in acupuncture. The energy flowing through the channels keeps the organs in harmony and helps in basic metabolic functions such as digestion. These subtle channels and the energy that flows through them also are intimately connected to consciousness.

6. The eight impediments or fetters (Tib. *kuntri gye*) are lethargy, sleep, excitement or agitation, regret, envy, stinginess, shamelessness, and indecency.

7. Analytical meditation is somewhat different from regular reasoned analysis, where one conceptually evaluates, for instance, the many logical arguments for why things are empty. At the Nalanda Institute for Higher Buddhist Studies, analytical meditation was taught by having the students face the wall and go into a deep shamata meditation. Then the teacher would read passages of the sutras or give the students thoughts to analyze. The students would contemplate this material one-pointedly with a minimum of discursive thought. This analytical meditation differed from placement meditation in that in placement meditation the mind would be examined with no intellectual mediation, or as the text says, by "looking at mind."

8. Hashang Mahayana is best known for his famous debate with Kamalashila in Tibet, which determined that the Tibetans would follow the Indian tradition of Buddhism rather than the tradition

emanating from China. Hashang said that it didn't matter whether a cloud covering the sun was black or white, it still darkened the world, and that, similarly, if one's thought is good or bad, it also doesn't matter because it is still a thought. He proposed that one could become enlightened suddenly by simply realizing the ultimate truth. Kamalashila on the other hand said that one can't develop realizations by doing mahamudra meditation if one hasn't first developed enormous good karma through a vast collection of merit.

9. The discussion of the main body of the practice of the view has two parts. The first is an analysis of other traditions, and the second is setting forth our own tradition. Thrangu Rinpoche leaves aside a great deal of material on others' traditions in the root text in order to focus on the view itself.

10. The tantras were brought to Tibet from India and translated into Tibetan. In addition, some Tibetans who went to India to master these practices brought back oral instructions from their gurus. They also developed their own oral instructions and passed these on as the quintessential instructions. The most well-known quintessential mahamudra instructions are the *Mahamudra Subtledrop Tantra* and the three spiritual songs by Saraha.

11. The vulture is considered auspicious in Tibetan culture.

12. When Thrangu Rinpoche gave these teachings, the Sixteenth Gyalwa Karmapa had passed away and a new Karmapa had not yet been discovered. The Seventeenth Gyalwa Karmapa Orgyen Trinley Dorje, since discovered in Tibet, is in his teens and studying in India.

GLOSSARY

Abhidharma (Tib. *chöngonpa*). The Buddhist teachings that discuss cosmology and classify phenomena into types and categories.

Avalokiteshvara (Tib. *Chenrezig*). The bodhisattva of compassion, regarded as the patron deity of Tibet. A common meditational deity, his mantra is *Om Mani Padme Hum*.

bodhichitta (Tib. *jangchub kyi sem*). The "mind of enlightenment." The aspiration to become a buddha in order to free all sentient beings from the suffering of samsara.

bodhisattva levels (Skt. *bhumi*; Tib. *sa*). Literally, "ground." The levels or stages a bodhisattva goes through to reach enlightenment. These consist of ten levels in the sutra tradition and thirteen in tantra.

Chakrasamvara (Tib. *Khorlo Demchok*). One of the five main tantric practices of the Kagyu Lineage. He is a meditational deity of the lotus (or Amitabha Buddha) family and plays an important part in the six yogas of Naropa.

clear light (Tib. *ösal*). A subtle state of mind that according to tantra is the state wherein highest realization is attained.

completion stage (Tib. *dzogrim*). In the Vajrayana there are two stages of meditation: creation and completion. During the completion stage, one dissolves the visualized deity into emptiness and rests in that sense of emptiness.

creation stage (Tib. *kyerim*). Also known as development stage. In the Vajrayana there are two stages of meditation: creation and completion. During the creation stage, one establishes and maintains the visualization of a deity and their mandala for the purpose of realizing the purity of all phenomena.

dakini (Tib. *khandroma*). A yogini who has attained realizations of the fully enlightened mind. She may be a human being who has achieved such attainments or a nonhuman manifestation of the enlightened mind.

definitive meaning (Skt. *nitartha;* Tib. *ngedon*). Teachings of the Buddha that give the direct meaning of Dharma and are not modified to suit the level of the listener. This contrasts with the provisional meaning.

dharmakaya. *See* kayas, three

disturbing emotions (Skt. *klesha;* Tib. *nyonmong*). The emotional obscurations (in contrast to intellectual obscurations) that drive us to do harmful actions. Also translated as "afflictions" or "delusions," the three main disturbing emotions are attachment, anger, and ignorance.

dzogchen (Tib. *dzogchen*). Literally, "great perfection." The highest of nine vehicles according to the Nyingma tradition, dzogchen is a meditation very similar to mahamudra, involving looking directly at the mind.

eight worldly concerns (Tib. *jigten chögye*). These divert one from the Buddhist path. They are four polar pairs: attachment to gain and aversion to loss, attachment to pleasure and aversion to pain, attachment to praise and aversion to blame, and attachment to fame and aversion to ignominy.

four noble truths (Tib. *pagpai denpa zhi*). The Buddha began his teaching career with a talk in India at Sarnath on the four noble truths. These are the truth of suffering, the truth of the cause of suffering, the truth of the cessation of suffering, and the truth of the path. These truths form the foundation of Buddhism, particularly in the Theravada school.

garuda. A mythical bird that hatches fully grown.

guru yoga (Tib. *lamai naljor*). The practice of devotion to the guru culminating in receiving his or her blessing and blending indivisibly with his or her mind. It is also the fourth of the preliminary practices *(ngöndro)*.

Hinayana (Tib. *tegmen*). The first of the three vehicles of the Buddha's teachings. The goal in the Hinayana is the cessation of one's own suffering through a realization of the four noble truths and the purification of one's conduct.

hungry ghost (Skt. *preta*; Tib. *yidag*). A type of being that incessantly craves food and drink but can never be satisfied. Products of excessive greed in previous lifetimes, they are usually depicted with enormous stomachs and thin throats.

interdependent origination (Tib. *tendrel*). The principle that nothing exists independently but comes into existence only in dependence on other factors.

jnana (Tib. *yeshe*). The wisdom that knows the true nature of phenomena.

Karmapa. The title given to the the head of the Karma Kagyu school of Tibetan Buddhism; the seventeen successive incarnations of Dusum Khyenpa (1110–93).

kayas, three (Tib. *kusum*). There are three bodies of a buddha: the nirmanakaya, sambhogakaya, and dharmakaya. The dharmakaya (Tib. *chöku*), the "truth body," is the completely enlightened mind, or the complete wisdom of a buddha, which manifests as the sambhogakaya and the nirmanakaya. The sambhogakaya (Tib. *longku*), the "enjoyment body," is an exalted aspect that manifests only to highly realized beings. The nirmanakaya (Tib. *trulku*), the "emanation body," is the body visible to samsaric beings. The historical Buddha, Shakyamuni, is an example of a nirmanakaya.

mahasiddha (Tib. *drubchen*). A practitioner with a great deal of realization and special powers. This term refers particularly to a group of tantric Buddhist yogis, often enumerated as eighty-four, who lived in India between the second and twelfth centuries.

mantra (Tib. *ngag*). (1) A synonym for the Vajrayana, or tantric, teachings. (2) Sacred Sanskrit syllables associated with a particular meditational deity that are recited as part of tantric practice.

mara (Tib. *dü*). Obstacles encountered by the practitioner that are sometimes personified as demonic forces.

nirmanakaya. *See* kayas, three

prajna (Tib. *sherab*). Wisdom, knowledge, or intelligence. *Prajna* usually it refers to the transcendent knowledge of the true nature of reality.

quintessential instructions. Also called oral instructions. These are instructions given directly from guru to student concerning meditation on the nature of mind. While some are written down, many are passed on only orally.

sambhogakaya. *See* kayas, three

sangha (Tib. *gendun*). Along with Buddha and Dharma, one of the three things that a

Buddhist practitioner takes refuge in. The Sangha are our companions on the path, especially the noble sangha, those who have realized emptiness directly.

Saraha. One of the eighty-four mahasiddhas of India said to have lived in the ninth century. He is known for founding the lineage of mahamudra by writing three spiritual songs *(dohas)*.

siddha (Tib. *drubpa*). A Buddhist practitioner who has attained siddhis.

siddhi (Tib. *ngödrub*). Spiritual accomplishments or powers of advanced practitioners. These include both the supreme accomplishment of enlightenment and such mundane powers as clairvoyance and flight.

spiritual song (Skt. *doha;* Tib. *doha*). A religious song or verse spontaneously sung by a Vajrayana practitioner telling of his or her realization. They typically have nine syllables per line.

sutra (Tib. *do*). A scriptural discourse of Shakyamuni Buddha. The sutras are often contrasted with the tantras, the Buddha's esoteric teachings.

Vajradhara (Tib. *Dorje Chang*). The exalted form in which the Buddha transmitted his teachings on tantra. A blue meditational deity that figures prominently in the tantras of the Kagyu, Sakya, and Gelug lineages.

Vajrasattva (Tib. *Dorje Sempa*). The buddha of purification associated with the vajra family of Akshobhya. Vajrasattva practice is also one of four preliminary practices *(ngondro)*.

Vajrayana (Tib. *dorje tegpa*). The tantric tradition of Buddhism, which began in India but now exists most fully in the Tibetan tradition. The Vajrayana practices are considered particularly expedient for attaining enlightenment quickly, as they rely on the transmutation of ordinary experiences and the transcendence of duality with the pure vision of a buddha.

TABLE OF TIBETAN TERMS

Pronunciation	Transliteration	Translation
bagchag	bag chags	latent disposition
bagyöpa	bag yod pa	attentiveness
chaggya	phyag rgya	mudra
chaggya chenpo	phyag rgya chen po	mahamudra
chamnepa	phyam gnas pa	smoothly abiding
chegom	dpyad bsgom	analytical meditation
Chenrezig	spyan ras gzigs	Chenrezig
chigcharwa	gcig car ba	sudden approach
do	mdo	sutra
doha	do ha	spiritual song
domsum	sdom gsum	three vows
dondam denpa	don dam pai' bden pa	ultimate truth
Dorje Chang	rdo rje 'chang	Vajradhara
Dorje Sempa	rdo rje sems dpa'	Vajrasattva
dorje tegpa	rdo rje theg pa	Vajrayana
drenpa	dran pa	mindfulness
drubchen	grub chen	mahasidda
drubpa	grub pa	siddha

Pronunciation	Transliteration	Translation
dü	bdud	mara
duje	'du byed	composite
dütsi	bdud rtsi	amrita
dzin	'dzin	hold onto
dzogchen	rdzogs pa chen po	great perfection
dzogrim	rdzogs rim	completion stage
gendun	dge 'dun	sangha
go	go	comprehension
gom	sgom	to meditate
gom	goms	habituation
göpa	rgod pa	excited mind
gyu	rgyu	primary cause
jangchub kyi sem	byang chub kyi sems	bodhichitta
jigten chögye	'jig rten chos brgyad	eight worldly concerns
jingwa	bying ba	dull or sinking
joggom	'jog sgom	placement meditation
khandroma	mkha' 'gro ma	dakini
khongdzin	khongs 'dzin	holding onto anger
Khorlo Demchok	'khor lo dbe mchog	Chakrasamvara
kuntri gye	kun dkris brgyad	eight fetters
kunzhi namshe	kun gzhi rnam shes	alayavijnana
kunzob denpa	kun rdzob bden pa	conventional truth
kusum	sku gsum	three kayas
kyeche	skye mched	sense fields; ayatanas
kyen	rkyen	secondary cause
kyerim	bskyed rim	creation stage
lada	la zla ba	transcendently determine
lagpa	lag pa	hand

Table of Tibetan Terms

Pronunciation	Transliteration	Translation
lamai naljor	bla ma'i rnal 'byor	guru yoga
lhagtong	lhag mthong	vipashyana
lhenchig kyepa	lhan cig skyes pa	coemergence
longku	longs sku	sambhogakaya
lung	rlung	wind; prana
masam jöme	smra bsam brjod med	inexpressible
mögü	mos gus	devotion
namtog	rnam rtog	discursive thought
nelug	gnas lugs	true nature
ngag	sngags	mantra
ngedon	nges don	definitive meaning
ngödrub	dngos grub	siddhi
ngondro	sngon 'gro	preliminary practice
nyam	nyam	temporary experience
nyingtig	snying thig	heart essence
nyong	myong	experiencing
nyonmong	nyon mongs	disturbing emotion; klesha
ösel	'od gsal	clear light
pagpai denpa zhi	'phags pa'i bden pa bzhi	four noble truths
Rangtong	rang stong	empty of itself
rigpa	rig pa	awareness
rimgyipa	rim gyi pa	stage by stage
ringsel	ring sel	relic pills
sa	sa	bodhisattva level; bhumi
salngar	gsal ngar	luminous sharpness
salwa	gsal ba	luminosity
sem	sems	mind
semjung	sems byung	mental factors

Pronunciation	Transliteration	Translation
semnyi	sems nyid	mind as it is
semtri	sems 'khrid	pointing out the mind
sherab	shes rab	prajna
shezhin	shes bzhin	alertness
shinjang	shin sbyangs	thoroughly processed
tamal gyi shepa	tha mal gyi shes pa	ordinary mind
tegmen	theg dman	Hinayana
tendrel	rten 'brel	interdependent origination
tigle	thig le	subtle drop; bindu
tingedzin	ting nge 'dzin	samadhi
tog	rtogs	realization
tögal	thod rgal	leaping over
tögalwa	thod rgal ba	one who bypasses stages
tongpanyi	stong pa nyid	emptiness
trullug	'khul lugs	confused manner
tsultrim	tshul khrims	moral discipline
yeshe	ye shes	wisdom; jnana
yidag	yi dvags	hungry ghost
yidam	yi dam	tantric deity
zangtal	zang thal	unobstructed clarity
Zhentong	gzhan strong	emptiness of other

INDEX

A
Abhidharma, 50–51, 58–60
action seal, 77
analytical meditation, 4–7, 63–66
analytical thinking, 2–6
anuttarayoga (unsurpassable yoga) tantras, 76–77
Asanga, 47–48, 50–51
Aspirational Prayer for Dzogchen (Jigme Lingpa), 10–11
Aspirational Prayer for Mahamudra (Rangjung Dorje), 10, 22, 212
Atisha, 190
Avalokiteshvara, 36, 80
ayatana, 34

B
bagchag, 62, 131
banishing, power of, 28
bardo, 238
basis, power of the, 28
bodhichitta, 17, 24, 169–71, 226–27
bodhisattvas, 50–51, 80, 91, 96
breathing, 25, 36, 43–44, 106–8
Buddha Shakyamuni (the Buddha)
  becoming like the, 20
  faith and, 6, 99–100
  four yogas and, 248
  generating devotion in the presence of, 28
  good qualities of, thinking about, 19
  prostrations to, 17
  on the realization of mahamudra, 76
  teaching style of, 94
  three bodies of, 81–82
  wheel of Dharma and, 47
  wisdom of, 88
buddha essence/nature, 2, 22, 23, 51, 75, 78.
  See also luminosity
butter lamp, flame of, 25

C
Chakrasamvara, 82
chammeba, 127
Chandraprabha, 84
Chandrakirti, 3
charya (performance) tantra, 76–77
chegom, 63
Chenrezig practice, 61
chigcharwa, 241
Chittamatra (Mind-Only) school, 6, 48, 50, 162
Chögyam Trungpa Rinpoche, 98
clear light, 202
coemergence, 151–68, 170, 198
coincidences, 144
collective unconscious, 62
compassion, 6, 32, 225–26, 253
  accumulation of merit and, 17
  emptiness and, 100
  four yogas and, 247
  traumatic experiences and, 117

wisdom and, 82
consciousness(es)
  alaya, 62, 116, 117
  as a composite, 56
  seventh, 116, 117
  six, 33–34, 104–5, 116–17
contemplating, power of, 40, 42
continually placing stage, 38

D
Dagla Gampo, 84–86
dark retreat, 2
devotion, 16–17, 89, 181–82, 228, 240–41
  power of the basis and, 28
  preparatory practices and, 96, 98
Dewachen, 61
Dezhung Rinpoche, 3
Dharma, 2, 4, 19–20, 28, 158
  devotion and, 181
  essential points of, 20
  faith and confidence in, 6, 254
  lada and, 220, 226
  motivation and, 239–40
  obstacles to the path and, 230
  prajna and, 20
  preparatory practices and, 93
  taming the mind and, 254–55
  wheel of, 47, 50, 78, 79
dharmadhatu, 56–57, 149–50, 234
dharmakaya, 10, 81–82, 90–91, 221
  coemergence and, 154–55, 160
  four yogas and, 244
  Zangpo on, 158
Dharmakirti, 61–62
dharmata, 25, 60, 65–66, 73, 152, 221
  levels of practice and, 241–42
  obstacles to the path and, 238
  seeing, directly, 88
domsum, 174
Dorje Gyalpo, 86
drenpa, 37, 105, 184
Drikungpa, 188
drops, practice of, 89, 118
Dudjom Rinpoche, 237
duje, 56
Dusum Khyenpa (First Karmapa), 87, 91
dzogchen, 9–11, 51, 74, 90, 220

E
emptiness *(shunyata)*
  analytical meditation and, 4
  appearance and, union of, 29
  buddha essence and, 23
  Buddha on, 94
  described, 22–23
  dreams and, 29
  four elements and, 58–60
  interdependence and, 54–56
  luminosity and, union of, 23–24, 126–27, 133–35, 142
  skillful methods and, 100
enlightenment, 1, 6, 65–66. *See also* nirvana
  accumulation of merit and, 17
  achievement of, 167, 170
  buddha nature and, 22
  goal of, 26
  heart of, 225–26
  meditation as a pathway to, 20
  Vajradhara and, 90–91
Entrance into the Middle Way (Chandrakirti), 3
essence, extracting, 2. *See also* buddha essence
ethics, 93
exertion, power of, 40–41, 42
extremely and thoroughly pure situation, 75

F
faith, 4, 89, 181–82, 228, 254. *See also* devotion
  the Buddha and, 6, 99–100
  preparatory practices and, 96, 98–100
familiarity, power of, 41, 42
fasting, 2
form
  bodies, 91
  Buddha on, 147
  in the *Heart Sutra*, 150, 210
  true nature of mind and, 22
fruition mahamudra, 75, 100

G
Gampopa, 10, 66, 78, 153–54, 161
  on clear light, 202
  on dharmata, 242
  four points of, 194

Index

on going astray, 212, 214–15
lineage of mahamudra and, 83, 84–88, 91
ordinary mind and, 176, 178
postmeditation and, 199
on removing obstacles, 216
sudden/gradual realizers and, 101–2
on sustaining meditation, 191
Gandavyuha Sutra, 7
Garab Dorje, 9
garuda bird, metaphor of, 5
generation stage, 103
Glorious Unblemised Tantra, 79
go, 241
gom, 183–84
Gom Tsultrim Nyingpo, 85
Gomchung, 86, 161
Gomtsul, 85–86
göpa, 20
great seal, 77
ground mahamudra, 74–75
Guide to the Bodhisattva's Way of Life (Shantideva), 75–76, 187
guru yoga, 17, 89, 96, 98, 120, 221. *See also* yoga
gya, 73
Gyalwa Karmapa, 237

H
healing
  nectar, 28, 234
  power of, 40, 42
Heart Sutra, 126, 127, 150, 210
Hevajra tantra, 120
Hinayana tradition, 21, 51, 94, 174

I
ill deeds, purifying, 27–28
illness, 23, 41, 216
  memory and, 68–69
  obstacles to the path and, 230, 236–37
impure and pure situation, 75
Indrabhuti (king), 1
interdependent origination, 69–70
interrupted engagement, 41, 42

J
Jamal Zangpo, 158

Jigme Lingpa, 10–11
jingwa, 20
Jivaka, 84
jnana, 26, 46, 60. *See also* wisdom
joggom, 63
Jung, C. G., 62

K
Kagyu lineage, vii–viii, 10–11, 85–86, 123, 128, 252
  emptiness of mind and, 211
  golden rosary of, 91
  mindfulness and, 187
  obstacles to the path and, 230
  preparatory practices and, 93
  songs of, 95
Kagyu Lineage Prayer, 160, 181
Kagyu Lineage Supplication (Jamal Zangpo), 158
Kalachakra Tantra, 77
Karma Nyingtig, 11
Karmapa, First (Dusum Khyenpa), 87, 91
Karmapa, Second (Karma Pakshi), 87
Karmapa, Sixteenth, 3, 4, 98
Karmapa, Third (Rangjung Dorje), 10–11, 22, 87, 51, 91, 212
Kham, 86
khongdzin, 117
King of Meditation Sutra, 83–84, 201
kleshas, 25, 32, 64
kriya (action) tantra, 76–77
kundzob denpa, 67
Kuntuzangpo, 74
kunzhi namshe, 62
kusali, 63
kyeche, 34

L
lada, 219–28
lagpa, 73–74
Lama Gotasangpa, 65
Lankavatara Sutra, 6, 242
lhag, 45, 119
lhagtong, 45, 119
Lhalungpa, Lobsang P., ix, 3
lhenchig kyepa, 151. *See also* coemergence
lineage gurus, 17
Lingrepa Pema Dorje, 86

Lodrö Taye (Jamgon Kongtrul), 5
Longchenpa, 11
lotus position, 102–3
luminosity, 57–58, 119, 123
   buddha essence and, 23–24
   coemergence and, 149–67
   emptiness and, union of, 23–24, 126–27, 133–35, 142
   going astray and, 212, 214–15
   meditation on, as a remedy for sleepiness, 19
   nature of mind and, 149–50
   obstacles to the path and, 235
   prajna and, 20
   use of the term, 30
luminous and knowing reasoning, 49
luminous and knowing states, 61–62

M

Madhyamaka school. *See* Middle Way (*Madhyamaka*) school
Mahamudra Subtle Drop Tantra, 76, 77, 79
Mahamudra: The Quintessence of Mind and Meditation (Lhalungpa), ix, 3
mahasandhi. *See* dzogchen
mahasiddhas (eighty-four great adepts), 1–2
Mahayana tradition, 51, 94, 174
Maitreya, 38, 51, 57–58, 65, 75
Maitripa, 74, 80–81, 82, 90
mandalas, 96–98, 103
Manifest Purification of Vairochana Tantra, 128
Manjughosha, 80
Manjushri, 80
mantra(s), 36, 98
   accumulation of merit and, 17
   garlands, 104
   Om Ah Hum mantra, 106
   preparatory practices and, 96
   six perfections and, 76
mara, 185, 216
Marpa, 10, 27, 97–98, 240
   lineage of mahamudra and, 81–84, 87, 90
   songs of, 247
Middle Way (*Madhyamaka*) school, 48, 51, 121, 150
   dzogchen and, 10, 11

   names for mahamudra in, 74
   texts on, 3–4
Milarepa, 10, 27, 240, 249
   lineage of mahamudra and, 83, 84, 87
   preparatory practices and, 97–98
   songs of, 157, 247
mind
   all dharmas as, 6
   all phenomena as, 5–6, 48–50
   awareness and, distinction between, 10
   nature of, reasons to meditate on, 4–7
   nondiscursive, 24
   problems from not meditation on, 7–8
   resting, nine stages of, 38–39
   use of the term, 36
   true nature of, 4–6, 123, 128–30, 149–50
   two aspects of, 21
Mind-Only (*Chittamatra*) school, 6, 48, 50, 162
mögu, 16–17
mudras, 73, 77

N

Nagarjuna, 1, 9, 47–49, 54, 80–82, 90, 121, 145–46
Nalanda, 50–51
Naropa, 65, 82–83, 87, 95–96, 240
ngondro practice, 36, 95–100, 116
nirmanakaya, 81–82
nyam, 131, 192, 227
Nyingma tradition, 9–11
nyong, 241

O

Om Ah Hum mantra, 106
one-pointedness, 40, 42, 44, 189–90, 244–45, 248, 253
Ornament of the Sutras (Maitreya), 38

P

pacifying stage, 39, 42
Pagmodrupa, 85, 86, 155
pandita, 63
paramitas, 75–76
pashyana, 45
path mahamudra, 75
perfections, six, 75–76

Index

placement meditation, 4–7, 38–42, 63–66
placing again stage, 38–39, 42
placing closely stage, 39, 42
placing (the mind) evenly stage, 40, 42
postmeditation, 8–9, 29–30, 181–207, 244–45, 254–55
prajna, 46, 115, 146, 147, 253
    as the fruition of vipashyana, 26
    luminosity and, 20
    six perfections and, 75–76
prajnaparamita, 47, 51
Prajnaparamita Sutras, 147–48
pramana, 65, 174
prana, fullness of, 106
Prasangika school, 150
preliminaries, four common, 96
prostrations, 20, 96–100

Q

Quintessential Instructions on the Middle Way (Atisha), 190

R

Rain of Wisdom, 95, 247
Rangjung Dorje (Third Karmapa), 10–11, 22, 87, 51, 91, 212
Rangtong tradition, 48, 51
Ratna Lingpa, 138
reincarnation, 50, 116, 238
reminders, four, 95–96
rigpa, 10
rimgyipa, 241
Rumtek, 87

S

Sakya Pandita, 66, 78, 174
salngar, 123
salwa, 149
samadhi, 15, 39, 130, 230
Samantabhadra, 74
sambhogakaya, 81–82, 90–91
Samdhinirmochana Sutra, 24
Samputa Tantra, 6–7
samya seal, 77
Sangha, 6, 17, 28, 121, 181
Saraha, 9, 80–82, 90, 121–22, 124
    on meditation, 109, 110
    on the mind, 132, 194
    songs of, 95
    on wildness, 111
seals, four, 77
sem (mind), 5, 10, 36, 104–5, 165. *See also* mind
semjung, 36, 104
semnyi, 66
semtri, 5, 123
Seven Yogas (Maitripa), 74
shamata (tranquility) meditation
    described, vii, 31–44
    four yogas and, 243
    lack of, mistakes due to, 173
    objects of focus in, 32–33
    obstacles to, 17–19
    qualities of good, 169–71
    root of, 16–17
    sequence for practicing, 24–26
    three primary causes of successful, 16–17
    true nature of, 21–24
    vipashyana and, shared tradition of, 15–30
Shantideva, 8, 37, 117, 184
    Guide to the Bodhisattva's Way of Life, 75–76, 187
    on shamata, 25
    on suffering, 122
Shavari, 80–81, 82, 90
Shawari, 9, 80
shezhin, 37, 105, 184
shila, 93
shinjang, 112
shunyata. *See* emptiness
siddhas, 24–26, 65, 247
skandhas (aggregates), 33, 126–27
skillful methods, 9, 100
spontaneous engagement, 41, 42
Stages of the Shravaka, 40
subtle body, 35–36, 89, 118
Sukhanata, 80
supreme nirmanakaya, 91
Sutra Requested by the Student Who Had a Jewel upon the Crown of His Head, 185–86
Sutra of Great Compassion, 128
Svatantrika school, 150

T
tamal gyi shepa, 176–77
taming (subduing) stage, 39, 42
tangkas, 82
Tashi Namgyal
  on analytical meditation, 64
  on the four ways of going astray, 211
  on illusion, 201
  on oral instructions, 101
  on valid cognition, 65
Theravada tradition, 124
Thoroughly Abiding Tantra, 79
Three Jewels, 28
throroughly pacified stage, 39–40, 42
Tilopa, 96, 145, 240
  lineage of mahamudra and, 80, 82, 87, 90
  on samsara, 122
  six points of, 192–93, 194
  songs of, 95
  on wisdom, 130
tingedzin, 15
tögal, 220
tögalwa, 241
Treasury of the Abhidharma (Vasubandhu), 7, 58–60
Tsangpa Gyare Yeshe Dorje, 86, 183
Tsawai Tsultrim, 50–51

U
Uttanratantra (Maitreya), 75

V
Vairocana, 102–3
vajra, 90
Vajradhara, 36, 82, 90–91
Vajrapani, 91
Vajrasattva, 28, 36, 76, 96–100
Vajrayana tradition, 27–28, 47, 94, 103, 120, 166–67
  coemergence and, 153
  completion stage, 78
  creation stage and, 35
  four sets of tantras in, 76–77
  mahamudra meditation as essential to, 4
  preparatory practices and, 99
  yidam practice, 17, 43, 89
valid cognition, 24, 65
variety of phenomena, 88
vase breathing, 106–8
Vasubandhu, 7, 50–51, 58–60
vipashyana (insight) meditation
  described, vii, 45–62
  eliminating doubts about, 63–70, 137–48
  lack of, mistakes due to, 171–72
  obstacles to, 17–19
  root of, 16–17
  sequence for practicing, 24–26
  shamata and, shared tradition of, 15–30
  three primary causes of successful, 16–17
  true nature of, 21–24

W
White Lotus of Compassion Sutra, 84

Y
yidam practice, 17, 43, 89
yoga(s), 76–77, 189–190, 225
  four, 242–50
  guru, 17, 89, 96, 98, 120, 221
  lineage of mahamudra and, 83

Z
Zangpo, 51
zangtal, 223
Zhentong school, 48, 51

ABOUT THE AUTHOR

Thrangu Rinpoche was born in Kham in 1933. At age five, he was formally recognized by the Sixteenth Karmapa and the previous Situ Rinpoche as the incarnation of the great Thrangu tulku. At Thrangu Monastery from the ages of seven to sixteen, he studied reading, writing, grammar, poetry, and astrology, memorized ritual texts, and completed two preliminary retreats. At sixteen, under the direction of Khenpo Lodro Rabsel, he began the study of the three vehicles of Buddhism while in retreat.

At twenty-three he received full ordination from the Karmapa, and at twenty-seven, at the time of the Chinese occupation, he left Tibet for India. He was called to Rumtek, Sikkim, where the Karmapa had his seat in exile. At thirty-five he took the geshe examination before 1500 monks at Buxaduar monastic refugee camp in Bengal and was awarded the highest degree of Geshe Lharampa. On his return to Rumtek he was named Abbot of Rumtek Monastery and the Nalanda Institute for Higher Buddhist Studies. He has been the personal teacher of the four principal Karma Kagyu tulkus: Shamar Rinpoche, Situ Rinpoche, Jamgon Kongtrul Rinpoche, and Gyaltsab Rinpoche. Because of his vast knowledge of the Dharma, Thrangu Rinpoche was appointed by His Holiness the Dalai Lama to be the personal tutor for the Seventeenth Karmapa Orgyen Trinley Dorje.

Thrangu Rinpoche has taught extensively throughout Europe, the Far East, and North America, and is the abbot of Gampo Abbey, Nova

Scotia, Canada. In 1984 he spent several months in Tibet, where he ordained over one hundred monks and nuns and visited several monasteries. In Nepal, Rinpoche has founded Thrangu Tashi Choling, a monastery in Bodhanath, Kathmandu, and a retreat center and college at Namo Buddha, east of the Kathmandu Valley. He has established a school in Bodhanath for the general education of lay children and young monks, as well as Kathmandu Tara Abbey, which offers a full Dharma education for nuns. He has also completed a beautiful monastery in Sarnath, India, a few minutes walking distance from where the Buddha gave his first teaching on the four noble truths. Presently, Rinpoche has begun to develop the Vajra Vidya Retreat Center for his Western students in Crestone, Colorado.

For more information on Thrangu Rinpoche's programs and teachings, please visit his website at www.rinpoche.com.

WISDOM PUBLICATIONS

Wisdom Publications, a nonprofit publisher, is dedicated to making available authentic Buddhist works for the benefit of all. We publish translations of the sutras and tantras, commentaries and teachings of past and contemporary Buddhist masters, and original works by the world's leading Buddhist scholars. We publish our titles with the appreciation of Buddhism as a living philosophy and with the special commitment to preserve and transmit important works from all the major Buddhist traditions.

To learn more about Wisdom, or to browse books online, visit our website at wisdompubs.org. You may request a copy of our mail-order catalog online or by writing to:

Wisdom Publications
199 Elm Street • Somerville, Massachusetts 02144 USA
Telephone: (617) 776-7416 • Fax: (617) 776-7841
Email: info@wisdompubs.org • www.wisdompubs.org

The Wisdom Trust

As a nonprofit publisher, Wisdom is dedicated to the publication of fine Dharma books for the benefit of all sentient beings and dependent upon the kindness and generosity of sponsors in order to do so. If you would like to make a donation to Wisdom, please do so through our Somerville office. If you would like to sponsor the publication of a book, please write or email us at the address above.

Thank you.

Wisdom is a nonprofit, charitable 501(c)(3) organization affiliated with the Foundation for the Preservation of the Mahayana Tradition (FPMT).